SCALE
FURNISHING | ZONING

SCALE

FURNISHING | ZONING

SPACES, MATERIALS, FIT-OUT

EDITORS
ALEXANDER REICHEL
KERSTIN SCHULTZ

AUTHORS
EVA MARIA HERRMANN
MARCUS KAISER
TOBIAS KATZ

Birkhäuser
Basel

EDITORS' FOREWORD

This fourth volume of the SCALE construction series, *Furnishing | Zoning*, focuses on the visual effect of space and its organisation, which together form a key aspect of architecture and the basis of interior design.

The emphasis is placed on the inhabitants: their perceptions, behavioural patterns and movements, as well as their proportions and dimensions as the basis of all space design and the associated complex interrelationships.

The ability to put together these various elements based on a comprehensive understanding of space requires an appreciation of the interrelationship between the factors related to design, function, technical services, building physics and hence comfort and use. The resulting requirements for walls, ceilings and floors – i.e. the components that enclose space and hence form rooms, define the construction details, the surface characteristics and materials – all follow from the architectural idea.

The *Furnishing | Zoning* volume therefore not only deals with the functional aspect of living in rooms and using them, but also with the linkage of processes and actions, resulting in spatial arrangements and architectural qualities. These qualities may be expressed in flexible, adaptable layouts or authentic space sculptures, in specific forms of use and interconnection, or in tailor-made solutions for special buildings in response to specific requirements.

In accordance with the tradition of the series, schematic diagrams and drawings at different scales clearly illustrate the logical sequence of design steps, the interrelationship between the idea of space and its construction, and details of how components have to be put together in order to achieve a unified whole.

The first chapter of the book explains fundamental room-forming elements, ordering systems and design principles. In interior design in particular, proportional relationships and scale, grids and dimensions are all essential to the functional and conceptual design, and these are illustrated here for a range of different space requirements. The tactile and emotional effect of the design elements is illustrated in the play of materials, colour and surface characteristics and in their effect on building physics and comfort levels, including acoustics and light.

The main part of the book details construction and conceptual design aspects of the different building components – floors, walls and ceilings. Exemplary solutions and the underlying principles are illustrated with explanatory drawings. These chapters on construction demonstrate how close the interfaces between architectural and interior design are, and how many decisions need to be made in consultation in order to integrate all of the design parameters and thus achieve the space qualities described. The focus in these three chapters is therefore on the method of jointing and the technical properties of building components and their conceptual expression. This becomes particularly apparent at the transitions between building components, for example at the skirting detail or joint design, air outlets or light fittings, modular components or fitted elements, and how they fit in from a technical and conceptual point of view.

At the end of the book, selected buildings and interiors illustrate how space concepts have been implemented in built examples. Detailed drawings and illustrations give a vivid impression of the atmosphere, both as drawn and as built.

This again clearly demonstrates the close connection between structure and the fitting-out trades – between architecture and interior design. The present volume eliminates the boundaries of these two disciplines and defines interface-straddling design principles dealing with the elements of interior spaces, their functional relationship to each other and their spatial/atmospheric effect. In this way this volume rounds off the other volumes of the SCALE series – *Open | Close*, *Heat | Cool* and *Support | Materialise* and continues the holistic approach to architecture with an emphasis on interior design.

We would like to thank the authors for their inspirational contributions to this book, Andrea Wiegelmann for her unwavering conceptual support of the series and Birkhäuser Verlag for a long and consistent working relationship. We hope that it will stimulate further discourse about the design and perception of interior space in all its facets.

Darmstadt/Kassel, 2 January 2014
Alexander Reichel, Kerstin Schultz

FURNISHING | ZONING
BASIS

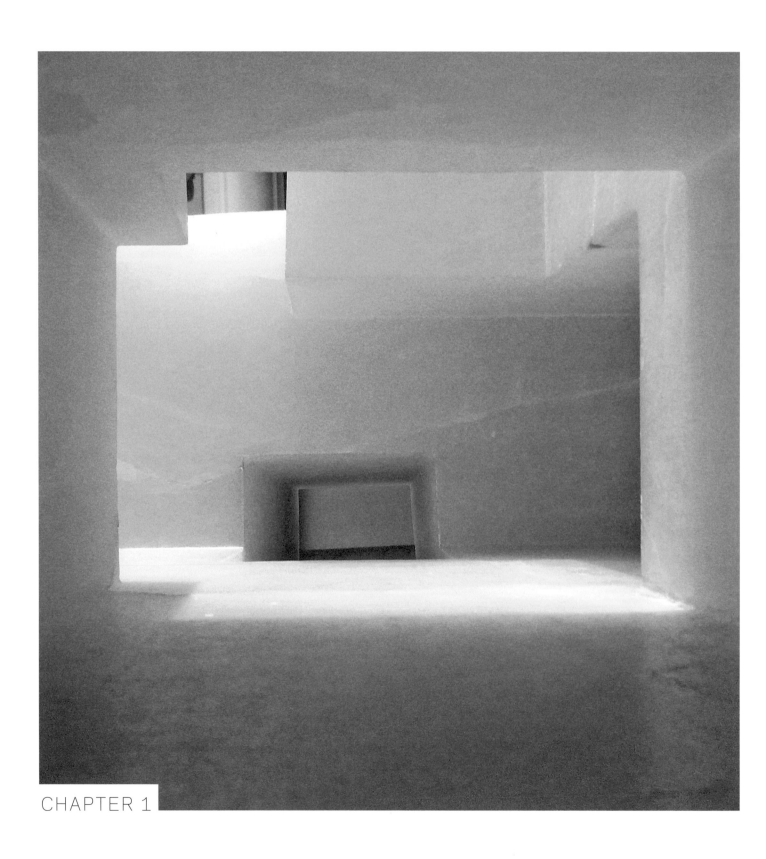

INTRODUCTION

Architectural space cannot just be understood in terms of a mathematical or physical definition subject to sociological and cultural changes. It is rather a structure in which the durable presence of material, function and urban design context, together with individual experience, memories and a web of relationships, is anchored and thus becomes what we call space. Our perception of space is not defined only by its footprint area, height and proportion. Likewise, the meaning of space is not determined solely by its function. Although it is important that a room functions well in terms of use and equipment, just naming it in accordance with the intended function says nothing about the real content – or the furniture and fittings – of a 'good' space. Its quality is determined much more by a range of other factors.

For example, the artists of the Renaissance used painted architectural impressions such as trompe-l'œils to change the aesthetical and proportional impression given by a room. Under the influence of art theory, the discussion focusing on the perception of space has developed over the last two centuries into an architectural debate on the concept of rooms and spaces, and has moved away from the pure description of rooms.

The examples discussed in this context do not represent a sequential development over time, but an illustration of certain approaches which inspired and had a lasting impact on the debate – approaches which are still relevant and being re-interpreted today. The most extreme contrast between two theories on space is that of the *Raumplan* versus the plan *libre*. In his *Raumplan* concept, Adolf Loos assigns a specific height to each room on the basis of its function, which creates a complex intersection of spaces on different levels. The centre of the building is the free mid-point around which the ancillary elements are grouped and aligned to create enclosure. Materials and surfaces are created individually for this specific space and vary depending on requirements – a clear commitment to the art of the craftsman. The unequivocal assignment of the rooms to specific functions is dynamic, but inflexible, since every room is assigned a specific height and mood and also requires generous circulation space.

The opposite theory to the *Raumplan* is Le Corbusier's plan *libre*, which he formulated in his manifesto 'Five Points of a New Architecture'. The spaces created by Le Corbusier are characterised by a maximum of freedom, achieved through the structural separation of the enclosing and the loadbearing elements in favour of an open plan layout. Modern technology and the possibilities of industrial production are the bases of his new architecture, which is not just the result of technical development, but also of the desire for freedom of architectural expression and the flexible use of space. → 1, 2

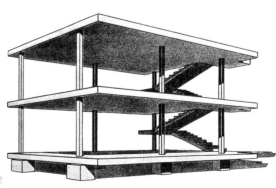

1 Villa Müller in Prague, 1928–30, Adolf Loos: Villa Müller is an example of the Raumplan principle. The 'living hall' extending across the entire width of the house on the main floor is the open centre around which flights of stairs provide access to the different levels. Rooms open and intersect and thus form a complex series of rooms.

2 Domino system, 1914, Le Corbusier: "3. Free layout design: the system of columns supports the intermediate floors and reaches to under the roof. The partition walls are placed wherever they are needed with no floor being tied in any way to the layout of another floor. There are no longer any loadbearing walls, only membranes of various thicknesses. As a result, the layout can be designed with absolute freedom; in other words, free disposal of the existing means, which easily compensates for the somewhat costly concrete construction." from *Vers une Architecture*, chapter "Five points towards a new architecture", 1923.

3 Möbius house, Het Gooi, 1993–1998, UNStudio: the opposite position to Loos' Raumplan. Rather than consisting of strictly functional separated rooms and intermediate areas, the Möbius house exemplifies the seamless transition of these spaces. Sculpturally and programmatically developed as an endless loop.

4 Rolex Learning Centre, Lausanne, 2004–2010, SANAA: For the new library of the EPFL (Ecole Polytechnique Federale de Lausanne), a model for future learning was designed rather than a conventional building. A continuous sequence of rooms is created with zoning based on artificial topographies to give maximum freedom of use to the individual.

3

4

In modern times, there is no longer a clear positioning in favour of one or other of these models, because the parameters for the construction of spaces have changed beyond a merely protective function. There rarely is a client these days who would commit to a complex system of specifically defined room components. Users and purchasers are not often involved in the design process and therefore the space created has to fulfil a variable set of room options and functions. For this reason, contemporary space concepts are much more differentiated in order to succeed in the market. Nevertheless, the desire for spatial effect and atmosphere is still there – unchanged. The lives of current and future generations are not static, but heavily affected by change. Rooms and their functionality have to remain flexible and convertible in order to meet these conditions. The quality of a room will always be defined by its aesthetic expression and atmosphere in addition to functional aspects and other relevant conditions. The subject is a difficult one to elucidate, because the sense and perception of space is largely affected by subjective attitudes.

Furnishing and zoning describes activities that are closely related and part of a permanent design process. 'Furnishing' refers to the design of the spatial environment as an expression of a way of life and work, of needs and of individual ideas as well as collective, social ones. Proportion, dimension, light, colour and type of material are dependent on functions and uses. 'Zoning' denotes the deliberate delimitation/separation of functional spaces and processes, either permanently or temporarily, using walls, room-height elements, room dividers, furniture and lighting, as well as changes in material, surface properties and texture – and the corollary, the deliberate joining of individual zones to create a room ensemble. This is interspersed with variable intermediate spaces as a type of filter, i.e. rooms in which several functions and processes can overlap in the course of time. Some examples of this are movable partition walls, which make it possible to link rooms in variable combinations, or the clever arrangement of built-in furniture, which accommodates various functions within minimal floor space. Does this change our concept of space, or do we perceive the changing fundamentals and requirements in a different way over time? What influences room quality? Which factors determine the quality of rooms and what constitutes the notion of value? These are complex issues, which will be examined in the following chapters.

ROOM FORMATION

Every room arouses a sense of comfort or discomfort – which is directly and individually perceived through our senses: through seeing, hearing, touching, smelling and the sense of balance. Rooms – and hence architecture – can be designed, constructed, observed and used. The perception of space is determined by the social and cultural background of the observer or user; it is shaped and influenced by use and continuous changes in use over time. What appears accidental and intuitive should, however, be part of a systematic design strategy that creates a relationship between the required conditions and their interpretation.

At the centre of all design considerations is the human being. The visual and tactile perception of space and atmosphere is the interface between the user and the building. The emphasis is less on short-lived trends than on design principles that promote the sustainable creation of space and the use thereof. A well designed architectural space creates tangible added value in the form of perception, quality of use, comfort and quality of life.

What are the factors that add to room quality or detract from it, and what affects the atmosphere and authenticity of a place? How can rooms be read and what design tools are available to endow rooms with different structures and qualities?

In order to comprehend a room and give it a certain atmosphere, a complex repertoire of measures and options is required. The basic structure of the building plays an important role in determining the characteristics of these rooms – use and movement processes – and hence the quality of the time spent in them. Decisions relating to dimension, shape and aesthetics depend on this. The properties and visual appearance of materials and surfaces trigger subjective responses. They contribute significantly to the lighting, orientation and connection (or separation) of room structures, as well as to identity.

Design principles such as 'lining' ➘ 2, 'separating' ➘ 3 and 'inserting' ➘ 4 are means of 'furnishing and zoning' space, irrespective of the particular room situation and structure. All these three instruments have the ability to change spaces and to imprint a specific note on a room. In addition to technical and structural considerations and the use of various materials, it is primarily the consideration given to zoning, function and use that mostly determines the quality of a room. The principal approach taken in this book, however, is to define different ways of handling space beyond the functional deployment of room-forming elements and to examine potential of various room ideas and related aspects in greater detail.

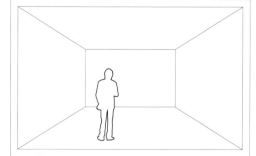

OPTIONS FOR MODIFICATION:
- Extending/reducing
- Limiting/stretching
- Adding/subtracting
- Lining/inserting/separating

EMOTIONAL COMPONENTS:
- Surprise/amazement
- Joy
- Well-being
- Dislike
- Feeling of oppression
- Sense of room dimensions

SCALE:
- Protection
- Sense of security

ATMOSPHERIC OPTIONS:
- Form
- Material/surface
- Light (daylight/artificial light)
- Colour

PARAMETERS GOVERNING THE DESCRIPTION
OF A ROOM / IMPLEMENTATION OF BASIC NEEDS:
- Cultural, ideological
- Local
- Economic
- Political
- Social

NATURAL FACTORS:
- Material factors:
  building material
  type of construction
  production

- Contextual factors:
  external influences, factors determined by use/processes and time
  > constant change/movement of parameters, sometimes for hours, sometimes for centuries

- Site/building
- Room schedule
- Budget

PERSONAL, SUBJECTIVE DECISIONS
- Trends
- Timelessness
- Specific perception
- Cultural background

1 In the detailed formulation of the styling of a room, a great many internal and external influences and dependencies have to be taken into consideration. The use and purpose are based on a subjective idea and are highly personal. The height of a space, its materials and lighting conditions determine a room in terms of functionality and emotional response.

2 'Lining' design principle
Kirschgarten refectory, Basel, 2010, HHF Architects: The lining covers the existing fabric of the listed structure like a second skin. Irrespective of the underlying spatial arrangement, zones are visually combined using identical materials and colouring to form one functional unit. The transition from floor to wall and ceiling is flowing and it makes the actual contours of the room merge into the background. Furthermore, acoustic elements and services installations for cooling/ventilation, lighting etc. are integrated without impacting on the appearance of the room.

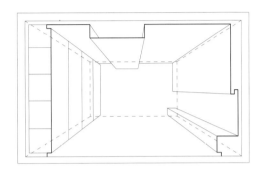

3 'Inserting' design principle
Conversion of the city and university library, Frankfurt am Main, 2006, Frankfurt Municipal Works Department: An independent structure was inserted into an existing building. The insertion of carrels creates zones within the space, defining public and private areas and providing spaces for private study. Depending on the intention, the installed fitments can be designed – using the appropriate material or colour scheme – to contrast with the surrounding space, or to blend in with it.

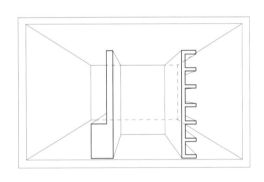

4 'Separating' design principle
Church youth club building in Thalmässing, 2005, Meck Architects: The room can be adapted to different uses owing to mobile, flexible elements that change its dimensions and feel. The continuity of the colour scheme from floor to ceiling unifies the adjoining spaces and allows the room-height sliding walls to merge with the background. Depending on the material of the separating elements – from solid to textile – the view to the other rooms is either opened up or closed off to the viewer.

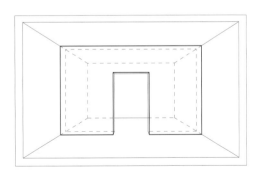

PROPORTION AND SCALE

The proportion of a room defines a certain dimension and relationship of width to length and length to height, and is affected by its function, shape and the overall layout concept. With the help of proportion, the formal and visual order can be defined or disrupted in a design concept. The building component is defined in terms of its relationship to the building and the user. Scale, room size, room delimitation and fitments are parameters for generating a proportion that is perceived as pleasant. While the process of creating a concept has strong subjective and emotional elements and is subject to aesthetic perception, there are nevertheless rational principles that can be drawn on for making decisions.

While the external appearance of the building is perceived in terms of its façade and the roof, interiors are primarily defined by the relationship between floor, wall and ceiling. The dimensions of the wall surface in relation to the ground surface create the relationship to the observer – the human scale. A square floor shape results in a different room perception to that of a narrow, rectangular room, a free shape generates different tensions than a geometric room does. The room height is one of the defining components in the description of space. It is associated with protection and intimacy, but also generosity. High rooms are perceived to be larger. If a room is too high, it appears monumental, whilst if it is too low, it generates a sense of oppression. On the other hand, a well-proportioned room is often actually lower than it seems. Areas used for the presentation of objects

and art usually require different dimensions than living spaces, or rooms for working in.

In addition to the types of activity and function taking place in the room, there are other factors that impact on its proportion and shape. In particular, the organisation of the layout and cross section in relation to the other rooms is just as important as the construction, structural elements, acoustics, climate, lighting and energy use, as well as the material properties and finish of the products used. The relationship between interior and exterior, and those between the rooms, are defined by pillars, structural and partition walls.

When circumstances such as structural limitations or listed building restrictions prohibit alterations to the fabric of an existing building, it can be modified using built-in furniture, claddings and room dividers. The dimension of these elements is determined by the needs of the user: height to width, eye level, fittings, handling, handle options, accessibility, cleaning or servicing. It likewise depends on human activities: conditions of movement and rest such as standing, walking, sitting, resting, eating, working and lying down. In addition, social habits have an impact on the perception of space and objects, because different cultures have different attitudes and sensitivities with respect to proximity and distance, for example. Architectural quality does not become apparent unless common scales are exaggerated by using deliberate contrasts of space and changes of material in the design.

In addition to the golden section, there are other theories of proportion used to provide a rational basis for the aesthetics of a room, including:

– Classical Orders
The Classical orders constituted the most important system of stylistic classification in ancient architecture. Revived in the Renaissance, it held sway through to the early twentieth century. References can be found in Vitruvius' *Ten books on architecture* and Vignola's *Rules of the five orders of architecture*.

– Renaissance theories
See Andrea Palladio, *The four books of architecture*.

– Leonardo da Vinci's Vitruvian Man illustrates the proportions of the human body.

– The Modulor, a proportional system developed by Le Corbusier between 1942 and 1955.

– The Ken
A Japanese system of measure that uses the basic module of the traditional tatami mat.

– Anthropometric proportions relate to the dimensions of the human body and can be transferred to the design of technical systems.

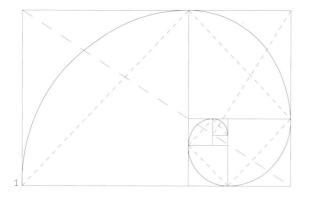

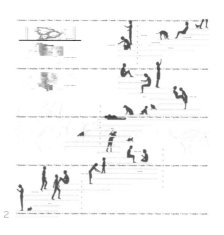

1   The golden section is based on the mathematics of Antiquity and results from the geometric definition of line segments to each other in the following algebraic equation: $a/b = b/a + b$.

2   Sou Fujimoto today bases his designs and room concepts on the module of 350 mm as a reference model between body and nature.

3 Scale
The general scale refers to the size of an element with reference to other sizes in the environment. Human scale describes the size of an element with reference to the dimensions and proportions of the human body.

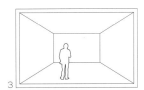 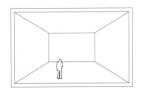 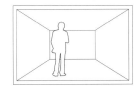

4 Room size
a   A room which is changed in its width by the factor × appears hardly any larger than
b   A room which is changed in its height by the same factor.
c   A room the footprint of which is increased disproportionally while maintaining the same height will appear significantly lower than the original.

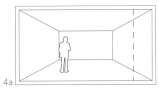 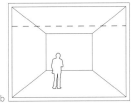 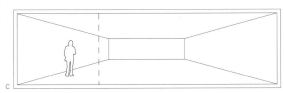

5 Room delimitation
a   with columns
b   with closed surfaces
c   merge the floor with adjoining walls
d   merge the floor with opposing walls

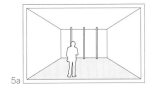 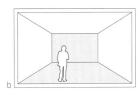 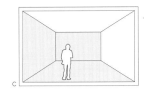 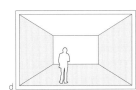

6 Depending on the size of the inserted element, it will either form a connection with the room or appear separate, in terms of the dimension, proportion, form, position, material and colour of the element, thus affecting one's perception of the room's delimitation and zoning.

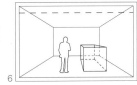 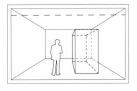 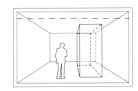 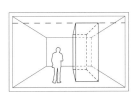

7 Producing a dynamic space and tension by
a   narrowing and widening areas – in a linear or organic manner
b   lowering or raising surfaces by addition or subtraction – geometrically or parametrically
c   using free-form elements.

  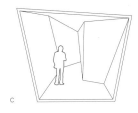

ROOM SEQUENCE AND ROOM CONNECTIONS

It is rare for a building to consist of just one room. Therefore the approach to the building and access to it are just as important as the connections between the individual rooms and functions within a sequence of rooms – both horizontally and vertically. Thought must be given to the arrangement of functions and uses and to the resulting dependencies, as much as to the accessibility and topographic conditions of the terrain. A suite of rooms in a building set on a slope incurs some restrictions which do not apply without such topographical limitations; building in the open countryside allows different connections to be made to the outdoor greenery than does a design in an urban setting.

The hierarchy defining the arrangement of rooms is defined by their functional relationship, the requirement either for rigid or for flexible use, and the desire either for a visible presence or for privacy. For exhibition venues, a linear arrangement of similar rooms that can be used flexibly is sensible ➘ 1, while rooms of a representational character should be located in a central position. Offices without an obvious hierarchy will function well as groups of rooms of equal room quality, while a radial system will guarantee short distances via a central distribution area. The circulation area between rooms can be designed as a buffer zone, or as a link area. It can lead directly to the objective, or offer a multitude of options with unexpected changes in direction; it can be a purely functional enclosure, or form part of the scenery. The individual room opens up to the observer through spatial continuity, intermediate spaces and the route. The perspectives and transitions that become apparent in this process are perceived subjectively. Adjacent rooms and areas can be enclosed or separated using material, texture, colour and dimension, and by omitting or emphasising the edges of rooms. The lighting arrangement can dissipate the flow of space or set dramatic highlights ➘ 2. Lowering or raising certain areas has an impact on the perception of the user when entering a room. For example, passing from a room with a low ceiling into one with a high one gives a sense of increased spaciousness, whereas coming from a room with a high ceiling into one with a low one is likely to create a more intimate or private impression.

In addition to the horizontal transition, the vertical one is important, e.g. circulation space which – as a void between different levels – blurs the room delimitations. This kind of link, however, can also create spaces with properties that go far beyond the merely functional ➘ 3. For example, the staircase hall of the Residence in Würzburg is shaped and decorated so as to transform a vertical access zone into a glorious space that provides exciting perspectives and communication across several levels ➘ 7.

A similar principle, albeit in a free, dynamic form, has been employed in the MAXXI: the central entrance area is crossed by access routes, which become part of the exhibition and the flow of space. ➘ 8

1 Lenbachhaus, refurbishment and extension, Munich, 2013, Foster + Partners.
The suite consists of a sequence of adjoining rooms. The colour scheme creates a rhythm and provides orientation.

2 House B, Stadtbergen, 2005, Titus Bernhard Architects.
The void creates a visual connection between levels . The play of dimensions and light generates a dynamic flow of space.

3 Boxhome, Oslo, 2009, Rintala Eggertsson Architects.
The materials and the light generate a dynamic horizontal and vertical spatial connection.

7 Würzburg residence, 1780, Balthasar Neumann.
The stairwell has been designed as a magnificent reception room. Together with the foyer and the galleries it forms a cohesive unit, setting the scene for reception and internal circulation.

8 MAXXI Museo nazionale delle arti del XXI secolo, Rome, 2009, Zaha Hadid Architects. The staged entrance to the museum doubles up as exhibition space.

1

2

3

4 Perception of space
a When entering a room, no direct connection is made to adjoining rooms.
b Inserted fitments; although the room can be perceived in its entirety, not all areas are actually open to view.
c Open space; all areas of the room are directly open to view.

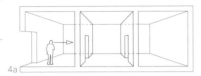
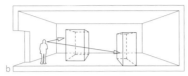
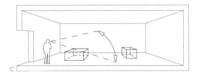

4a

5 Horizontal transitions
a A low zone merges into a higher one; the increase in height intensifies the perception of space.
b Transition from a high, open room to a lower room zone; the lower area creates a sense of intimate space.
c Separating two areas of a room by a connection zone with a lower ceiling; the two areas are clearly defined.

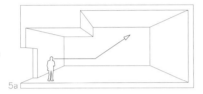
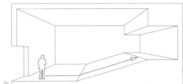
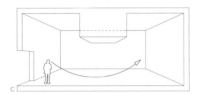

5a

6 Vertical room connections
a Two floor levels are separated from each other; there is no visual connection. Access to the upper level is provided by a separate circulation area.
b The circulation elements are located in a void that connects the different floor levels. This connection enhances communication across several levels.
c A highly expressive statement of vertical circulation: a range of different vistas is created by open spaces, hidden staircases and other sight connections.

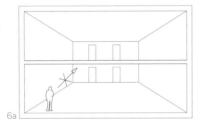
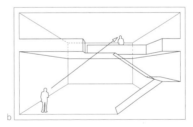
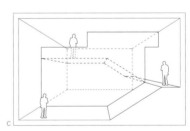

6a

7

8

INTERIOR AND EXTERIOR

It could be said that interior and exterior are not opposite terms, but in fact refer to positions that are mutually dependent and exist through interaction. Without an exterior there can be no interior, and likewise the interior of a building cannot exist without exterior space. The relationship between inside and outside, looking inwards and outwards, and the spatial consequences result from the degree of openness, as well as the fixed or accidental relationship between rooms. There are many spatial concepts that seek to blur the boundaries between inside and outside in architecture – not only in an attempt to display the life within in an extrovert fashion, but also as a design technique to extend the interior space visually by including the surroundings. Depending on the type and position of the opening, the filter zones and the layers between interior and exterior, a number of parameters determine the effect of the visual relationships. These are as follows.

Visual relationships can emphasise the experience, but they can also limit it, or prevent it altogether. A residence with hidden, introverted access conveys a desire for privacy, whereas a place of congregation with full-height openings at ground level onto the forecourt announces its openness to the public. A landscape that can be seen through an unspecific opening that takes up the whole side of a room has a different effect to one that is glimpsed through a single incision in the building envelope, similar to a picture on the wall. The degree of openness varies depending on the function and activity concerned. The window display of a shop and the movable glass facade of a restaurant serve the purpose of presentation and communication. In this case, transparency and the ability to look in are desirable – even necessary. In residential buildings, in contrast, the private sphere can be protected by the careful control of visibility and the direction of view, while still providing the benefit of generous openings with views to the outside.

When the boundary can no longer be perceived with the senses owing to the continuation of materials and surfaces, the delimitation between interior and exterior space also disappears. Conversely, a deliberately installed threshold marks different room zones by accentuating the visual and tactile difference in terms of finish, surface property or colour. Distinction and transition, interruption and continuity, boundary and passage are expressed in thresholds, filter zones and transitional spaces used as a means of symbolic zoning and delimitation of specific areas. Differentiation is achieved in the form of steps, ramps, lowered or raised areas and changes of material or surface finish. Transitions are created between the sequence and functions of rooms. Public-to-private filter zones can be designed as spatial transitions involving both compositional and functional aspects, e.g. in the form of a glazed bay that projects into the exterior space, or as a piece of Nature that grows into the interior.

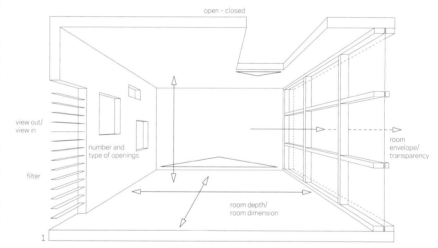

1

2 Residence in Leiria, 2011, Aires Mateus & Associados. The introverted house stands as a monolithic block on the site. There is no direct visual connection from the inside to the outside. Private open spaces and light-wells are created by deep incisions.

1 Interior/exterior
A range of factors influence spatial perception and the relationship between inside and outside.

2 Residence in Leiria, 2011, Aires Mateus & Associados. The introverted house stands as a monolithic block on the site. There is no direct visual connection from the inside to the outside. Private open spaces and light-wells are created by deep incisions.

3 Wetzlgut Health Centre, Chalet, Bad Gastein, 2013, Kuehn Malvezzi. Large-format windows at various levels provide specific views of the landscape.

4 The geometry of openings
The type of opening and its geometry in a facade direct our view
from the inside to the outside and
thereby influence the sense of the
space and degree of privacy.

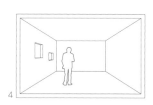 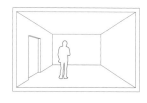 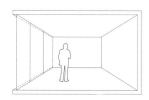

5 The position of openings
The position determines the
amount and direction of daylight,
the degree of privacy and the
furnishing options.

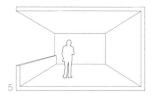 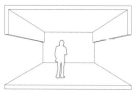 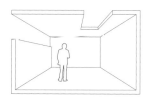

6 Screening
The building fabric and construction elements define the transition
between inside and outside. The
transparency between the inside
and outside – and vice versa – can
be controlled using appropriate
screening.

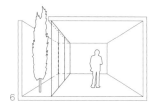 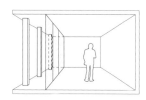 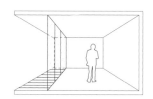

7 Exterior space
With light-wells and incisions it is
possible to blur the boundaries
between inside and outside.

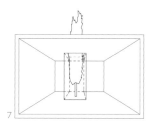 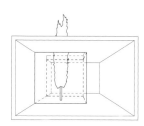 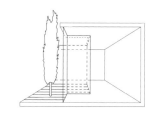

8 Pawson House, London, 1999,
John Pawson. There is fluidity in the
transition between inside and outside. The row of kitchen furniture
inside the house continues outside
in the form of a long table. The profiles used for the full glazing are
reduced to a minimum. At the same
time the relationship between the
inside and outside is restricted
to the private space, which is separated from the public realm.

9 Toledo Museum of Art, Toledo,
2006, SANAA. Under a continuous
roof the walls, corridor zones and
exterior envelope are formed by
full-height glazing panels. The transitions between interior and exterior spaces disappear.

SCHEDULE OF ACCOMMODATION

All building briefs are developed from a schedule of accommodation which structures the requirements for space and circulation and assigns rooms in accordance with the proposed use and function, the number of users and how long they spend in them. This abstract functional scheme is the starting point for the design work.

Higher order dependencies between functional areas, as well as direct relationships between individual rooms, can be graphically illustrated.

This schedule is expressed in the inner layout, in openings and closures, in the connection or separation of rooms, in the grouping or isolating of functions and, not least, in routes and visual connections – from communicative to private, from publicly accessible to restricted access and from bustling to quiet. In this context, it is not only the specified minimum sizes – such as for workspaces, bathrooms, kitchens, sanitary facilities or lecture halls – that play a role, but also the requirements of individual users.

For example, one person might wish to have a house with a small, separate kitchen so as to allow a larger dining or living room, while another might favour the kitchen as the centre of communication in an open-plan living and dining space. In addition, multiple uses and interchangeable functions should be part of the considerations. A study could also be used as a guestroom, for example, or a working area could be annexed to a living area as needed.

Further important aspects are the ability to extend a room schedule and to change the function of individual rooms when there is a change in the users' personal circumstances. For example, how can a children's area be used once the children have moved out? Can it be assigned a new function, or possibly be let out separately? The way rooms are arranged in relation to each other affects the way they are used. Rooms arranged on one level, i.e. with purely horizontal connections, allow for a different use than those arranged on a vertical basis over several floors.

The composition of individual room sequences for the creation of communicative, personal or service areas does not depend only on functional requirements and aesthetic considerations. In addition to the purely functional requirements and the personal preferences of future users, it is also necessary to take into consideration structural aspects, physical performance requirements and governmental regulations.

What has been described here using the example of housing – with the diagrammatic arrangement of functions ⟶ 1, the classic implementation ⟶ 2 and its reinterpretation based on uses overlapping in the course of a day ⟶ 3 – also applies to all other room typologies. Architecture expressed in the form of room sequences is not successful unless there is a harmonious interplay between the function/use as perceived by the user and the contextual design.

1 Diagram of the functions required in a house.
Considerations::
– rooms (number and size)
– relationships of rooms to each other
   (connections, position, flexible use/multi-functional rooms)
– hierarchies (relationship between rooms, size of rooms, secondary/primary rooms, service/serviced rooms)

Rooms with specific uses are grouped together. Reference lines represent functional and spatial dependencies. In addition there are orientation according to the compass, access, sight connections, shading etc.

2 Layout of a traditional apartment building
All main rooms are accessed via the corridor but are also interconnected via internal doors. The rooms lend themselves to flexible use and can be interconnected in different ways.

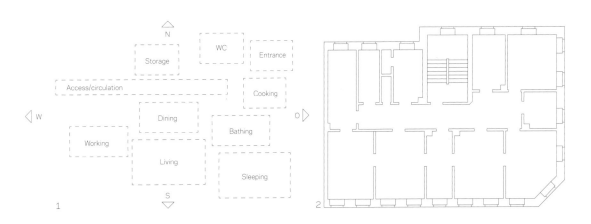

FUNCTION AND USE

'Architecture is the thoughtful making of spaces – it is the creating of spaces that evoke a feeling of appropriate use' is what Louis I. Kahn once said in an interview to describe his approach to design. On this basis he used the principle of ordering rooms into served and servant spaces, in which a higher level of order defines the room for the respective function. With the Salk Institute laboratory building in California (1959-1965), Louis Kahn created the prototype of today's modern building typologies. The separation of alternating served and servant areas allows for flexible rooms free of technical installations and other rooms with a high concentration of services.

This contrasts with Louis Sullivan's 'form follows function', which propagates programmatic emptiness in favour of maximum flexibility. Or Ludwig Mies van der Rohe, who countered Sullivan's principle with the term 'structure', in which the functions behind the envelope can be flexibly interchanged while the form remains the same. Nowadays, these three different approaches are not seen as opposites, but are used instead – in deliberate combination – to find a solution for a range of spatial requirements. This is becauseroom schedules and functional specifications no longer constitute a viable strategy for producing designs that will remain usable. Instead, flexibility and neutrality of function are in demand.

Rather than by its dimensions, type and position of openings and the connection to other rooms, a room is primarily defined by the type of use and the user. Whereas in former times there was still the client whose personal requirements and representational preferences could be systematically expressed in space, this kind of typical user no longer exists today. In spite of comparable demographic characteristics, the differences in cultural heritage, personal preferences, economic and personal resources are too large.

However, all users share a need for safety and physical protection against climatic conditions. Communication with others and the active or passive participation in social and cultural activities is equally as fundamental for the individual, depending on his or her stage of life and the external circumstances. Irrespective of the requirements and restrictions imposed by building control or listed building authorities, there are nevertheless some overarching principles which are important for the success of functional room compositions.

What is the target group for the design? Families with children have different priorities to those of an art collector; different lifestyle concepts require spaces that can be used in different ways, spaces that can grow and shrink with a family and the users' age, and in that way adjust to the requirements of the generational change. What are the processes over time? Are there overlaps in terms of time and space at peak times – e.g. in canteens, libraries and communication centres – and how can these be accommodated by providing back-up space? What options are offered by arranging functions according to concepts for flexible change, facilitated by openable annexes, movable elements, furniture inserted as room dividers? What size and proportions should a room have? A concert hall has different requirements in terms of vertical layering and proportions than a gymnasium and it requires different technical installations, lighting and access provisions. What solutions for the arrangement and alignment of functions and uses result from orientation in terms of the points of the compass, from lighting or shading, from separate accessibility or privacy? The tendency towards more personalised styling in recent years is apparent from the variety of concepts that are continually being created.

3 Illustration of Möbius house, Het Gooi, 1993-1998, UNStudio The family home as an experimental project for a new style of living. The circulation and living areas overlap in the course of the day and are superimposed in the room schedule, internal circulation and structure.

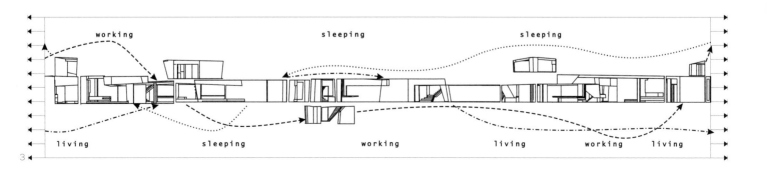

working   sleeping   sleeping

living   sleeping   working   living   working   living

PRINCIPLES OF ORDER

The formation of space as architecture almost always serves a certain need or user. Once the schedule of accommodation, functions and uses have been defined, the complex requirements for a building are consolidated into a recognisable and comprehensible structure. Depending on the underlying approach, this can be done using an orderly, rigid principle, or an irregular, flexible one. In a place of worship, for example, the space will often be arranged in a dramaturgical fashion, heightening the atmosphere both visibly and on an emotional level. As the focus is on the main space, the secondary rooms in the hierarchy are grouped around a central area. When creating rooms for work or manufacturing, the spatial organisation follows the functional requirements for business expansion and contraction, while at the same time maintaining the existing systems and installations.

'Order without diversity soon turns into monotony and boredom, diversity without order soon turns into chaos' (Francis D. K. Ching). Both principles – order and chaos – have their place. The fixed parameters of three-dimensional order are the requirements of the structure: construction, structural system, spans, loads, room height and geometry, openings and zones. The elements creating the atmosphere and identity – such as materials, surface and styling – are the means with which to create order as well as flexibility.

Depending on the requirement profile, spatial order can dominate the room visibly or subconsciously. The strict symmetry of Villa La Rotonda by Andrea Palladio ↘1 dominates the space and at the same time establishes a hierarchical sequence of rooms. In contrast, the open plan layout of Le Corbusier's ↘2 residences allows for maximum flexibility and the rearrangement of room sequences. The monotony of a rigid rhythm of rooms in linear order, which is required for presentation in museums and galleries, can be interrupted by design elements such as fittings and surfaces. Rigid order and simultaneous flexibility of use create an imaginary axis in House K ↘3, which separates the living space into served and servant rooms using structural wall slabs and roof lights. Spaces and volumes can serve as a pattern for order, helping to organise, enclose or separate secondary functions ↘5, as in the 'Schwarzer Laubfrosch' experimental dwelling, whose functionally neutral central volume creates both maximum flexibility and order.
For all principles it is necessary to use order – rigid and/or flexible – to create a user-oriented base that fits into the context, functions and substance of a building. The clearer this system is in terms of readability and usability, the easier it is to accommodate changes and flexibility of use in the existing structure when the requirements change.

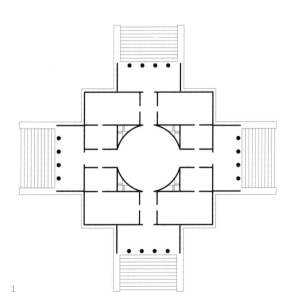

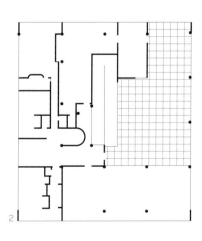

1 Villa La Rotonda, Vicenza, 1566–1570, Andrea Palladio. Working from the basic geometric shapes of a square and a circle, the layout is subdivided into four identical parts. The facade reflects the totally symmetrical base arrangement and provides views to the four cardinal directions via four identical porticos.

2 Villa Savoye, Poissy, 1928–1931, Le Corbusier. Built in accordance with his manifesto *The Five Points of Architecture*, the facade is fully independent of the loadbearing structure. The freestanding columns allow for a free design and hence changeability of the layout - to suit the requirements of the users.

3   Zoning through screening
Residence in Gmund, 2005, Titus
Bernhard Architects. The house
design is based on the screening
principle. The secondary rooms and
storage space are placed along a
linear circulation axis following the
slope of the terrain, while the important zones of the house open
out towards the lake.

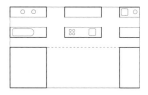

4   Defining space using flexible
walls
Residence at Lake Constance,
2010, se(arch). The space can grow
or shrink in line with the number
of occupants without sacrificing
room quality. The overall space is
defined by the building envelope,
within which individual spaces can
be freely arranged. Full-height
sliding elements create maximum
flexibility – adding or subtracting
rooms.

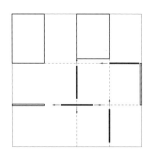

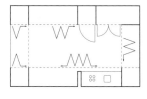

5   Separation of space and
function
Schwarzer Laubfrosch, Bad
Waltersdorf, 2004, Splitterwerk.
The building consists of a neutral
central area which is enclosed
by peripheral zones. These accommodate minimalist equipment for
everyday functions, behind sliding,
turning and folding elements. When
the peripheral areas are accessed
(by opening doors, flaps etc.), the
central zone becomes part of the
respective function and augments
the usable space. A high degree
of flexibility is thus achieved by
superimposing space.

CHANGE OF USE

Work on existing buildings is becoming an important part of architecture. Owing to the differences in the service life of various building components (structure: 50–100 years, envelope: 20–50 years) and the content (room functions and surfaces: 5–10 years), it is clearly important to deal responsibly with existing buildings. In refurbishment projects, it is possible to use many different concepts.

Everything is possible in such cases, from a radical conversion to a sensitive transformation. Working with existing buildings requires an intensive design effort, so as to accommodate the brief along with imposed factors such as listed building and building control legislation, the intended use and the budget. Existing building substances not only impose structural limitations, but also have an existing shape and layout of rooms, which have to be reconciled with the new user requirements. Quite often this leads to somewhat peculiar spatial configurations, which draw their attractiveness from the juxtaposition of the existing fabric with the new functions. The re-establishment of the historic style with careful reconstruction and repair of existing period features is as legitimate a strategy as the complete reinterpretation and reorganisation of the space to accommodate the functional brief. Every change of use involves modification of the existing building fabric, the degree of which depends on how easily the building's typology, its substance and the new function match. Many specialised buildings undergo remodelling, be it for economic or structural reasons, or because the space requirement has changed. For example, in the recent past some church buildings have been converted into youth centres, venues, hotels or libraries. ⟶ 1

In other cases, the transformation consists in accommodating a new function in an existing building. For example, the Tate Modern gallery in London was the result of a deliberate decision to use a defunct power station for the display of modern art. The alterations and additions to the built fabric and the design are clearly discernible, while the identifying elements of the existing building – for example, the oversized turbine hall and the defunct oil tanks – remain a seminal feature of the new ensemble. Cheap brownfield sites in up-and-coming areas of the city are often used for hotel schemes, exploiting the charm of the past for relatively short periods of between five and ten years in a tightly timed market. ⟶ 2

The change in requirement is not only limited to spectacular special uses. The world of living and working is also subject to change, which needs to be accommodated in the built environment. Sophisticated concepts with open loadbearing structures and neutral functional zones to permit short and long-term reconfiguration can retain flexibility in furnishing and zoning for many quite different purposes, well beyond the initial period of use.

Period of time for which elements affect the design:

Place, town, context	>100 years
Structure, construction	50–100 years
Bldg. envelope and installations	20–50 years
Function and use	5–10 years
Surfaces and interiors	5–10 years

1   Boekhandel Selexyz Dominicanen, Maastricht, 2007, Merkx + Girod. Conversion of a former Dominican church into a bookshop. The fitments placed into the church interior and the flat presentation elements are subdued in terms of colour and material, giving prominence to the historical face of the building.

2 New element – room within
a room
Atelier Hall A, Munich, 2013,
Designliga designers. The former
metalwork building of a power
station was converted to offices.
In order to preserve the basic character of the 10 metre-high building,
individual boxes and fitments are
inserted, which divide the room into
zones, accommodating all work and
service areas.

3 Reorganisation of space
House Z, Königsstein, 2012,
Meixner Schlüter Wendt. A 1920s
house was reorganised and extended with a new building. While
the interior spaces of the existing
building allude to the time at
which it was built, the architecture
of the extension is defined by the
functional needs and space
requirements.

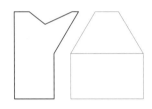

4 Change of use of an existing
structure
Bogenallee residence, Hamburg,
2005, blauraum architects. A
former office building with garag-
ing, dating from the 1970s, was
transformed into open-plan urban
residences using the skeleton
structure of the former offices.
The installations necessary for
domestic use are added with the
help of inserted boxes, which
are placed into the stripped-out
loadbearing structure, or in projections on the outside.

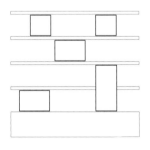

GRIDS AND DIMENSIONS

The human anatomy, with its dimensions of body and movement, defines our space requirements. The height and distance of everyday items, the space required for moving, sitting, working, sleeping etc. and the dimensions of the volumes in which these are arranged, are based on an idealised average dimension and proportion of the human body. There are numerous standards and regulations which define a basic framework of ergonomic criteria for barrier-free integrated design. In planning specific projects, it is also necessary to take the respective dimensions into account, in particular the body's dimensions and the resulting space requirements.
The following activities and dimensions have to be considered when designing interiors and furnishings:

– Space requirement
Sitting, walking, standing, during sleep, performing ablutions, when cooking, sitting at a desk or working on a production line – the human dimensional relationship is different for different movements and functions.

– Movement radius
Assumed reach and operating heights – as well as eye level and perspective – are different for different functions, and they should also reflect demographic change.

– Space and volume
Free-standing and fitted furniture, equipment and personal items all require space, which has an impact on the provision of living and working environments. How much storage space is required for books and office material; how big are chairs and armchairs, tables, desks or shelves; what is needed for a reception, back office etc. down to the washing machine?

– Furnishing and zoning
What heights and dimensions should chairs and tables have for them to be universally usable?
What is the minimum or maximum distance needed between various items in order to be able to perform daily tasks? In which position, or in which order, should the various items be arranged in relation to each other in order to ensure optimum utilisation?
How should horizontal and vertical connections be designed: the width of corridors, the size of door openings, the ratio of goings to risers in staircases?

While the human scale and smooth processes can be deemed to provide a general orientation for the selection of dimensions, there are other parameters the designer has to take into consideration that depend on the desired function and the building component. Circulation areas, the width of openings, the height of seats and the height of work surfaces all have to be matched to the requirements of the human body and optimised for the average user. In addition, it is necessary to take into account the size limits of transportable items, manufacturing processes and the specific properties of various materials, such as the format of panels. The modular assembly of industrially produced components thus has an impact on the design.
The dimensions of furniture and fitments are not subject to standardised rules. Nevertheless, since the beginning of industrial furniture production, a grid and modular principle has developed which has proven useful for ubiquitous functions such as cooking, storage and working, but which can also be modified. The grid dimension is the smallest unit by which an element can be increased incrementally in width and height.

Another criterion is the compatibility of a primary, i.e. structural grid, with an interior fitting grid, which determines the basic dimensions of interior fitment elements such as partitions, suspended ceilings or raised floors. If it is intended that the grid should be visible in the finished building as a distinctive design pattern throughout all areas of use and construction levels – i.e. from the envelope through to the interior fitments – this can only be achieved in a systematic fashion when the building design is developed from the inside out and the chosen grid takes into account the details of interior fitting-out components throughout the design stage. Another design strategy would be to use superimposed grids, or surfaces without joints.
Currently, design concepts tend to combine functional modules that can be used in an intelligent, flexible way and refined modifications thereof within the available space by creating bespoke interior fitment solutions.

Variables to be considered for a grid and ordering principle:
– the human anatomy and the space required for various activities, such as sitting, standing, gripping
– the dimensions of the space required for objects to be accommodated
– the size of equipment and services installations
– standard dimensions required for various functions
– international applicability
– the creation of a dimensional system that is free of overlaps and residual space.

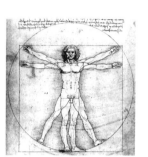

Leonardo da Vinci's Vitruvian Man shows the human body's system of proportions.
➔ p. 14

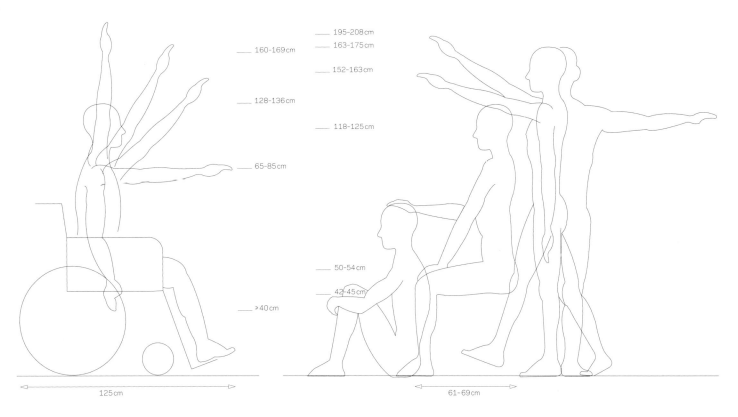

160-169 cm

128-136 cm

65-85 cm

≥40 cm

195-208 cm

163-175 cm

152-163 cm

118-125 cm

50-54 cm

42-45 cm

125 cm

61-69 cm

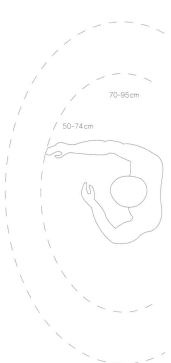

70-95 cm

50-74 cm

The radius of movement of the human body is the basis of all interior designs. While average values can provide a general orientation, the designer should always take into account for whom he is designing. For example, the work surface in a kitchen for a person who is more than 2 m tall should be significantly higher than that for a very small person. The following dimensions can be used as a design guide. Scale 1:20

Dimensions of a standing person
Upwards reach
(grasp axis): 195-208 cm
Body height: 163-175 cm
Eye level 152-163 cm

Dimensions of a seated person
Upward reach 160-169 cm
Height of seated body 128-136 cm
Eye level, seated 118-125 cm
Forward reach
(grasp axis): 69-74 cm
Buttocks to knee 61-69 cm
Knee height 50-54 cm
Height of seat 42-45 cm

Movement radius
Forward reach
(grasp axis): 50-74 cm
Sideways reach 70-95 cm

RECEIVING AND ARRIVING

Reception areas designate a transitional zone between outside and inside. They represent a climatic buffer and are an intermediary space between the public and private sphere. Reception areas represent the company and organise the building. They can vary in size from a small space, created by a curtain behind the entrance door, to huge entrance halls such as those in airports. The route to and the position of the entrance are critical points, which impact on the circulation and zoning of the interior. Should the reception area be entered frontally along a central axis, or discreetly from the side? Does the lighting and choice of materials provide intangible orientation? Is the facade closed or largely transparent? Does the reception area permit a view into the adjoining suite of rooms, for example in museums, galleries or retail areas? Or does a wall protect against intrusive glances and ensure the necessary privacy? How does the horizontal and vertical circulation connect with the reception and waiting area? How much space is needed for representational purposes and at what distance should the auxiliary rooms in the background be? These are just a few short questions intended to stimulate ideas about bespoke solutions for various building types.

This type of question has to be asked in the design of all types of building, although there are large differences in the contextual diversity that go beyond the purely functional aspect of access spaces. Even in residential buildings, reception areas can vary from an introverted, functional space for the purpose of providing access and distribution, at one end of the spectrum, to a representative hall with additional functions at the other.

In public buildings, offices, hotels, restaurants, educational establishments, shops and health centres/hospitals, the number of parallel and connecting functions is much larger: they include waiting, informing, distributing, socialising, presenting, managing, delivering, collecting, depositing and storing.

The reception desk of an office building is the point of arrival for visitors with different purposes – from the delivery man to the business customer who wants to deposit his luggage. Depending on these requirements, space may be needed for a temporary sojourn, for the safe intermediate storage of deliveries, for luggage, a cloakroom etc. Furthermore, the reception in a hotel or restaurant is affected by the change in daytime and nighttime use: during the day visitors arrive with their luggage to check in; in the evening the reception area is a meeting and service point, sometimes including access to a bar. In shops and museums, it is necessary to provide retail space. The reception in health establishments needs to manage patient registration, patient files and other day-to-day activities.

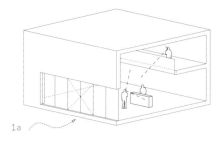

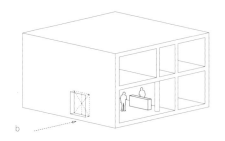

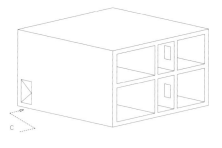

1   Arriving and receiving
The position of the entrance and the design of the reception area can be the visiting cards of a building.

a   The generous transparent entrance has an inviting feel; the open interior with central reception area and a two-storey atrium offers open views and hence allows perfect orientation.

b   The restrained central entrance door creates a natural distance and feeling of enclosure. The single-storey room height presents a limitation to the reception area and only allows views into the publicly accessible zones.

c   The exterior, with a discreet entrance to the side, does not offer any view into the interior and the expected reception area or disclose any generosity that may be offered by room height and interior views.

2   Schematic layout of functional relationships

3   AachenMünchener Versicherung, Aachen, 2011, kadawittfeld-architektur. The reception area of the insurance building features full-height glazing that allow the exterior to flow into the interior. The multi-storey atrium conveys a sense of openness and orientation, in spite of the limitation on access. The colour scheme and materials are subdued, yet prestigious, and are intended to express the company philosophy.

4   VIP wing, Munich, 2011, Erich Gassmann, Tina Aßmann. The reception desk of the VIP lounge within the security area of the airport fulfils a double function: it is both an image-builder for the Munich destination and a service point for transient guests. Instead of an anonymous style of corporate architecture, the lounge has a distinctly local feel even though the guests may not leave the airport.

2

Schematic zoning of a reception area

Layout and section
Scale 1:50

a   Space requirement
The dimensions and height of the reception counter as the work surface behind the information area depends on the user's requirements.

b   Movement area
The distance between the counter and work area, the height of handles and the legroom are defined by the current Workplaces Guidelines. To accommodate the height of the reception counter and the lower height of the work surface for the receptionist whilst still allowing eye contact, it is possible to raise the receptionist area on a podium.

c   Furnishing and zoning
In addition to technical installations such as telephone system, computer, printer, cash point and security devices, it is possible to integrate a cloakroom and stationery storage area in the reception fitment.
The reception area may lead to further secondary zones such as cloakrooms, sanitary facilities, storage areas, a back office and a waiting area.

The reception area serves as a point of orientation and distribution to the subsequent functions such as conference and office areas, exhibition areas, reading rooms and library, auditoria, lounge areas and social rooms, wellness and fitness areas, restaurants, consulting and treatment rooms and circulation space such as staircases and lifts.

Depending on the type of building, reception areas can also be used for several different functions at the same time - temporary exhibitions, assembly, gastronomy etc.

3

4

WORKING AND MEETING

No sphere of life has changed so much in recent decades as that of work. The development of the service society has generated increased demand for office space. At the same time, work itself has changed. The spread of technology, in particular electronic media, has made work more flexible in terms of time and less dependent on place. Home offices and laptops have the effect of blurring the boundaries between work and leisure time. In theory, this means that work can take place anywhere, which leads to new building typologies.

At the place of work too, there is a trend towards more openness and flexibility. The conventional classification as cellular, open-plan, or combination offices has been modified to include desk-sharing, flexible project zones and open communication areas. This allows for a greater degree of adaptation of space to the type of activity – be it group work, project work, or individuals working without disturbance in a concentrated fashion.

Depending on the size of the business, the space required for work is supplemented by rooms for secondary functions such as staff rooms, fitness rooms and even in-house day nurseries. These are peripheral functions which contribute to the attractiveness of the working environment.

Similarly, individual workplaces and the space required for them have also changed. On the one hand, there is the paperless office with an increased need for technical equipment and, on the other hand, there are work areas with large presentation, storage and archiving requirements. Irrespective of the activity, the design of any workplace requires a focus on functionality and ergonomics. The arrangement of shelving and technical equipment (distance to the monitor/depth of desk), comfortable seating, leg room, work height and line of vision, acoustic measures and glare protection are important factors that impact on well-being (and hence productivity) and which are controlled by regulations. The adaptation of work processes to take older employees into account includes personal control of the height and incline of the desk.

Of special importance at work is the lighting and illumination. Uniform background lighting at the workplace is supplemented by individually controllable functional lighting that suits the activity, independent of the level of daylight. ↘ p. 42, Light

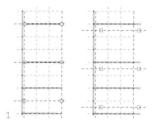

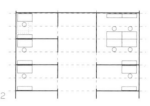

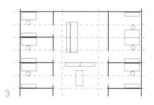

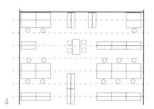

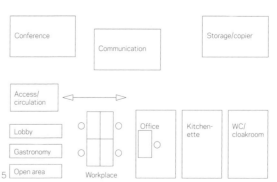

Minimum size of an office layout (depending on room volume):
8 m² normal office use
12 m² primarily sitting occupation
As the floor area of an office increases, the height should also increase:

up to 50 m²	2.50 m
51–100 m²	2.75 m
101–2000 m²	3.00 m
from 2000 m²	3.25 m

1 Grid
Construction and facade grids ideally overlay the fitting-out grid (basic dimension for fitting-out elements such as partitions, suspended ceilings, raised floors etc.). A common grid dimension offering maximum flexibility of use for the implementation of office concepts is 1.35 m between axes.

2 Example of cellular offices
Cellular offices are suitable for activities requiring a high degree of concentration. This type of layout requires more space per workplace as well as individual control of light, heat and ventilation.

3 Example of shared offices
This type of office provides spaces for individual work and team work, communication areas and offices for concentrated work. Each room has its own controls for light, heat and ventilation.

4 Example of open plan offices
Open plan offices are the most efficient way of using office space. Advantages are the variable allocation of space, desk sharing, short communication paths and flexible project areas; on the downside there are no individual controls and a high distraction potential.

5 Schematic layout of functional relationships

6 LHI campus, Pullach, 2010, Landau + Kindelbacher. Individual offices for activities requiring concentration are located around a glazed atrium. A workplace system with flexible storage elements provides an organisational framework for everyday office life and was especially designed for the requirements of the company.

7 Cargo, 2010, Geneva, group8. A former industrial building is used for an architectural experiment. The 'room within a room' principle allows for a range of different workplaces. The cargo containers have been cut open, providing meeting rooms and shared areas overlooking the office landscape.

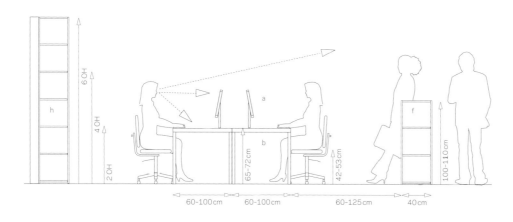

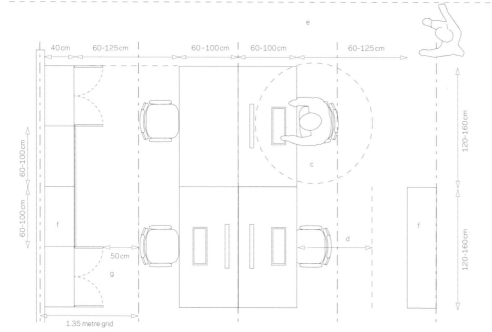

Schematic zoning of a work area

Layout and section
Scale 1:50

a   Work surface:
Standard size 1.28 m²
160 × 80 cm/min. 120 × 80 cm for
purely computer-based workplaces

b   Height of work surfaces:
Table/desk height 65 to 72 cm
Height of counters/sideboards
from 105 cm.

c   Movement area:
minimum 1.50 m², min. 100 cm
depth
Standing: minimum 80 cm depth.
Visitor traffic: 80 cm depth or
60 cm where the area underneath
the table/desk is also available.
The movement areas of adjacent
workplaces should not overlap.

d   User area:
results from adding the furniture
function area to the safety
distance.

e   Circulation areas:
Access to the workplace:
1 user min. 60 cm wide
2 to 5 min. 80 cm
6 to 20 min. 93 cm
21 to 100 min. 125 cm etc.

f   Furniture deposit/function area:
In the case of furniture elements
that move outwards (doors, drawers), the overlap of furniture function areas may only occur in the
movement area of the personally
allocated workplace.

g   Safety distance:
Follows on from the furniture function area and is a place where the
person can put things, min. 50 cm.

h   Cupboard height:
The height of cupboards/cabinets
is stated in multiples of folder
height (1 folder height = 33 cm).
Common heights are for between
2 and 6 folders; sideboards for at
least 3 folders are suitable as
standing workplaces.

6

7

COOKING, EATING, DRINKING

Nowadays, cooking has become a social, communicative and even representational function. The role of the cooking area as the social centre of the house has gone through various changes throughout history since the late Middle Ages, in close connection with technological advances. In the modern era, cooking lost its function as a means of heating the dwelling, which meant that it became separate from the social life taking place in living rooms. Specifically furnished show kitchens now served the purpose of representation. Industrialisation and social change amongst the working population led to the development of functionally optimised kitchens →1, with minimised space requirements and only elementary functions. In the latter half of the twentieth century there was a rediscovery of the representative character of a kitchen, as contemporary social developments found expression in modern kitchen design.

The design is based on the number of inhabitants as well as the logic of processes that have to be carried out. Wherever possible the functions of storing, pre-preparation and preparation, as well as cooking and clearing up, should be arranged as a continuous workflow. Depending on personal lifestyle, the kitchen can be separately accessible, or combined in a cooking/dining area. A flowing transition between cooking, dining and living areas creates maximum openness and avoids the need to create separate circulation space. →2

An important interface that requires design consideration is the transition between the cooking zone and dining area. A flexible solution that prevents odours spreading and affords visual protection can be installed in the form of folding or sliding elements as room dividers, with the help of which it is possible to open a room up to the kitchen or separate it.

Again, the trend towards more openness and flexibility has been supported by technical advances. Modern refrigeration facilities and air conditioning have made it unnecessary to locate larders and other cool rooms to the north, which previously was accepted practice. Flexible cupboards and changes in the supply structure (shop opening hours, delivery services etc.) means that the space required for storage is much reduced.

Similar ergonomic and functional criteria apply to the design of restaurants and commercial kitchens. Refrigeration and storage rooms are located directly adjacent to the kitchen and the areas for pre-preparation, preparation, food dispensing and washing up are strictly separated. Owing to the complexity of these functions and the relevant hygiene standards, it is not possible to cover such areas in the appropriate depth in this book.

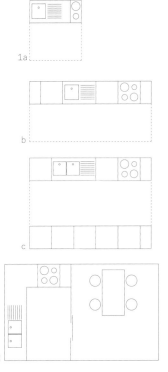

1 Dimensions of cooking areas
Scale 1:100
a Kitchenette/galley kitchen
Minimal solution 60 × 150 cm with reduced standard and space requirement for essential functions.

b Galley kitchen
Single row of kitchen furniture for small households, usually in a separate room.

c Galley kitchen
A double row of kitchen furniture where the functions are arranged on one side and the other side is used for storage. Saves space since movement areas can overlap.

d Dining kitchen
Kitchen and dining areas can be used in open-plan fashion or separated by sliding doors.

e Overlap of functions
Depending on requirements the cooking, dining and living functions can be arranged flexibly using sliding elements. The principle can be developed further by establishing a separate preparation kitchen so as to leave the actual cooking area free for more representational entertaining.

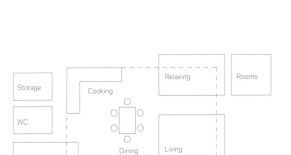

2 Schematic layout
Functional relationships

3 The Frankfurt kitchen, 1927–28, Margarete Schütte-Lihotzky.
Designed akin to an industrial work place, this compact and rationally designed minimal space has all items within easy reach. The Frankfurt kitchen is considered the archetype of the modern fitted kitchen.

4 Penthouse Munich, 2009, Landau + Kindelbacher. The open two-storey room integrates different functions, which include cooking and eating, with an island block creating a distinction between the zones.

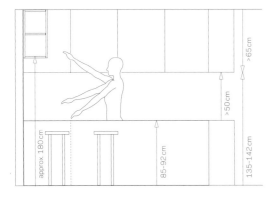

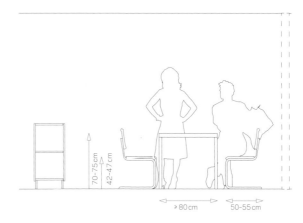

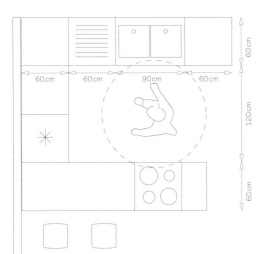

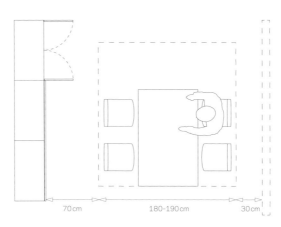

Schematic zoning of a cooking and eating area

Layout and section
Scale 1:50

a Movement area:
The required minimum distance between depositing areas and walls/enclosing furniture, doors and windows is min. 120 cm; for wheel-chair/barrier-free use it should ideally be 150 cm.

b Furniture grid:
The following widths are common for kitchen cabinets: 30/40 (45)/ 60/90/120 cm, and for kitchen equipment, 45/60 cm. The height of base cabinets varies between 77/82/87 and 92 cm (> DIN EN 1116).
The worktop height should be selected in accordance with ergo-nomic principles: 80/85/90/95 cm. The longstanding recommendation of DIN 18022, which is no longer in force since 2007, was 92 cm; the recommen-dation of the Arbeitsgemeinschaft Die Moderne Küche (AMK) is for 70–105 cm, depending on a per-son's height.
The reach height for wall-hung cabi-nets depends on a person's height; the maximum top level of wall-hung cabinets is at 225 cm, the minimum distance to the worktop is 50 cm.

c Kitchen fittings/furniture:
Base/wall cabinets and tall units
Refrigerators and freezers
Worktops and shelving
Hobs and ovens
Sink units
Eating area with sideboard

d Services:
Depending on the equipment used, an electricity or gas outlet must be provided. The number of electric sockets and outlets for light fittings depends on the positioning in the room.

Conclusion
The standard sizes of equipment should always be taken as basic dimension.
In order to optimise the space for activities and processes in accor-dance with individual ergonomic requirements, it is possible to modi-fy the height and depth of work areas, movement areas between the work areas, the reach height for handles and the leg room below units etc.

3

4

ABLUTIONS AND BODY CARE

Just like the kitchen, the bathroom has also gone through significant modification as part of social change.

On the one hand there were the baths of antiquity, the bathhouses of the Middle Ages and the marble baths of the Baroque era, which were patronised for leisure and socialising as well as physical cleanliness and fitness, and on the other hand, there has always been the functional aspect of bodily hygiene, with washstands, bath tubs and outside toilets. Personal bath facilities were considered a great luxury, because the water supply and the heating of the water involved considerable effort. In today's fast-moving times the focus has shifted to reflection on essential elements such as light, air and water. Minimalism and purism in design convert bathing into a ritual.

In terms of physical space, bathrooms vary from purely functional sanitary cells to generous suites designed for lingering in. Within the general layout, bathrooms are normally linked with bedrooms or suchlike. The toilet is often in a separate room from the bathroom. Trends from the hospitality and wellness branches are increasingly being adopted in private homes. For example, the en suite bathroom, which is a typical feature of hotel rooms, has become increasingly popular in private residences: either in the form of a master bathroom, a guest bathroom, or a separate bathroom for children. In the zoning of a floor plan, a bathroom can be used as a divider between public and private areas. Likewise, sanitary elements can be integrated into a separate room, or into an open plan layout. In this context, bodily hygiene is no longer considered a strictly private affair and the bath becomes a wellness facility in the home, with bathing being part of living and increasing the quality of life.

A very important aspect of situating the bathroom is the availability of daylight, which also makes it possible to arrange for natural ventilation. The close functional dependence of the service lines makes it important to consider the location of private and/or public sanitary facilities within a building or unit. Healthcare and care facilities require special attention in terms of barrier-free design and allowing access for care staff.

In buildings with public access such as workplaces, places of congregation and educational establishments, the number and size of toilet facilities and washrooms has to reflect the number of persons predicted to use them. Here, barrier-free access is mandatory.

1a

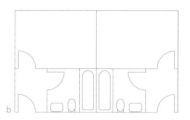

b

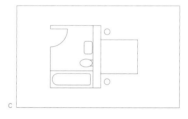

c

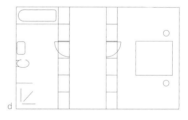

d

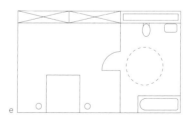

e

f

1 Dimensions of sanitary facilities
Scale 1:100

a Bathroom with dual access
This bathroom can be accessed from two different rooms. In addition, a separate WC is available.

b Hotel bathroom
Each bedroom has its own bathroom with bath, shower and separate storage cupboards.

c Bathroom box in a room
A bathroom box placed into a room allows flexibility for other uses in the room.

d En-suite bathroom
This bathroom is accessed via the dressing room. En-suite bathrooms may include a shower, sauna etc. which are intended for the sole use of the occupants of the respective bedroom.

e Care bathroom
This bathroom is large enough for the movement radii needed by disabled users.

f WC facility
In public WC facilities, a separate lobby has to be included in front of the WC cubicles. Where this is not possible due to lack of space, special doors can be fitted that act as an odour barrier.

2 Bathroom in London around 1900: with the advent of gas boilers and running water in the cities, separate bathrooms were installed in English middle-class houses. Although fitted with bathtub and washbasin, the interior styling with the timber panelling and furnishing is more reminiscent of an opulently appointed salon than a functional bathroom.

3 Town Hall Hotel, London, 2010, Rare Architecture. The 98 bedrooms that have been created in the listed building of a former town hall feature individual fitments for sleeping and bathroom functions. In line with the current trend to make body care into a cult and wellness occupation, the bathroom becomes a more ritualised place, occupying a prominent position in the room.

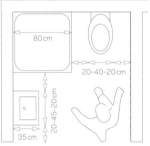

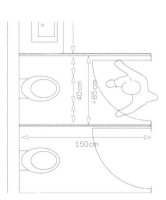

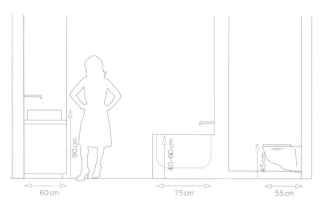

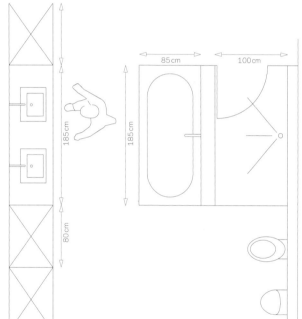

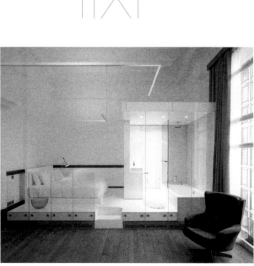

2

3

Schematic zoning of sanitary areas

Layout and section
Scale 1:50

Movement area
The required minimum distance between depositing areas or walls is 75 cm from walls and 90 cm in front of equipment such as washing machine, dryer etc. The distance between a depositing surface and the door reveal should be 10 cm.

Dimensions of sanitary equipment
Washbasins – top height guideline: 85–105 cm
Individual washstand:
width > 60 cm, depth > 55 cm
Double washstand:
width > 120 cm, depth > 55 cm
Hand washbasin:
width > 50 cm, depth > 40 cm
Vanity unit with two basins and base cabinet:
width > 140 cm, depth > 60 cm

Bathtubs and shower trays
Ideal height 59 cm. Movement space min. 55 cm, ideal 105 cm
Bathtub:
width > 170 cm, depth > 75 cm
Shower tray:
width > 80 cm, depth > 80 cm

Toilets
Seat height of 40 cm standard dimension
Upward movement area: 145–155 cm
Wall-mounted WC with pressure flushing:
> width 40 cm, depth 75 cm
WC with concealed cistern:
> width 40 cm, depth 60 cm
plus 20 cm for cistern

Washing machine and dryer
width/depth 60 cm + connections

Decisions to be made:
- Position of sanitary elements in relation to window areas (lighting, ventilation, privacy)
- The position of installation ducts (accessibility, noise)
- Installation walls or services installed within the wall thickness (dimensions, inspection openings)
- Heating (integrated wall or floor heating, towel rail heater etc.)
- Tiles/surface finish
- Installation of fittings (surface-mounted or under plaster)
- Access to sanitary elements (with or without a step)
- Electric installations (routing of wires, safety measures)
- Position of mirrors and furniture elements

MATERIAL AND CONSTRUCTION

The design of rooms is significantly affected by structural considerations. Is the building to be of solid or lightweight construction? Is the shell going to remain exposed to view, as in the case of fair-faced concrete, or is the interior fitting-out separate from the building envelope? Are fitments integrated into the building fabric, or are they meant to be independent and reversible, for example in the case of listed buildings? The production processes have to be taken into consideration just as much as the surface texture and finishes in order to be able to make the best use of the design potential and technical properties of the materials and construction. In addition to the typology and design of a building and considerations of cost-efficiency, context is also of significance. The choice of a certain type of construction may also be determined at an early stage by the construction process in confined inner city situations, or by the loadbearing capacity of existing structures or the ground.

A solid building made of concrete or brickwork has to be conceived of in a different way from a lightweight structure made of wood. In timber construction, the wooden elements that enclose rooms can also take care of the loadbearing function, which has an effect on the layout of rooms, their geometry and their atmosphere. The ongoing technical development of concrete leads to new properties regarding processing and use of the material. By varying the aggregate in concrete it is possible to produce high-strength construction materials for difficult ground conditions or construction times, to integrate energy-efficiency aspects such as activating the thermal mass, to produce prefabricated components such as sandwich elements that include conduits for the installation of pipes and cables, and to create special visual effects in terms of colour and surface texture. The design specification determines whether a monolithic material can be chosen for a certain project. In order to be able to create a homogeneous, uninterrupted surface, an early

decision must be made with respect to form, visual and tactile appearance and the technical installations (electrical, lighting, cooling, storage areas etc.). Subsequent modifications can only be achieved with great technical effort and financial outlay. ⟋ 1

Apart from the visual design aspect, lightweight construction has advantages in situations where there is a restriction on the load that can be imposed and where short construction times are required. This type of construction can be prefabricated to a high degree – both in skeleton designs and where the walls come as timber panels – and buildings can be occupied very quickly, offering great flexibility.

Timber construction has recently been the focus of increased attention for the purpose of increasing the residential density of inner city areas. This is supported by a new interpretation of this traditional material in terms of space and expression, as well as its good energy-efficiency and sustainability values. ⟋ 2

Here too it is possible to use the advantages of prefabrication, provided the room structure, surface quality and technical installation requirements are defined at an early stage. In addition, it is possible to retrofit functions and fitments in the loadbearing structure and building envelope of buildings in lightweight construction. The system allows an overlay of uses in both neutral and specific areas, as well as complete dismantling after a certain period of use.

Extensive interaction with experimental technologies and design strategies has an impact on the development of architectural space. New compound materials, 'smart' materials and changes in complex computer-aided production processes lead to new design options. The fact that it is easier to produce prototypes and apply tailored designs to surface finishes in small series opens up opportunities for a wide range of experiments in construction and aesthetics. ⟋ 4

1 Rolex Learning Centre, Lausanne, 2004–2010, SANAA. For the new library of the EPFL (Ecole Polytechnique Federale de Lausanne), a model of future learning was designed rather than a conventional building.
The envelope largely consists of two free-spanning concrete shells; the formwork for the shells was prefabricated using complex computer technology and installed on site using GPS technology. Subsequent adaptations such as barrier-free access across the curvatures and access control are therefore always visible.

2 Ipark, Stavanger, 2012, Helen&Hard. For the new entrance portal between two existing buildings, the architects used an innovative system of industrially prefabricated components.
The basic components consist of prefabricated hollow box elements that together form long narrow units and which were installed in a twisted, fan-shaped fashion over a period of ten days. The dynamic shape determines the roof, facade and openings and gives the entrance portal a sculptural character.

3 Leonardo Glass Cube, Bad Driburg, 2007, 3deluxe. An organic, sculptural element is placed within the cube envelope, imparting a sense of drama and quality. The separate zones of the building are connected by three white sculptural structures. The organic shape is made of two moulded acrylic half shells, the substructure of which is placed on a steel and wood structure. The interior of the showroom also contains purpose-made lounge furniture, a counter and exhibition areas.

4 HygroSkin project – Meteorosensitive Pavilion, 2013, Achim Menges Architekt BDA, Institute for Computational Design (ICD), University of Stuttgart, Prof. Achim Menges. The reactive properties of wood as a material, i.e. swelling and shrinking in response to relative humidity were used for the construction of a "weather-sensitive" architectural skin using material-oriented, computer-based design and robotic manufacture. The envelope opens and closes in accordance with weather conditions, without requiring any energy for operation.

2

3

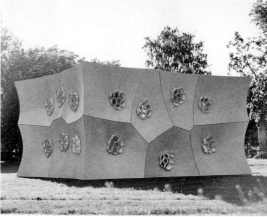

4

MATERIAL AND SURFACE

Materials enhance the atmosphere and effect of a room. In addition, they play an important role in the determining the acoustic, climate and energy factors. Materials can allow the ingress of light and they enable a room's functionality. They can be used in short-term applications (exhibitions, shops), or may last sustainably for several generations. A distinction should be made between the material itself and its surface, which is the result of processing or finishes. ➘ 3-7 While, some time ago, designs depended on the regional availability and processing options of materials, the technology of today offers a large and varied selection of materials with a very diverse range of finishes. The perception of materials is also modified by cultural and social influences. While at Corbusier's time concrete was still considered as brutal and coarse, today's perception of the material – given a special finishing process – is that it is velvety and refined. Marble, which today is a ubiquitous material, at one time represented luxury and elegance.

The requirements for functionality have changed over time. They may relate to specific purposes in neutral rooms, sanitary areas, functional and production zones etc., or to a material's use in floors, walls, ceilings and fitments. Depending on its intended application, the selected material has to fulfil different requirements: some of the criteria are durability and wear, resilience paired with stability of shape, loadbearing capacity, breathability, anti-slip and abrasion resistance properties, to name but a few. The technical properties of the material and its application methods impact on the size of panels/ plates/tiles, the joint patterns and the methods of fixing.

Likewise, time is an important factor when selecting materials. Changes in colour due to the effect of light or wear are considered to adversely affect the quality of some materials, whereas others improve in quality through ageing, something that is often the case with timber floors.

Therefore surfaces are more than just a decorative element. The physical composition of a compound element today is determined by building physics standards whereby its component materials, structural properties, structure and texture function as a unit. The appearance of many materials is not consistent with their properties. For example, laminates are usually a cheaper imitation of another material, without possessing the latter's physical performance or tactile properties. Some innovative materials can be efficiently cut for a certain room and can also change their form due to the effects of light, temperature, pressure, electricity etc. In addition, ecological aspects and energy parameters are becoming increasingly important in the processing of materials.

As products used in building, materials can be used in different ways according to the design approach, such as creating a distinction between different components. In this context, the relationship of the materials to each other is very important; on the other hand, the intention may be to deliberately merge components in order to achieve seamless transitions. In all these considerations, the choice of material is not the only issue, but also the fundamental relationship between the room's surfaces where they meet and the ensuing spatial impression.

➘ p. 14, Proportion and scale, p. 94, Wall cladding

1 Church youth club building in Thalmässing, 2004, Meck Architects
The combination of the materials used and their haptic and optical properties create a calm, quiet room. The low, long wall to the left is lined with woven willow. In combination with the ceiling and partition walls it creates a contrast with the dark concrete floor which has a ground finish. Different atmospheres are created depending on the time of day and the quality of daylight.

2 Regional Centre of Contemporary Music, Nancy, 2011, périphériques. The public areas of the building are finished in red throughout, thus unifying the various functions and elements. Contrasts arise from vistas, views and proportions, and the various uses of the rooms.

3 Owing to their specific grain patterns, different kinds of wood natu-
rally have very different appearanc-
es. The effect of light changes the
appearance of wood over time, with
some species becoming grey. The
surface can be textured in different
ways. Various colour finishes are
possible.
a Smoked oak, rough sawn
b Spruce, weathered
c Walnut, embossed
d Walnut with 3D texturing

4 Concrete and natural stone
surfaces can be processed manually or mechanically. With the help of
modern processing methods such
as water-jet cutting, it is possible
to produce a wide range of shapes
from stone material.
a Concrete, sandblasted
b Concrete, acid-treated, letters
manually produced by stonemason
c Natural stone, routed
d Natural stone, ground and 3D
routed

5 Metal finishes can be modified
by alloying or weathering (patina),
mechanical polishing, brushing or
grinding, embossing, stamping,
cutting and complex forming processes. Lightweight metal sheeting
is suitable for a range of interior
fit-out requirements
a Copper, oxidised
b Ground metal sheet
c Rolled metal sheet with pattern
d Metal sheet processed with
laser cutting

6 The surface of glass can be
modified in the manufacturing process, using different casting
shapes, and with subsequent chemical or mechanical processing as
well as various printing and laminat-
ing processes.
a Molten glass granulate with
colour pigments
b Glass mosaic
c Satin glass with anti-slip finish
d Glass with 3D laser inscription

7 The texture of textile materials
is primarily created by the manufacturing process. ⟶ p. 66, **Textile floor
coverings** Fabrics can be modified in
various ways either by additional
processes or by combining them
with backing cloth.
a Coarse woven fabric
b Felt with perforations
c Sound insulation fabric
with fleece
d Fitted carpet with thermal
embossing

COLOUR AND COLOUR EFFECT

Colour creates zones in a room; it can heighten the effect of a space or distort it. It can alter our perception of a room in a variety of ways, although the actual dimensions stay the same. Bright colours with little contrast create an impression of size and openness, whereas dark and contrasting colours convey an impression of enclosure, density and depth. Independently of surface and texture, the use of colour creates a distinct impression of space – and can also enhance texture and atmosphere. Depending on the way it is used, it can create irritation or optical illusion, and it can impart emotional overtones to the architecture and structure. The choice of colour can also influence the perception of interior climate. Warm colours suggest a higher room temperature than is actually the case.

For this reason, consideration should be given to colour as an architectural element at an early stage of the design process.

Colour also changes the character of interiors – and the colour scheme affects the time that people consciously or subconsciously spend in a room. Colour is not a property of an object, but a subjective perception. In turn, these memories are linked with associations and emotions depending on a person's cultural background. Le Corbusier, for example, not only places his spaces in a relationship in terms of sequence and volume, but also uses a specially developed colour palette in order to transform room volumes and make them more dynamic. Colour can be used to give orientation and to establish a certain order. It can also be used to make activities and factory work more pleasant, and to engender a certain psychological effect – e.g. in medical and care environments.

The natural colour of the materials, textures or surfaces (concrete and plaster areas in a natural colour or enhanced by a pigment, warm wood colours, shiny/matt metal surfaces etc.) may be used, or colour can be applied in the form of paint or varnish on materials and textiles, or as a coating. Colour does not reveal its effect unless it is in a certain context. In that, some impacting factors should be taken into consideration, such as the type of room (whether it is intended for living in, or other purposes, whether it is for private or public use) and the room functions (whether it is an area for relaxation, or for dwelling; whether it is a place of communication, or of physical or mental activity). Each room of a building needs a colour scheme that suits its function. In sports venues, colour is used for orientation and zoning, whereas in private dwellings the occupants' well-being is the primary concern. The colour scheme of an exhibition area or shop with a short service life will look different to that of a social room in a hospital. The existing dimensions and room proportions are affected by the colour scheme as much as by other elements such as the number of openings, raised or sunken areas, inclines or fitments. Likewise, the ingress of natural daylight – either direct or indirect – or constant artificial lighting with its intensity and shadow formation, can direct one's vision and bring out the shape of building components. In the design of colour schemes, consideration must be given to existing colour elements, historic painting styles and colour shades, as well as to the surface finish. Colour is subject to considerable change during the course of the day. The spectral composition of artificial light has a big impact on colour.

Luminosity refers to the degree of reflection of a certain colour shade. White surfaces (degree of reflection = 100%) reflect a great deal of light; dark surfaces (degree of reflection = 0%) absorb much light. In front of a neutral white background, colours appear differently than if placed in contrast with other colours. Here too the principle applies that the greater the colour contrast, the more intensive the luminance.

Examples of surfaces and colour shades with reference to the degree of reflection:
Wood, white coated 84%
Solnhofen slab 50%
Wood, pale fir 50%
Wood, oak, light 33%
Concrete, light 32%
Asphalt, dry 20%
Red brick/tile 18%
Wood, oak, dark 18%
Dark clinker 10%
Wood, walnut 8%
Asphalt, wet 5%

Lemon yellow 70%
Lime green 50%
Light blue 40–50%
Salmon pink 40%
Silver grey 35%
Orange 25–30%
Beige 25%
Grass green 20%
Scarlet red 16%
Turquoise blue 15%
Carmine red 10%
Violet 3%

1

2

1 Johannes Itten, *Die Begegnung*, 1916: even before the Bauhaus was founded, Johannes Itten had already used many of the subsequent hallmarks of Bauhaus art, including an abstract vocabulary of geometric shapes such as the circle, square and spiral, and light/dark contrast and varied colour schemes.

2 Casa Gilardi, Mexico City, 1975–77, Luis Barragan. Colour as a direct reflection of context, climate and vegetation and as an expression of regional architectural identity. The sun penetrating from the inner courtyard through yellow glass panes reinforces the yellow of the walls that lead to a new world of colour with red and blue surfaces.

3 Spatial effect and colour surfaces
Colour can enhance an interior or detract from it. By emphasising surfaces and transitions for orientation in a room, a rhythm is created that overlays room sequences. Likewise, colour can link functions and content and also create highlights.

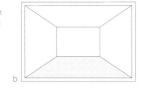
3a

a   A room with the same colour on all sides appears without direction and homogeneous. This causes individual structures, fitments or installations to merge into the background.

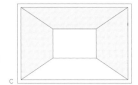
b

b   The coloured floor surrounded by light wall and ceiling surfaces conveys a sense of openness as well as a certain solidity and groundedness.

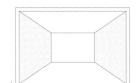
c

c   The floor surrounded by dark walls and ceiling creates the effect of a room that is focused on a central fixed point.

d

d   Coloured surfaces opposite each other create a focus on a central point. Vertical or horizontal areas are emphasised.

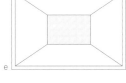

e   The coloured back wall is the clear reference surface and conveys a definite sense of enclosure as well as a signal effect.
e

f   Adjoining coloured walls convey a sense of enclosure with an impression of expansion to the top and bottom. The horizontal surfaces are emphasised and framed.

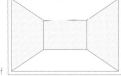

f

g   Floor and back wall form a seamless continuum. No angle is visible and the rear delimitation of the room appears to be dissolved.

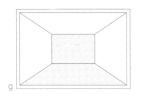

g

4

5

4 Davos sports centre, 1996, Gigon/Guyer with Adrian Schiess
Colour as an identification device controlled by the underlying architectural structure. The colours determined for the exterior space penetrate to the interior via the openings and are further supplemented by other colours.

5 Architects' offices near Madrid, 2009, SelgasCano
Zoning of functional areas with the help of colour and incoming daylight. The structure of the building recedes in favour of a strong linearity.

6 Apartment in Stockholm, 2008 Tham & Videgård Architects
The colour scheme emphasises the existing sight lines and creates a flowing transition between social and private spheres. The colour code is clearly identifiable and renders the visual barriers of solid room boundaries nearly superfluous.

6

LIGHT AND LIGHT DIRECTION I DAYLIGHT

Light is one of the most important design tools in architecture. Light and shadow are means of accentuating colour, texture, surfaces and proportions, or for blending them with the background. The three-dimensional sense of the room changes continually depending on the respective artificial and natural lighting situations – both in the course of the day and the seasons. Often direct and indirect light sources are deliberately used to create a certain atmosphere in a room, e.g. in sacral spaces or buildings with a representational role. ➔ 6, 7

The deliberate orientation and position of a room and its openings towards the sun is important in order to achieve the best possible utilisation of daylight and to protect the interior against overheating and glare, if necessary, by suitable construction measures. By using dedicated shading components, e.g. brise-soleil, it is possible to filter and reduce direct solar irradiation. ➔ SCALE, vol. 1,

Open | Close

A differentiation is made between daylight and artificial light, the colour of light and its direction – light from directly above, light from underneath objects, light from the side and glancing light – as well as between direct and indirect lighting.

In terms of quality (illumination and light colour) and atmosphere, natural light is superior to any artificial light. However, it is subject to the natural rhythms of day and night and of the seasons, and of the location itself; these cannot be influenced, so the design must take them into consideration.

The significance of daylight has many facets in architecture. While the requirement for thermal comfort demands that overheating is avoided, a view to the outside and sufficient brightness are important for psychological wellbeing. Another health aspect is the biological effect of daylight. The change in the spectral composition of daylight throughout the day (the blue component of light during the day stimulates vital functions and alertness, while the high content of yellow and red in the evening promotes relaxation and sleep) is used to enhance medical treatments in the health service and in care homes.

There is also an important energy aspect to the use of light: the more daylight can be used, the less energy has to be consumed for artificial lighting.

The perception of space and atmosphere depends heavily on the intensity of the lighting, and hence the design of the light direction. Most interior illumination takes place in the form of lateral lighting, the optimum use of which depends on several factors: the arrangement of the windows in relation to the points of the compass; the size and position of openings in the walls (full room height or with a lintel) and the degree of reflection from materials and surfaces. In addition to lighting from the side, which results in a poor distribution of light, it may be possible to use rooflights, subject to the geometry of the building and the design concept. Light from above is brighter – while the light entering through a side opening only includes about 33% of light emitted from the sky, a rooflight may admit up to 100%. Zenith brightness, room proportion and height, room reflection, the rooflight opening and its incline all have an impact on the optimum use and architectural feel. For uniform light distribution and a balanced light level for day/night and the seasons, directed light is required; direct and indirect glare and shading should be avoided.

The need for visual comfort – for even levels and distribution of daylight – varies according to the different uses of a room and the activities in it. Depending on the visual requirements for a certain activity, the standards specify certain levels of daylight illuminance.

Minimum requirements for the general provision of daylight are specified relative to the depth of a room, the size of the opening and the distance to the window. A measure for this is the daylight factor (D). A value of D > 3% for the daylight factor means that a work place is supplied with sufficient daylight for between 50% and 70% of the day. Where a room does not receive sufficient daylight, artificial lighting has to be added.

Daylight inside buildings is evaluated using the following parameters:
- Intensity of illumination and brightness
- Evenness of distribution
- Daylight ratio D_{min}/D_{max}
- Reflection
- Colour rendering
- Glare
- Room geometry
- Shading

Design criteria for the provision of daylight:
- DIN 5034 Daylight in interiors
- State standards for computer workstations
- D (daylight ratio) Dmin ≥ 2%
- G (evenness of distribution) D_{min}/D_{max} ≥ 1:6
- Ø window sizes for room depth (m) divided by floor area (%):
  ≤ 8 m, approx. 16-20%
  ≤ 8-11 m, approx. 25%
  ≤ 11-14 m, approx. 30%
  ≤ 14 m, approx. 35%

Sunny day - bright	100,000 lx
Sunny day - overcast	20,000 lx
Summer day - in the shade	10,000 lx
Illumination - operating theatre	10,000 lx
Winter day - overcast	3,500 lx
Office/room illumination	500 lx
Corridor illumination	100 lx
Street illumination	10 lx
Candlelight	1 lx
Night sky - full moon	0.25 lx
Night sky - new moon	0.001 lx
Night sky - cloudy	0.0001 lx

Illumination intensity
Illumination intensity is measured in lux (lx). The illumination intensity of certain interiors is determined by guidelines. ➔ p. 159

1 Solar irradiation consists of a direct part and a diffuse, non-directional part which consists of an even, low-contrast light (cloudy or overcast sky).
The maximum horizontal illumination intensity when the sun is shining is up to 100,000 lx; when the sky is overcast – depending on the weather – it is between 5,000 and 10,000 lx.

2 Illustration of the daily orbit of the sun at different times of the year. The most important factors dominating the amount of solar energy received are the conditions in the building, its location/latitude and the daily and annual variations in the position of the sun.

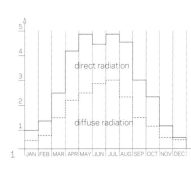

1 JAN FEB MAR APR MAY JUN JUL AUG SEP OCT NOV DEC

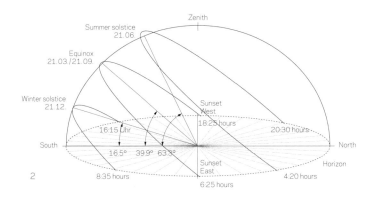

2

3 Factors influencing the amount of lateral daylight inside buildings:
DH = proportion of light from the sky – daylight incidence <α°
DV = proportion of area closed by building fabric
DR = amount of interior reflection
DH = degree of light transmission of the glazing (4–7)
τ = angle of daylight incidence
Window position and size

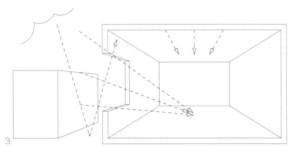

3

4 Room height, room proportions, size of opening and angle of the rooflight influence the amount of daylight received from above. The ideal illumination level is achieved with a ratio of 1:2 representing the distance between rooflights divided by the height of the room.

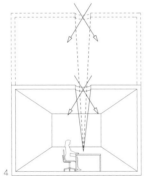
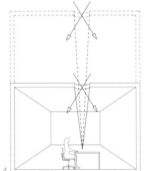

4

5 Light control and solar screening systems are used for the control of incoming light (depending on angle of incidence and lateral light/over-head light) to increase the light yield, especially for deeper rooms, and to avoid glare and overheating.

a Light control within the facade/coating of the glazing in order to filter unwanted parts of the radiation spectrum. Pale surfaces increase reflection and cause light to penetrate deeper into a room.

b Controlling the direction of sunlight with horizontal louvres/a curved reflective surface.

c Light from the roof illuminating the interior rooms, partly directly and partly indirectly via deflection from other surfaces. This effect is enhanced by bright surfaces.

5a

b

c

6 Moritz Church, Augsburg, 2013, John Pawson
The incidence of daylight into the pure white church interior provides illumination but also creates a sacral atmosphere.

7 Church of Light, Ibaraki, 1989, Tadao Ando
The daylight reaching the otherwise dark interior via a very specific, symbolic opening – the cross – creates a very dramatic effect in the church interior.

8 Skyspace, James Turrell
Light is used as a means of setting the scene and amplifying the perception and proportion of the walk-in installation, making use of the natural changes in daylight.

9 Exhibition pavilion of the Nordic countries, Venice, 1962, Sverre Fehn
Thin vertical slabs of light-coloured concrete are used for solar screening and as a construction grid. In order to retain the intensity of daylight, the entire building was lined with a material consisting of a mixture of white cement, sand and marble.

6

7

8

9

LIGHT AND LIGHT DIRECTION I ARTIFICIAL LIGHT

Artificial light can change the perception and atmosphere of a room without any physical impact. In contrast to natural light, which is subject to continual change depending on the time of day and the season, illumination by artificial light remains constant – although it does of course require a source of energy.

Artificial light may be used purely functionally to raise the level of brightness but, with its different facets and options, it can also become a means of creating an atmosphere and setting a scene.

The general lighting in a room provides an even background brightness, whereas task lighting is used wherever a specific task has to be carried out: at the desk, in the laboratory, in the kitchen etc. Accentuated lighting uses one or several adjustable light fittings to create spotlighting and contrasts: either for picking out a certain object, or for defining a certain area in a room through a difference in light intensity. The type of use of a room is one of the main criteria for selecting lighting. Depending on the activity taking place, a certain light intensity must be provided. Office work places (300 lux for work places close to windows and daylight, otherwise 500 lux) require a different level of illuminance compared to circulation zones and entrance areas (50 to 200 lux). Exhibition rooms may require temporary lighting arrangements as well as permanent ones and therefore are subject to a different range of criteria compared to restaurants and hotels, where the focus is on differentiated, individually switchable atmospheric lighting scenarios.

The quality of colour plays a very different role in the sale of goods than in a care situation, where task-related specific additional light sources increase the visual comfort of staff while the health-promoting effect of certain light spectrums is used for the benefit of patients.

In order to achieve a balanced lighting design, it is necessary to take into consideration the size of the room, the materials and textures, the openings and the natural lighting situation, as well as the correct positioning and selection of light fittings. It is possible to create the impression of a larger room by the even illumination of wall and ceiling surfaces – without the source of light being visible – when using pale, matt finishes. Technical factors that determine the selection of light fittings are the luminous efficiency and luminous flux, the colour of light emitted, its colour rendering, the expected service life, dimmability etc. The consumption of energy in a building and the quality of the interior climate are not only affected by the correct choice of light fitting and by appropriate user behaviour: the energy required and the amount of heat generated can also be optimised through intelligent design and the use of efficient control systems. In order to achieve improved cost-efficiency and dimensions for artificial light sources – incandescent lamps, discharge lamps and LEDs – development is constantly being carried out. Modern building management systems automatically regulate the balance between natural and artificial light, including shading mechanisms, according to programmed scenarios for certain times of day and seasonal conditions.

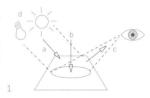

1

1 Interaction of technical parameters

a Luminous flux
Luminous flux (measured in lumen (lm)) describes the overall perceived power of light coming from a light source.

b Illumination intensity
Illumination intensity (measured in lux (lx)) is defined by the ratio of luminous flux falling on a surface over the size of that surface.

c Luminous intensity
Luminous intensity (measured in candela/m² (cd/m²)) refers to the power of light emitted from a surface, which can be a light source or a transmitter/reflector of light.

d Sources of light – electrical:
- Thermal radiators:
  incandescent lamps
  halogen lamps
- Discharge lamps:
  high-pressure lamps
  low-pressure lamps
- Electroluminescent lamps: light-emitting diodes (LEDs) organic light-emitting diodes (OLEDs)

Colour temperature ⟶ 3
The colour temperature of a light source is measured in kelvin (K).

Colour reproduction index Ra
This refers to the quality of colour reproduction of the light from a given light source in deviation from a reference light source.

Technical architectural selection criteria:
Luminous flux and light yield
Service life
Colour of light/colour rendering
Start-up time/re-ignition
Dimmability
Size and shape of light source
Method of light generation (ballast or transformer)

2 Museum of the Bavarian Kings, Hohenschwangau, 2011, Staab Architects/Licht Kunst Licht. The ornamentally decorated glass ceiling panels with integrated LED lights and special lenses to achieve the specific radiation effect were specially developed for this atmospheric background lighting.

2

3 Colour temperatures (Tep)
a Warm white light with a higher proportion of red generates a sense of comfort
Tep < 3,300 K
b Neutral white light generates the character of artificial light
Tep 3,300 K–5,000 K
c White daylight with an increased proportion of blue generates a cooler room atmosphere
Tep > 5,000 K
As a comparison:
60 W incandescent lamp: 2,680 K, average sunlight: 5,500 K

4 Combination of light sources
a By lighting the wall surfaces/coving it is possible to emphasise the delimitations of the room
b Accented light generates small light patterns
c Evenly illuminated surfaces provide diffused lighting

5 Types of glare:
a Direct glare from light fittings and/or solar irradiation.
b Reflected glare from surfaces or equipment, vertical and horizontal. Reduction of the reflected glare through indirect lighting.
c Mirror effect
By arranging lamps on two sides it is possible to avoid shadowing and the direct reflection of the light in the mirror.

6 Architect's office, Munich, 2012, Landau + Kindelbacher. The neutrality of the white room is further enhanced by the lighting scheme which includes downlights, accent lighting and coving lighting at the ceiling.

7 Schorndorf Town Hall, 2012, Ippolito Fleitz Group/Lichtwerke. A continuous acoustic ceiling, which is curved at the edge, integrates directional light fittings and downlights which can be controlled to provide the necessary additional illumination as required by the situation.

3a

b

c

4a

b

c

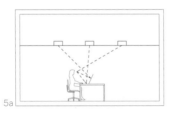
5a
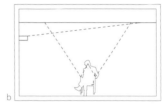
b
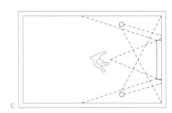
c

6

7

ACOUSTICS

ROOM ACOUSTICS

Room acoustics are a further factor in the comfort and usability of a room. This is particularly evident in rooms that are used by many people simultaneously, or where there is a certain expectation, such as quietness in sacral rooms. Poor acoustics render a room unusable. During the design stage it is necessary to check the volume, geometry, proportions and surfaces of a room with respect to acoustic properties. The room acoustics are determined by the materials and surfaces used in the room; these can be either an integrated part of the fabric or inserted as an additional measure. A general rule is that the softer and more porous a material is, the more airborne sound it can absorb. However, any given material will react differently to different frequency ranges. Sound can be directed and its effect influenced by a wide range of variously shaped ceiling and wall structures: diffusers and reflectors. This is particularly important in concert halls, where finely tuned and controllable room acoustics are crucial.

NOISE CONTROL

The arrangement of rooms in relation to each other has an effect on the amount of noise they are exposed to. Depending on the function of adjoining rooms, the building components involved need to comply with certain requirements. For example, in apartment blocks the requirements for an apartment door are more stringent than those for a door between individual rooms.
It is therefore necessary to define the hierarchy of requirements for building components at an early stage. The construction of elements such as floors, ceilings and walls and their joining details must be designed with a view to avoiding sound transmission to adjoining rooms or other facilities. This can be achieved by inserting joints for decoupling adjoining building components, by air layers, or by elastic materials as separating layers.

AIRBORNE SOUND AND IMPACT SOUND

Generally, a distinction is made between two types of sound: airborne sound, which – originating from one or several sources – spreads in all directions, and impact sound, which is transmitted by a building component following the impact from a mechanical force. The impact sound is not audible in the building component itself, but when emitted from surfaces it is converted into airborne sound and becomes audible. A special form of impact sound is that caused by footfall. There are several options for improving footfall sound insulation: de-coupling building components; increasing the weight per unit area of the separating floor/ceiling; installation of resilient floor finishes or floating floor constructions on the structural floor. ⟶ Chapter 2, Floor

SOUND ABSORPTION

The term 'sound absorption' refers to the attenuation of sound energy when sound waves impact on surfaces in a room. By modifying the sound absorption surface it is possible to influence the reverberation time and thereby improve the room acoustics. This is most commonly done by cladding ceilings and walls with absorption panels. A distinction is made between two types, which are effective for different frequencies: absorbers and resonators. Absorbers consist of mineral and organic fibrous materials, foam plastics or textile curtains, which are available in a range of different forms. Resonators are made up of enclosed or partially open air spaces, which can be penetrated by the sound waves and thereby absorb the sound energy. With a combination of these two types of absorbers it is possible to cover the entire audible frequency range.

The German standard DIN 4109 (Sound insulation in buildings) defines minimum requirements for sound insulation in buildings. ⟶ Appendix, p. 160, 168

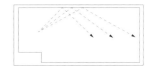

1 Types of sound transmission and degree of absorption
a Airborne sound
b Impact sound
c Degree of absorption

2 The effect of the room shape and reflector surfaces in a concert hall

3 Agora Theatre, Lelystad, 2007, UNStudio. Prismatic folded surfaces in positions which have been determined by simulation can ensure a balanced listening experience at every seat, in spite of the different acoustic requirements – from theatre to opera.

4 Ørestad College, Copenhagen, 2007, 3XN Architects. The design idea for this school building aims for a new flexibility and openness. Agreeable room acoustics are created using various absorption surfaces such as a multi-layered acoustic plaster system, a suspended acoustic ceiling, and the 'resting islands' with fitted carpet and bean bags.

5 Room acoustics are assessed on the basis of human hearing. With the help of integrated or added measures it is possible to modify and optimise rooms with respect to their acoustic properties. It is also possible to play background noise in order to mask individual sounds.

a Sound-absorbing wall cladding
b Sound-absorbing ceiling lining made of gypsum panels with random perforations
c Expanded metal grid ceiling
d Multi-layer floor structure with impact sound insulation and textile floor covering
e Undulating wall elements with felt surface
f Acoustic panels with fabric lining
g Flat sound-attenuation element consisting of a soft material, suitable for digital printing
h Suspended acoustic element, either flat or in the form of vertical slats or honeycomb elements
i Adaptation of the room geometry
j Curtain
k Upholstery
l Carpet

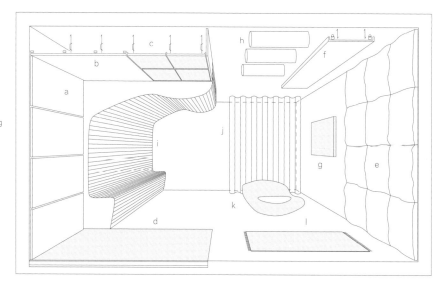

6 Sound pressure level
The sound pressure level (dB) denotes the level of audible sound. Guide values for sound pressure levels depend on the type of activity taking place in a room.

Sound levels (dB) in different environments with reference to guide values

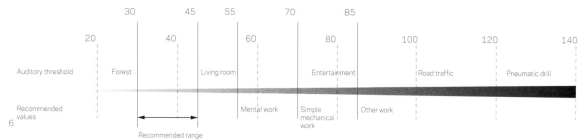

7 Reverberation
The acoustic properties of a room are determined by its reverberation time T (s) and the degree of sound absorption (α). The reverberation time defines the time it takes a sound to reduce its level by 60 dB after emission of the sound has ended.

a Reverberation time
b Optimum average reverberation times for various room functions depending on room volume
c Curve of the frequency of optimum reverberation times for speech (0.5–1 s) and music (1–2 s).

8 Architect's office, Munich, 2006, Landau + Kindelbacher. Acoustic panels with a perforated surface and a sound-absorbing fibre-fleece backing regulate the room acoustics. In addition, the large pin-board walls consisting of soft fibreboard have a sound-absorbing effect.

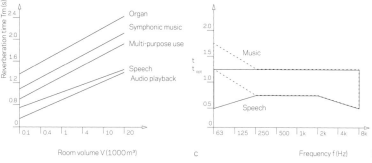

ROOM CLIMATE

Although people's sense of comfort varies from person to person, some of the main contributing factors, such as temperature and relative humidity can be measured. A good room climate is determined by parameters such as lighting, hygiene and psychological factors and thermal comfort. It is an essential prerequisite for users to be able to concentrate and work, but also for their health and comfort. Because the perception of these factors is subjective there is no uniform measure but only a range of guide values that can be applied.

The quality of air depends on a balance between the factors of air temperature, relative humidity and air speed. When the difference between the air temperature in a room and the surface temperature of the enclosing elements (floor, wall, ceiling, windows and doors) is too great, the resulting air movement (owing to the convection of air between elements with different temperatures) can soon be perceived as uncomfortable. Ambient temperature and relative humidity – both when it is too dry and too humid – affects people's sense of comfort.

Likewise, air changes have an impact on the occupants' wellbeing. Inappropriate ventilation habits by users can be just as counter-productive as the installation of materials and technical equipment with emissions that a detrimental to health. Where the natural boundaries are reached, man-made heating and cooling devices are introduced to control the room climate. ⟶ SCALE, vol. 2, Heat | Cool, ⟶ Chapters 2, Floor, and 4, Ceiling

Intelligent concepts reduce technical solutions to a reasonable minimum and integrate technical installations so that, for the most part, they cannot be seen. Environmental protection and increases in the cost of energy lead to a focus on renewable energy sources and a re-appreciation of the qualities of natural materials (e.g. clay) and their storage capacity and filter functions. ⟶ 8 Classic products, such as radiators, can have a negative impact on the flexibility of a room. This negative impact is avoided in alternative developments, such as wall and underfloor heating, or by activating the thermal mass of materials. Although these devices may cost more to purchase and install, these disadvantages have to be weighed up against the greater flexibility achieved – e.g. in positioning furniture. Advances in technology offer many possibilities that can be helpful in refurbishment projects of existing and listed buildings where costly energy upgrades are required to make these buildings viable again. ⟶ 7

The relationship between room volume and enclosing envelope is as important as the proportion of open and closed areas. The more compact a room is, the greater is the influence of the surface temperature on its room quality. Conversely, in order to achieve a similar degree of comfort in large rooms with high ceilings, the surface temperature has to be raised artificially or the area has to be subdivided into zones with the help of fitments and a choice of surfaces. Conventional devices can be supplemented by multifunctional elements such as radiators that double up as furniture elements, or cooling panels that provide thermal comfort and also integrate lighting, acoustic and fire safety functions. ⟶ 9

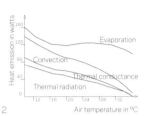

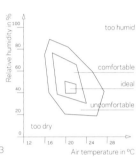

2   The air of a room that has been heated by the body can be cooled using controllable devices (fresh air intake, cooling ceiling, air conditioning system etc.) to regulate the room climate and contribute to comfort levels.
It is also possible to heat rooms to an average temperature of 20-22 °C without visible apparatus in floors and walls.

Air temperature (°C)	Relative humidity (%)
20	80
22	70
24	62
26	55

3   Recommended relative humidity depending on the air temperature

Prerequisites for a good room climate:
Perceived temperature: 18-21 °C
Room air temperature: 20-22 °C
Wall surface temperature: 17-19 °C
Floor temperature: 18-20 °C
Air movement, maximum: 0.2 m/sec
Temperature differentials in vertical direction not more than: 3 °C
Ceiling temperature: 18-20 °C
Relative humidity approx.: 50%

Heat is generated by solar radiation, work/technical equipment as well as by people, both resting and during activities:
Resting, sleeping: 60 W
Light work, sitting: 120 W
Sports activities: up to 500 W

Air change recommended for hygienic reasons:
0.5-1.0 change/h in living rooms and bedrooms
4-5 changes/h in internal sanitary rooms
0.5-25 changes/h in kitchens (peak loads)

External factors:
Climate zone
Orientation
Solar irradiation

Ratio of open to closed surfaces:
Construction method
Material properties
Finishing standards

Arrangement of heating surfaces:
Convectors
Panel heating
Radiators

Internal factors:
Type of use
Intensity of activity
Clothing, age, gender

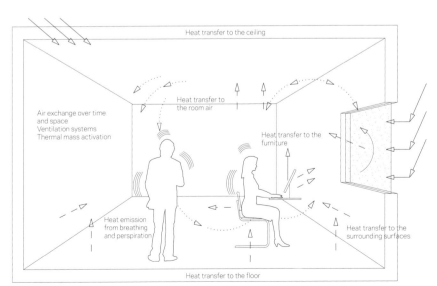

1   Heating/cooling schematic diagram

4 Room climate – controlled by:
a Material: surfaces with air-enhancing properties (plaster, paint, textiles etc.)
b Nature: ability of plants/water to clean the air
c Natural thermals: using the physical flow characteristics resulting from temperature differentials between interior and exterior and within the building

5 Room air – controlled by:
a Manual, individual controls
b Ventilation via floors, ceilings and installations
c Using the energy cycle in addition to simple air ventilation, i.e. ground heat exchanger, heat recovery etc.

6 Room temperature – controlled by:
a Panel systems for heating and cooling
b Multifunctional heating/cooling elements such as ceiling sails/panels etc.
c Using the natural storage mass of building components, e.g. brickwork and clay

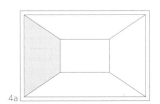
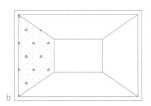
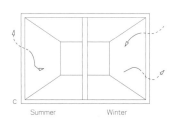

Summer   Winter

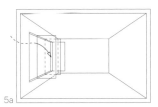
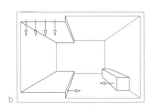
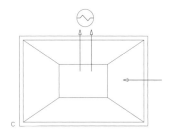

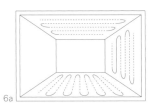
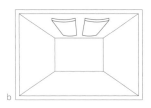
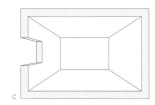

7 The wall panel heating in a drywall system heats the room air through comfortable radiated heat and can be used both in timber construction and in refurbishments and loft conversions with sloping panels.

8 House in Deitingen, 2009, Spaceshop Architects. Control of room climate through the selection of material: Clay construction with straw added to the prepared clay, produced without shuttering.

9 AachenMünchener Versicherung, Aachen, 2011, kadawittfeldarchitektur. Increasing the thermally active surfaces by inserting a ceiling sail increases absorption and is also useful for the installation of light fittings, sprinkler system, fire alarm etc.

FURNISHING | ZONING
FLOOR CONSTRUCTION AND FINISHES

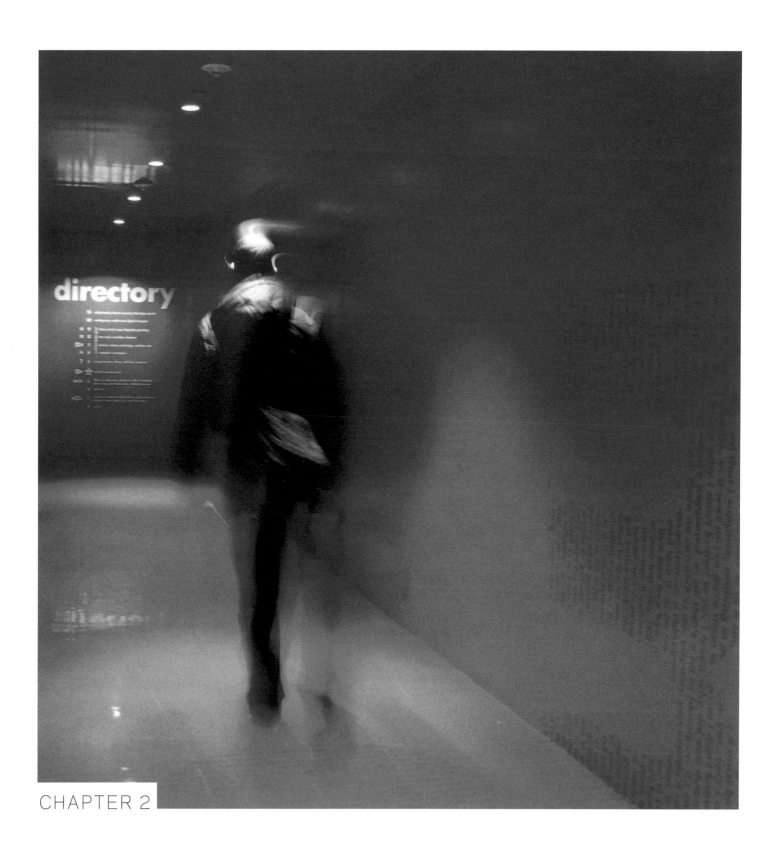

CHAPTER 2

REQUIREMENTS

The floor of a room creates an important first impression. The actual physical contact created by stepping on to a floor finish leads to a very direct perception. In addition to the visual impression, we primarily perceive the tactile, acoustic, visual and also the olfactory properties of a floor surface. Floor surfaces always have to be considered together with the supporting floor construction – which has be designed for the specific requirements – and the structural floor. p. 54

New construction methods and technologies have spawned a nearly limitless variety of products, which provides an appropriate floor finish for all kinds of applications. The selection of a floor finish is determined not only by the intended design concept and the overall atmospheric feel, but also by technical and functional requirements. For example, parquet and wooden floor finishes are suited to use in the home, whereas resilient floor finishes are better for offices, and screeds are the ideal material for surfacing the floor of production facilities. The advantages and disadvantages of a floor finish must be considered in relation to the intended use, and also in terms of ecological parameters such as emissions into the air indoors, compatibility of adhesives and recyclability of the material.

REQUIREMENTS

In addition to atmospheric considerations, the floor designer has to answer a number of functional questions: What is the intended and possible height of the floor construction? How often is a room used, and how many people will use it daily? What type of wear will the floor be exposed to? Will the flooring be exposed to special loads, for example special machinery or equipment? How quickly will the floor become soiled and how well can it be cleaned?

The thermal comfort of a room, for example, is significantly affected by the floor finish. Owing to their much lower thermal conductivity, textile floor finishes are perceived by users as being much warmer than stone flooring. As with other building components, the measurable parameters for classifying a floor are its thermal resistance and its thermal conductivity. These have to be weighed up against each other according to the situation: for example, any floor finishes installed over underfloor heating should not have too high a thermal resistance.
As with other building components, the fire assessment classification of a floor finish and the entire floor construction is determined by the classifications contained in DIN EN 13501 and DIN 4102. Another design aspect is the protection of the building fabric against dampness.

Consideration has to be given to sealing the floor as a whole against rising damp and in wet rooms, in accordance with DIN 18195 Waterproofing of buildings. Noise control, above all footfall sound insulation , can be optimised through the selection of a suitable floor construction. The impact sound improvement factor of a floor covering indicates its ability to minimise impact sound. Smooth floor coverings such as laminates and lino only achieve a reduction of about 5 to 15 dB, whereas textile floor finishes achieve between 25 and 35 dB. The provisions on sound insulation in buildings in DIN 4109 however represent only minimum requirements and should be bettered. Chapter 1, p. 46

All textile and resilient floor finishes, as well as laminates, should carry a CE mark. 1 This certification mark, which is applied uniformly throughout Europe, provides the manufacturer's information on various physical properties of a flooring material. Users are given information on fire resistance, the content of pentachlorophenol (PCP), the emission of formaldehyde, the waterproof properties, the friction resistance, the electrostatic properties and the thermal conductivity of the material. EN 14041-2011 contains the provisions for testing such materials and the formalities of CE marking.

Flooring materials used in public and commercial premises must be slip-resistant. To clarify the issue, all flooring materials available in the market are divided into various slip resistance groups and two application areas. The flooring of work rooms and work areas with greater slip hazard (DIN 51130) is assigned to slip-resistance classes (R 9 to R 13), while that of wet-loaded barefoot areas (DIN 51097) is classified as either A, B or C. When choosing floor finishes for private residences, it is advisable to look for slip-resistant finishes even though this is not a legal requirement. p. 163, 164

1   Standard symbols for floor coverings

a   Duty: domestic
b   Duty: commercial
c   Comfort value
d   Fade resistance
e   Fire resistance
f   Slip resistance
g   Suitable for underfloor heating
h   Suitable for damp rooms
i   Anti-static
j   Electrical conductivity
k   Sound absorption
l   Impact sound insulating
m   Suitable for castors
n   Suitable for stairs
o   Fray resistant
p   Dimensional stability

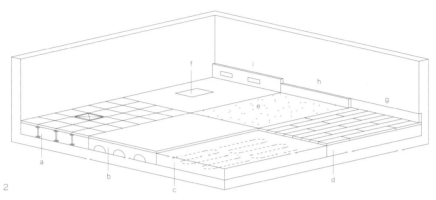

2

2   Types of floor construction
a   Raised floor
b   Cavity floor
c   Underfloor heating
d   Floor with wood covering
e   Floor with textile covering
f   Inspection opening
g   Skirting board integrated in wall
h   Skirting board surface-mounted
i   Skirting used for services

3   Formats impacting on design
a   Tile and joint dimensions
b   Dimensions of floor boards
c   Panel dimensions
d   Width of rolls

4   Kustermann Park, Munich, 2011,
Oliv Architects. In the canteen of
an office building, the timber floor
laid at a different level serves to
distinguish a private seating area in
the open-plan space.

5   Audi Terminal, Munich, 2009,
Allmann Sattler Wappner Architects. Outside the racetrack, the
banked corner theme is adopted
for presentation of the vehicles.
A homogeneous surface rises up
from the ground such as could
be achieved with asphalt, extending
into a dynamically shaped wall.

DIMENSIONS AND INSTALLATION PROPERTIES

The production and delivery formats of a material define its suitability for installation in a room. With homogeneous floor finishes that are installed in situ – such as
terrazzo – and with floor coatings, one only needs to provide the appropriate expansion joints, whereas with all
other types of flooring, the material properties and production method determine the dimensions and hence the
layout or joint patterns in a room. In the latter case, the
direction of a layout can have the effect of making a room
look larger or smaller. The transition between floor and
wall also has to be taken into consideration, for example
with stone or tile flooring, in coordination with any objects
that have to be installed.

CLASSIFICATION

In addition to the distinction made in the DIN standard
between hard, resilient and textile floor finishes, they can
be classified further according to their raw material, the
production method, or the installation method.

3a   b   c   d

4

5

FLOOR CONSTRUCTION

As a rule, floor constructions consist of several layers which perform different functions and which are designed to suit the intended use of the room. Design criteria for the construction details are defined by the requirements for protection against dampness, for sound and thermal insulation and any installations that may have to be accommodated, as well as structural and functional loads. For this reason, the flooring material always has to be considered in combination with the structura floor. There are three distinct functional levels defining the various layers: structural floor, substructure and floor finish. In addition, it may be necessary to take into account an existing or required ceiling lining beneath the structural floor. ⮕ **Chapter 4, p. 96 seqq.**

STRUCTURAL FLOOR, EVENNESS TOLERANCE

The condition of an existing structural floor can vary greatly. Structural systems can be roughly divided into solid and lightweight decks, such as timber beam floors. The main criteria for the quality of the construction are the amount of deflection, the connecting details with adjoining building components and the surface properties of the structural floor. If a floor or slab is in contact with the ground, the substructure must be protected against rising damp.

When refurbishing an existing building, it is possible that the structural floor is very uneven, or perhaps not altogether level, so that this defect has to be compensated for by adding either loose or applied material.

In new buildings too, the structural tolerances permit a degree of unevenness that may have to be compensated for when building up the floor.

DIN 18202 Tolerances in buildings specifies the angle and evenness tolerances for the execution of buildings and building components. ⮕ **Tab. 1, Fig. 2, p. 162**

MOISTURE PROTECTION

Floor structures must be appropriately sealed to protect them against moisture. This is particularly true of floors that are in contact with the ground and floors of sanitary facilities. A damp-proofing layer protects the structure from dampness, which may penetrate from the ground or adjoining building components, or which may be the result of the use of water in the room, particularly in sanitary areas. The type and source of the dampness defines the position of the damp-proofing layer within the floor construction. DIN 18195 Waterproofing of buildings contains provisions for the different types of exposure of floors in contact with the ground; the Additional Technical Contract Conditions (ZTV) for tilers can be used to specify requirements for interiors.

SUBSTRUCTURE

The task of the substructure is to provide a loadbearing base for the floor finish and ensure that imposed loads are evenly distributed. The substructure is composed of different functional layers. The complexity of the construction depends on the existing structural floor and the functional and building physics requirements for the floor. Each layer performs one or more functions within the overall construction. In this way it is possible to improve impact sound insulation, to introduce damp-proofing in sanitary areas, to optimise the distribution of loads on the structural floor and to level out any discrepancies in the shell construction. In sanitary areas where much water is used ('wet rooms'), it is also necessary to provide a fall, normally of 1.5 to 2%. As a rule, this fall is created as a monolithic screed directly on the structural floor beneath the insulation layer. Alternatively, it is also possible to install sloping insulation.

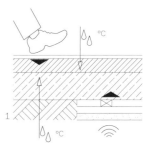

1 Requirements for floor/ceiling construction
The construction of floors depends on a range of functional and building physics requirements. The layers of the floor structure must meet these requirements. Depending on the situation, the following layers may be required:
– levelling layer
– layer to create fall
– damp-proofing layer
– thermal insulation
– sound insulation
– separating layer
– vapour check/vapour barrier
– load distribution layer

2 Haus PQ, Deggendorf, 2012, Hiendl_Schineis Architektenpartnerschaft. The connection to the natural world through a framed opening continues in the minimalist interior of the house in timber construction; warm larch wood planks are used to line floor, wall and ceiling.

3 Visitor Information Centre at Messel mine, 2011, Landau + Kindelbacher. In order to achieve the effect of a rough shell in fairfaced concrete, all the functional and aesthetic requirements for the floor have to be determined prior to the start of construction.

2

3

4 Timber floor: The construction of floors based on timber floor joists varies according to whether the joists are fully exposed, partially exposed or concealed, and has to meet the functional and building physics requirements.
a   Timber joist floor with joists exposed; the insulation layer is used for the integration of installations.
b   Timber joist floor with joists partially concealed; covering layer: floorboards on bearers with loose perlite between the bearers
c   Timber joist floor with a floating screed construction and a continuous plasterboard ceiling lining underneath

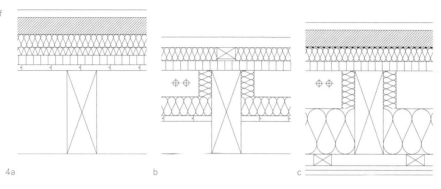

4a   b   c

5 Reinforced concrete floor: As with timber joist floors, the detailing of layers is primarily determined by building physics requirements. The stricter the sound insulation requirements, the more layers are needed.
a   Concrete floor with fair-faced ceiling finish and screed on a separating layer
b   Reinforced concrete floor with plaster ceiling and floating screed
c   Reinforced concrete floor with floating screed and a suspended ceiling with sound insulation layer

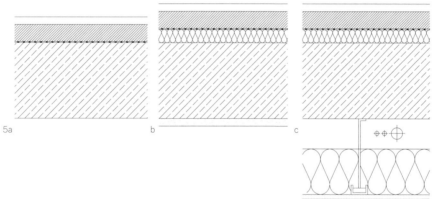

5a   b   c

IMPACT SOUND
In the detailing of a floor construction, the reduction of impact sound is an important objective. On its own, a floor finish with a good sound insulation value does not normally achieve sufficient improvement in impact sound insulation. Laying screed with a high weight per unit area increases the sound insulation value, but as a rule it is preferable to install a floating floor construction of several layers. This involves laying impact sound insulation beneath the screed, which reduces the transmission of sound to the structural floor. Suitable materials are between 15 and 60 mm thick, have different densities and are available as slabs or as rolled material. Mineral and plant-based insulation materials are commonly used, as are rigid foam slabs made of polystyrene or polyurethane. It is also important to decouple the lateral contact to vertical elements by inserting insulation strips of at least 5 mm thickness. In existing buildings, the floor construction is often made of timber; when its sound insulation is improved as part of a refurbishment or modernisation programme, the floor surface usually ends up higher. This means that connecting elements such as doors have to be adjusted. Where this cannot be done, it is possible to install rubber granulate or rubber foam mats, which separate the flooring from the substrate and reduce the risk of crack formation. → p. 71, fig. 3 In residential developments, floating screed is a standard solution, owing to the strict sound insulation standards.

TRANSITIONS
Expansion joints, the junctions between the floor and adjoining building elements, and the joints between different flooring materials all have to be taken into account when designing the flooring substructure. It may be possible to avoid a threshold at the junction between different materials, for example between textile flooring and wooden parquet, by combining different substructures. Where there are big differences in the combined thickness of the substructure and floor finish, it may be appropriate to counteract this by providing a corresponding change of level in the structural floor. → p. 56, p. 72

SCREED AS SUBFLOOR

The term 'screed' in floor construction refers to the layer that prepares the structural floor for the actual floor finish. This layer evens out any tolerances and unevenness in the structural floor and helps to spread imposed loads. Screed is laid either directly on the structural floor, or on a separating membrane, or in floating construction on insulation layers for impact sound decoupling; it can either be used directly as the base for a variety of floor coverings, or it can be mechanically processed or coated to serve as the final surface ⟶ p. 60. It follows that screeds play a vital role in all floor constructions. They do, however, fulfil a range of different tasks and they have to be modified to suit the intended purpose. DIN 18560 Floor screeds in construction and DIN EN 13813 regulate the material requirements and installation of screed. Screeds are distinguished on the basis of their construction, the manufacturing method and the binder. Depending on the binder used, reference is made to: cement screed (CT), calcium sulphate or anhydrite screed (CA), mastic asphalt screed (AS), synthetic resin screed (SR) and magnesite screed (MA). ⟶ Tab. 3, p. 162

CONSTRUCTION

There are three principle construction methods for screed. In bonded screed construction ⟶ 1a the screed is applied directly on to the loadbearing floor. In order to prevent the formation of cracks or the penetration of dampness, it is possible to install screed on a separating membrane ⟶ 1b. This layer is comparatively thin so that the screed is fully supported by the loadbearing floor, although it is decoupled by the separating membrane. The screed can be used directly or in combination with a subsequent coating. Another option is to install the screed on a layer of insulation. This is referred to as floating screed. ⟶ 1c In order to prevent impact sound being transferred to adjoining building elements, the screed is separated from these by foam perimeter strips. Special forms of screed are those integrated with heating systems. In order to prevent any damage from thermal expansion and contraction, a continuous surface must be no larger than 40 m², with the proportion of length to width not greater than 2:1 and no side longer than 8 m. This means that movement joints may have to be provided to limit the size of fields, which in turn affects the appearance; it may also be appropriate to provide dummy joints to accommodate any cracks where this fits in with the design. Where there are joints in the building fabric, a similar joint also needs to be provided in the screed. ⟶ 2a

PRODUCTION

In the production of screed, a distinction is made between wet and dry processes. Wet screed can be supplied ready-mixed to the building site, or produced on site. Ready-mixed screed can be pumped and – due to the addition of appropriate admixtures – is largely self-levelling. By contrast, screed mixed on site is rather stiffer in consistency and is installed by laying it, levelling the surface, compacting and smoothing it. Dry screed is installed in the form of prefabricated material slabs that come in modular sizes. ⟶ 4

NOMINAL THICKNESS
AND FLEXURAL STRENGTH/HARDNESS CLASS

Depending on the composition of the screed, it is subdivided into different hardness classes, which are specified in DIN 18560. The minimum nominal thickness of screed is defined in relation to its hardness class (DIN EN13813 Bending tensile strength class or hardness class). The nominal thickness varies depending on the type of screed and its intended use. For example, mastic asphalt only requires a minimum thickness of 25 mm, whereas a cement screed of hardness class F4 requires at least 45 mm. For higher point loads and spread loads, the minimum thickness must be increased appropriately. The standard short designation for screed is made up of the code for the type of screed and the strength/hardness class; for example, the screed designation DIN 18560 - CT - C30 - F4 - T35 refers to: cement screed (CT) with a compressive strength class C30, flexural strength class F4 and screed on separating layer, nominal thickness 35 mm (T35).

CURING REQUIREMENT

Before screeds are covered with a floor finish, they have to cure and dry out so as not to damage the flooring. Possible damage includes the flooring separating (due to vapour pressure), discolouration or, (in the case of too-rapid drying) cupping. The screed will be ready for a flooring material when it has reached its nominal strength and has dried out to the degree specified for the flooring material to be applied. The degree of moisture content is normally measured with a CM device (calcium carbide method).
Owing to the time pressure on construction sites, so-called fast-setting screeds are becoming more and more popular. These screeds cure faster and are ready for a covering material in a shorter time, owing to the addition of a mixture of binding agents, such as calcium alumina cement and Portland cement, or calcium sulphate. However, the processing time (including levelling) is not reduced below roughly 30 minutes. ⟶ Tab. 3, p. 162

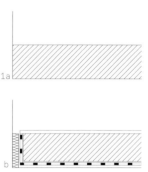

1   Different types of screed construction
a   Monolithic screed
b   Screed on a separating layer
c   Screed on an insulation layer (floating screed)
d   Dry screed consisting of chipboard panels, gypsum slab or cement-based panels on an insulation layer

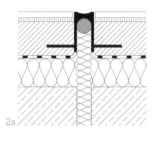

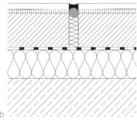

2 Floating screed joint details
a Construction joint continuing in the screed
b Movement joint

3 Installation of a ready-mixed screed on a separating layer provides a smooth and level base for further finishes/processing.

4 Installation of dry screed panels on a level surface or layer of levelling material. The dry screed can be walked on immediately following installation; no curing time is required as with wet screed.

5 The installation of mastic asphalt has to be carried out while the material is liquid, which means that it is hot and therefore requires the substrate and any installations to be heat-resistant.

CEMENT SCREED

The most frequently used type of screed is cement screed. It has very good strength values and – in its cured state – can be used internally and externally as it is not affected by dampness. It consists of standard cement, sand, water and optionally granular aggregate. When hard aggregates have been added, cement screed is called granolithic screed. Owing to its high water content it takes a long time to dry out and, without admixtures, requires 20 to 30 days to fully cure.

CALCIUM SULPHATE SCREED
(ANHYDRITE SCREED)

Calcium sulphate screed can be exposed to load soon after installation, it is low-stress, keeps its form, is free from cracks and has low shrinkage characteristics. If it is installed with underfloor heating, the heating can be used within seven days. Assuming that the drying-out process can proceed unhindered, the screed is ready for a floor finish within one to two weeks. It consists of the components anhydrite, sand or gravel, water and any admixtures. The disadvantage of calcium sulphate screed is its susceptibility to dampness. It therefore cannot be used in external applications. In areas where dampness must be expected, the screed needs to be sealed or a vapour barrier has to be installed.

MASTIC ASPHALT SCREED

The installation of mastic asphalt screed is independent of the external temperature and weather. It can be walked on after just one day. It is impervious to water vapour diffusion, offers good impact sound insulation and relatively thin layers can support loads. It is installed in thicknesses of between 25 and 40 mm. Mastic asphalt screed is composed of bitumen, limestone or quartz sand filler, natural sand and stone chippings. The material must be laid manually in liquid form, which requires temperatures of between 200 and 250°C. This means that the materials and installations it comes into contact with have to be heat-resistant. Due to its high degree of elasticity in the cured state, it is very suitable for refurbishment applications.

SYNTHETIC RESIN SCREED

Screeds made of synthetic resin are highly wear-resistant, are not susceptible to dampness, frost and many chemicals, and have a high electrical resistance. They have a short curing time (can be walked on after 8 to 12 hours, suitable for exposure to mechanical loads after 3 to 8 days), can be installed almost without any joints and have low shrinkage characteristics. Synthetic resin screed consists of synthetic resin mortar and a synthetic reaction resin as binder. The cost of the material and its installation is very high because producing the material composition is an expensive process and the material must have certain temperature conditions during installation and the curing period.

MAGNESITE SCREED

Originally, around 1900, magnesite screed was a mixture including wood flour and small pieces of wood which was installed as 'xylolite screed' over timber beam floors. It is still used in this form today in ecological refurbishment projects. Magnesite screed can achieve great strength and can be used as the top flooring layer, for example in industrial and commercial buildings where the floors are exposed to particularly high loads. As magnesite screeds are electrically conductive, they are suitable as floors with antistatic properties. As a binder they contain caustic magnesia, usually in combination with an aqueous solution of magnesium chloride. As an aggregate, organic and/or inorganic materials are used. The screed readily accepts pigment for colouration. In view of the fact that it is susceptible to dampness, it can be used neither in external applications nor in sanitary and wet rooms; furthermore, it reacts aggressively with metals.

DRY SCREED

Dry screeds (or prefabricated screeds) are manufactured from prefabricated floor panels, which are installed with a structural edge connection to form a structural layer that can distribute imposed load. The materials used include plasterboard panels, gypsum fibre panels, wood-based panels, cement-bonded woodchip panels and sandwich screed panels with insulation. They can be installed on a substructure, on a layer of dry-poured material to even out differences in level, or directly on the structural (or existing) floor. Because dry screeds do not require any drying time (in contrast to wet screeds), they can be covered with flooring material immediately following installation. Furthermore, because the installation of dry screed does not involve any water, it is often used in the refurbishment of existing buildings. Compared to conventional screeds, dry screed panels are less thick; this can be an advantage, but it also means that the loadbearing capacity is reduced and less impact sound insulation is achieved. Another important factor is that many of the materials used are susceptible to dampness.

UNDERFLOOR HEATING SYSTEMS

A special form of floating screed is that with underfloor heating, i.e. screed incorporating heating pipes or mats for heating the room above. The pipes may be installed within the loadbearing layer, or beneath it. A distinction is made between two systems, depending on the heating elements used. In the hot water option, hot water pipes are laid in loops in the floor; in the electrical option, heating mats are installed. Hot water systems are regulated by DIN EN 1264, and electrical installations by DIN EN 50559, both in combination with DIN 18560-2. A distinction is made between different types of installation, depending on where the heating elements are positioned in the screed.

WET-INSTALLED HOT WATER SYSTEM

In this system, the heating pipes are installed in the screed. The pipes are held in position by spacers, or special installation mats, above the insulation layer and are enclosed all round by the screed – usually ready-mixed screed. The heating pipes may optionally be installed in a levelling screed, also known as a protective screed. The final screed layer, which has a load distribution function, has to be separated from the levelling screed by two layers of separating membrane. 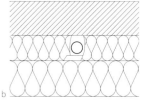 2

DRY-INSTALLED HOT WATER SYSTEM

In this system, the heating elements are installed in the insulation layer beneath the screed, which can also be combined with a dry screed. One variant consists of dry screed panels with grooves cut into them, into which the heating pipes are laid before being covered with a thin layer of wet ready-mixed screed. ⟶ 6

The thickness, strength classes and hardness classes of screed used with underfloor heating are specified in DIN 18560. The thickness of coverage above the heating pipes must be at least 25 mm. The screed temperature must not exceed 45°C in the case of mastic asphalt screeds, and 55°C in the case of calcium sulphate and cement screeds. Once the screed has fully cured ⟶ p. 56 it must be heated up twice as part of a recorded test procedure. The first heating cycle is a functional test, and in the second cycle the screed must be heated up to test whether it is ready to be covered. If the guide value for moisture content has been reached, which can be measured using the CM method, the floor finish can be laid.

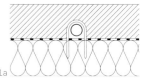
1a

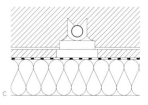
b

c

1 Details of pipe fixings for underfloor heating installed in wet screed
a Heating tube held by brackets on thermal insulation and separating membrane
b Heating tube in castellated profile panel
c Heating tube fixed to carrier mesh

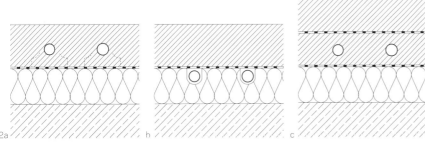
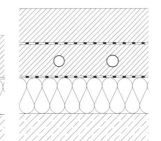

2a b c

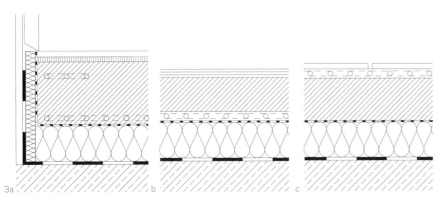

3a b c

ELECTRIC UNDERFLOOR HEATING SYSTEMS

In electric underfloor heating systems, the heating elements are installed either directly under the floor covering, within the screed, or beneath it. A distinction is made between electric underfloor storage heating, which heats up the screed during the night and gives off the stored heat to the room during the course of the day, and direct electric underfloor heating, which gives off the generated heat directly, although this latter method is rarely used these days because of the inefficient use of energy.

FLOOR FINISHES

Most floor finishes are suitable for installation over underfloor heating. The critical parameter of a flooring material governing its suitability is thermal resistance, which also determines the flow temperature of the heating system. A value of $0.15\,\text{m}^2\text{K/W}$ should not be exceeded, since otherwise too much heat escapes. It is therefore advisable to discuss the floor construction with the manufacturer. Stone, ceramic and resilient floor coverings have good values. Not all wood and textile floor coverings are suitable for installation over underfloor heating. They therefore have to be labelled accordingly by the manufacturer. In the case of wood parquet, it is necessary to use shear-resistant adhesive and to provide an expansion joint of at least 15 mm width all round the perimeter.

2 DIN 18560-2 distinguishes between three types of screed and heating screed:
a Heating tubes installed within the screed (installation type A1-3)
b Heating tubes installed beneath the screed (installation type B)
c Heating tubes in a protective screed layer (installation type C)

3 Installation options for electrical underfloor heating
a Electrical underfloor storage heating with direct heating around the edge
b Electrical underfloor storage heating
c Direct electrical heating under ceramic tiles

4 Heating loops installed in carrier mesh

5 Heating loops in a castellated profile panel on insulation layer

6 Heating loops in grooves cut into dry screed panels

4 5 6

SCREED AS FINISHING LAYER

Provided a screed has sufficient strength, it can also be used without an additional floor finish. This option is often used in industrial and commercial buildings. In recent years, however, owing to their homogeneous surface – which is easy to maintain – and appearance, these floors have also become common in residential and office buildings. In industrial applications, these floors are usually exposed to heavy mechanical loads, temperature fluctuations and frequently also chemicals, which means that they must hard-wearing and resistant to abrasion. Suitable screeds for these applications are primarily high-strength cement screeds, mastic asphalt screeds and screeds based on synthetic resin. For some purposes, their surfaces must have anti-slip properties, which is achieved, for example, by adding appropriate aggregate to the screed.

GROUND SCREED AND CONCRETE

Conventional screeds such as cement and calcium sulphate screeds, but also mastic asphalt screed and concrete, can be ground. The finished appearance depends on the aggregate used in the screed. It is also possible to use pigments to produce a coloured screed. In its type, hardness and composition, the screed should be specifically formulated for the subsequent grinding process and its use as a floor finish. The grinding process leads to silicification of the surface, making it harder and more robust. By sealing the floor with polyurethane, epoxy resin or brick oil, the surface becomes more resistant to the penetration of grease and liquids. However, with excessive sealing the screed will lose its natural character.

TERRAZZO FLOOR

Traditionally produced Terrazzo consists of broken marble, limestone or dolomite, with water and lime as binder, whereas modern methods usually use white or grey Portland cement. The floor is built up in two layers. On a concrete sub-base, a wet layer of 15 to 35 mm is applied, the thickness depending on the grain size and on the strength and load requirements; it is compacted by tamping or rolling and then divided into small panels in order to avoid shrinkage cracking. After it has cured, it is ground in several steps and the open pores are closed. Finally the floor is finished with wax, oil or polymer. This produces a very hard-wearing, easily maintained floor, the colour of which can be adjusted to suit a specific design; however, it is very expensive to produce.

FLOOR COATINGS

There are many different options for applying a finishing coat to screed, with the choice depending on the intended use. Screed coatings are often used in industrial applications. A coating system must be selected according to the functional requirements. As a rule, reaction resin is used, which cures chemically on its own; the curing process can also be accelerated by using appropriate admixtures. Coatings are usually applied in several layers. Depending on the intended purpose, coating systems may include impregnation, priming, sealing and coating layers. Coatings may be applied by roller, may consist of self-levelling compound or mortar and may be finished with an additional sprinkled aggregate ➔ 6-9

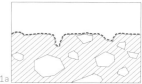
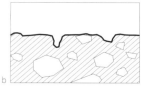
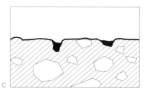
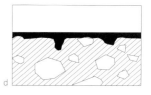

1   Schematic of floor coatings
a   Impregnation
b   Priming
c   Coating
d   Sealing

2 Elaborate patterns installed manually in terrazzo

3 Example of an historic terrazzo floor

4 Family residence in Engelberg, 2009, Andreas Fuhrimann, Gabrielle Hächler Architects. Ground concrete dominates the service areas. → p. 138

5 Conversion of industrial building, Frankfurt/Main: large expanse of dark, mastic asphalt floor

6 Klassikstadt, Frankfurt am Main, 2010, Lengfeld & Wilisch. Coated industrial floor in a centre for classic cars with showroom and workshop

7 Office, Aachen, 2003, kadawitt-feldarchitektur. Screed with epoxy resin coating

8 Co-working office in Darmstadt, 2011, H2S Architects. The screed is coloured with sprinkled aggregate.

INSTALLATION FLOORS

These days, offices and administration buildings, research and laboratory facilities and commercial premises are all expected to allow easy changes of use and adaptation of rooms. In addition to spatial alterations, the technical needs of work places are also subject to constant change. Services therefore have to be adapted to the new functions and the latest technology. To accommodate this need, raised floors have been developed, which create a cavity between the structural floor and the finishing layer. This cavity can be used to install power and IT lines, for example, as well as ducts for ventilation, cooling, or heating. This type of floor is referred to as an 'installation floor' and can be divided into three main types according to the construction used: underfloor duct, cavity floor and raised floor systems. Where modular walls are used, it is possible for installations to span several rooms. For all floor systems, the requirements in terms of technical installations, room zoning and adaptability should be determined at an early stage in the design. Modular floors should be designed in combination with the wall and ceiling systems. Depending on the system, the floor covering either consists of small elements to allow for the joints in the structure, or is continuous. This affects the choice and appearance.

UNDERFLOOR DUCTS

In this system, prefabricated ducts with various inspection and installation openings are placed under the floor and connected to each other. The duct system is installed directly on the structural floor. As a so-called 'open system', it is not encased by screed on all sides and can therefore easily be accessed from above at any point for subsequent installations. However, systems that are covered by screed are more common. In these systems, ducts may be encased on all sides by the screed, or they may be installed beneath the screed and separating layer, within the insulating layer of a floating screed. When laying screed over duct installations, it is important to provide the minimum coverage which, depending on the type of screed, is between 35 and 45 mm; these dimensions therefore need to be taken into consideration at the design stage.

In this system, access to the ducts is only possible at the outlet points and floor boxes, which cannot be changed subsequently. For this reason, this system has limited flexibility and is primarily suited to rooms with a defined function in which a cost-efficient installation upgrade option is to be provided. ➘ 3

CAVITY FLOOR

Cavity floors offer significantly more extensive options for accommodating change. These floors can be used for the installation of electric and communication wiring, as well as of ducts for ventilation, cooling or heating. Cavity floors can be constructed using three different methods: monolithic, multi-layered and with dry construction slabs. A monolithic cavity floor is constructed by placing moulded plastic elements on the structural floor or the insulation layer, which are linked with each other using sealing tape and then encased with ready-mixed screed. A resilient foam strip has to be inserted between the edge of the screed and the surrounding walls. The installation space created with this system is limited by the spacing of the moulded plastic elements. Similarly, the achievable height of the space is limited to 20 cm. Multi-layered cavity floors are constructed using adjustable pedestals which support a carrier panel, usually consisting of gypsum fibre board. This is finished with a ready-mixed screed on a separating layer. Dry cavity floors are likewise constructed using adjustable pedestals, but with several layers of gypsum fibre or wood-based panels laid on top. This type of construction is quick to install and avoids introducing moisture into the building. Again, inspection openings and installation points need to be planned with care in advance. ➘ 4

RAISED FLOOR

Raised floors are the most expensive of the installation floors, but also the most variable and flexible. The system uses adjustable pedestals which can be raised to create installation voids up to 180 cm high. These support industrially produced floor panels which are available in finishes to suit a range of requirements. Since every single panel of the floor can be removed, the installations beneath can easily be inspected or modified. Similar to cavity floors, raised floors can be used for the installation of wiring as well as of ducts for ventilation, cooling and heating, albeit with much greater flexibility. Furthermore, raised floors tend to be designed for greater loads. ➘ 5

1   Bavarian Landtag, Munich, 2008: as part of the conversion of the Senate Hall in the Bavarian Landtag (regional assembly) to form a multifunctional events room, a raised floor was installed which is also sound-absorbing.

2   Neues Museum, Berlin, 2009, David Chipperfield Architects. A special heavy-duty hollow-floor system was installed in the exhibition areas, which has to carry the weight of gravestones weighing up to 40 tonnes.

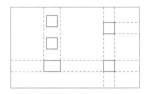

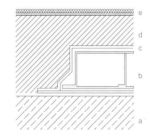

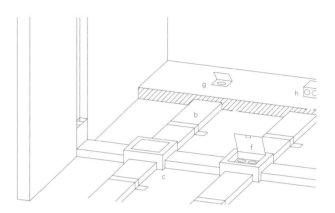

3 Underfloor duct system
Floor with ducts covered by screed
(closed system)
a Structural floor
b Underfloor duct
c Fixing brackets
d Screed
e Floor finish
f Installation element
g Installation socket with cover
h Surface mounted installation element

3

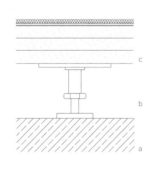

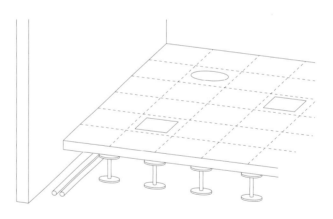

4 Cavity floor system
with dry screed or prefabricated
monolithic elements
a Structural floor
b Height-adjustable stand with
connection elements (20–30 cm)
c Support panel

4

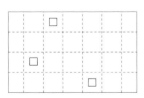

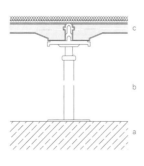

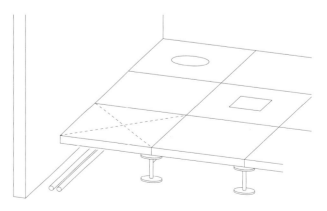

5 Raised floor system
a Structural floor
b Adjustable stand with
connection elements, sometimes
with grid profiles
c Floor panel, 60×60 cm

5

RESILIENT FLOOR COVERINGS

Resilient floor coverings are suitable for heavily trafficked areas as an alternative to screed, floor coatings and stone finishes. They are available in a number of different types. Since no covering is suitable for all kinds of wear, it is necessary to take a closer look at the properties of each material. EN ISO 10874 classifies the different coverings by the amount of wear they can withstand. Tab. 5, p. 163

Coverings are available in rolls or in the form of tiles. Some other coverings, for example cork, are supplied on carrier panels which are installed like engineered parquet flooring. Although the general appearance of the finished floor is homogeneous, it is nevertheless necessary to consider the pattern and direction of joints at the design stage. Depending on the material and the application, the joints between off-the-roll lengths or tiles have to be seal-welded after installation. The market offers synthetic coverings made of polyvinylchloride (PCV), polyolefin (PO), quartz vinyl or elastomer, and coverings based on natural materials such as linoleum, natural rubber and cork.

PVC

PVC floor coverings (thickness 1 to 3 mm) are based on polyvinylchloride as a binding agent, which is given the necessary resilience required for floor coverings through the addition of plasticisers, stabilisers and fillers. This is processed in different ways to produce coverings with or without a backing layer, or coverings of a foam consistency. Those without a backing layer are divided into homogeneous coverings consisting of a continuous layer, and heterogeneous coverings with a high-quality surface finish and a second layer with filling material. PVC coverings that are attached to a backing layer of jute, polyester fleece, expanded material, or cork are called compound coverings, whereas foam/cellular coverings with a textured face are referred to as cushioned vinyl (CV) coverings. PVC coverings are available in the form of rolls, tiles or panels and in many different colours; they are generally the simplest and most economical of resilient floor finishes.

In recent years, PVC has been subject to doubt regarding its health and environmental effects, which has led to the development of alternatives free of plasticisers – the polyolefin (PO) coverings – which are produced in a similar fashion to PVC coverings, but are much less sturdy.

Quartz vinyl floor coverings are suitable for particularly heavy duty applications. They contain a large proportion of quartz sand and fillers, and a small PVC component.

RUBBER COVERINGS

Rubber coverings (elastomeric floor coverings, 2.5 to 3.5 mm thick) are produced from synthetic or natural caoutchouc and various admixtures. They are extremely robust and have short-term resistance to solvents, acids and alkalis; they are resistant to cigarette embers and have low flammability. The edge of the material is pre-cut by the manufacturer, which means that no seal welding is required. In view of the fact that caoutchouc, although soft, has good anti-slip properties, it is often used in sports and multipurpose halls. Owing to their wear-resistance, rubber coverings are also used in highly trafficked areas such as airports or industrial premises. In addition to homogeneous smooth coverings, there are numerous textured coverings and form pieces for a wide range of requirements.

LINOLEUM

Linoleum (2 to 4 mm thick) was developed prior to 1900 and is therefore one of the oldest resilient floor coverings. It consists of linseed oil, natural resins, wood and cork flour, mineral fillers and colour pigments. A thick linoleum compound is produced in a number of manufacturing steps, then applied to a jute backing layer and rolled out under heat and pressure. Linoleum is available in many colours, in both monochrome and mixed colour versions. Initially the material has open pores, but is offered with factory-applied transparent surface sealing. In addition to jute-backed linoleum, the material can also be purchased with a cork backing to improve its thermal insulation properties. As the covering consists of natural raw materials, it is prone to discoloration or yellowing due to the effect of sunlight; this must be taken into consideration when selecting colours.

CORK COVERINGS

Cork (4 to 8 mm thick) has many favourable building physics and ecological properties. It has good thermal and sound insulation, is resilient to impact, hard-wearing and, as a natural product, can easily be recycled. There are quite a number of different colours and surface textures on the market, ranging from fine to coarse-grained. Cork coverings are available in the form of tiles or as prefabricated flooring. Cork tiles come in a range of thicknesses from 4 to 8 mm. They are attached directly to the subfloor using adhesive. In the case of prefabricated cork flooring, the cork facing layer is attached to a backing material. The 12 mm thick elements are tongue-and-grooved all round and are laid as part of a floating construction similar to engineered wood flooring.

1 EN ISO 10874 contains a classification system for resilient floor coverings; this specifies the correct covering for various requirements, including moderate to very heavy wear.
a Residential (classes 21/22/23)
b Commercial (classes 31/32/33/34)
c Industrial (classes 41/42/43)

2 Installation methods
When selecting a resilient floor covering, it is important to consider the format and installation method. Both off-the-roll material and tiles come in certain specific dimensions which have to be considered early on in the design (joint layout drawings).
a Off-the-roll material
b Tiles

3 Kustermann Park day nursery, Munich, 2012, Oliv Architects. Resilient flooring for day nurseries has to meet the requirements of classes 32 to 34.

4 Hamburg Museum, Hamburg, 2013, arge gillmann schnegg consortium. The floor covering installed in the auditorium, which is listed as an historic building, is hard-wearing, easy to maintain and will be attractive to look at for a long time.

5 Regional Centre of Contemporary Music, Nancy, 2011, Agence Périphériques. The flooring meets the requirements for heavy wear as a circulation area with gastronomy function; its colouring is continued on walls and ceiling to create a flowing continuum. The resilient material is flexible enough to form rounded edges.

6 Sports hall, Tübingen, 2004, Allmann Sattler Wappner Architects. The multifunctional use of the sports hall by professionals, schools and sports associations means that the floor has to withstand heavy wear (class 33/34).

7 BMW Leipzig, 2005, Zaha Hadid Architects. Requirements for production facilities and industrial premises are the most demanding. Depending on the use, floors have to meet the requirements of classes 41 to 43.

5

3

6

4

7

TEXTILE FLOOR COVERINGS

Owing to the use of fibres and the air spaces between them, textile floor coverings are extremely warm under-foot and have a soundproofing effect within a room and on any rooms beneath. The properties of such coverings depend on their construction, the materials used and their quality. Textile floor coverings can be distinguished according to the form in which they are offered (runners, rugs, carpet tiles, fitted carpet), by the manufacturing process (tufting, woven or needle felt), or by the fibres used (natural or synthetic). Owing to the numerous types of fibre and production methods, there are a great many products available – a range that is best narrowed down by considering the specification needed for the proposed use. For example, a carpet with a long pile provides a greater level of comfort and is therefore suitable for living areas, whereas it is not very suitable for heavily traf-ficked rooms such as offices. For representational pur-poses in commercial premises, it is possible to process textile coverings using different methods: for example, digital printing or motif stencilling.

MANUFACTURING METHODS

There are three main manufacturing methods for textile floor coverings: pile carpets, flat carpets and needle felt coverings. Pile carpet consists of a textile surface layer (pile layer) which is supported by a base layer. They are produced using different tufting methods (cut or loop pile, Berber and Saxony carpet), or the wire weaving process. ➘ 3-5a Flat carpet or flat woven fabric does not have a layer of pile and is created by weaving fibres. Frequently used fibres are sisal, jute and coir. As a rule, flat carpet has two usable sides, but it can also be produced with a backing layer, which increases its slip resistance and the stability of the fabric. ➘ 5b In the production of needle felt, one or several layers of fibre material are reinforced by needling. Needle felt floor coverings can be supplied with or without backing. As they are hard-wearing, they are suitable for offices. ➘ 6

NATURAL FIBRES

Natural fibres are distinguished according to the source material: plant fibres include cotton, sisal, jute and coir, and animal fibres include wool, hair and silk. Natural fibres have a balancing effect on interior air because they can absorb moisture and give it off again when the room air is dry. It is important to ensure that the relative humid-ity in rooms is adequate. Wool fibres tend to fluff on the surface of the fabric. Natural fibres should not be used in damp rooms because they have a tendency to rot in those conditions. Furthermore, natural fibre flooring should be impregnated against insect attack.

SYNTHETIC FIBRES

Synthetically produced fibres are also known as chemi-cal fibres. They can consist of polyamide (PA), polyester (PE), polyacrylics (PC) or polypropylene (PP). Depending on their chemical composition, they are used for differ-ent purposes. In general they are colour-fast, are highly abrasion-resistant, do not soil easily and are therefore easy to maintain.

1 Comfort characteristics of textile floor coverings
Textile floor coverings can vary substantially in their degree of soft-ness. In order to classify these degrees of softness, comfort class-es have been defined throughout Europe using the LC (luxury class) value, which is in addition to the load classes specified in EN ISO 10874 Resilient, textile and lami-nate floor coverings – classification (replaces DIN EN 685). The higher the value, the softer the surface. For example, a needle felt covering has an LC value of 1, whereas pile carpets are classed between LC1 and LC5. Pile carpets are also dis-tinguished by the thickness of the pile layer and the weight, which determine the wear characteristics; the categories are L, M and N.
➘ Tab. 5, p. 163

2 Classification of textile floor coverings by type of fibre

CARPET FIBRES			
NATURAL FIBRES	Fibres from plant sources		Cotton
			Jute
			Sisal
			Coir
	Fibres from animal sources		Wool
			Hair
			Silk
ARTIFICIAL FIBRES	Cellulose fibres		Viscose
			Others
	Synthetic fibres		Polyamide
			Polyacrylics
			Polyester
			Polypropylene

7 Fraunhofer Headquarters, Porto, 2011, Pedra Silva Architects. The new headquarters of the Fraunhofer Society symbolises both innovation and dynamism and – with its range of different floor coverings – creates a differ-entiation between room qualities for different requirements.

8 Rolex Learning Centre, Lausanne, 2004–2010, SANAA. The free form of the building is further enhanced by the selection of the textile floor covering. Instead of rigid work places, the entire complex can be used for working.

9 Restaurant, Stuttgart, 2008, Ippolito Fleitz Group. The tables of the restaurant are allocated to in-tersecting circles of dark needle felt, which create a distinct zoning of the space.

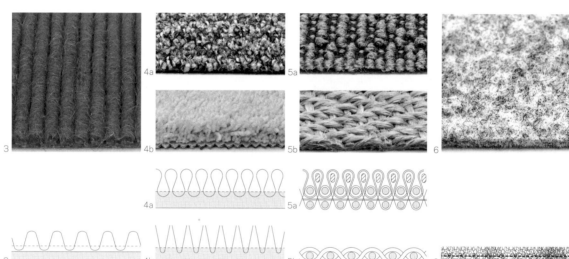

3   4a   4b   5a   5b   6

Selection of textile floor coverings, schematic illustration of production methods

3   Bonded pile process
In the bonded pile process a folded or pleated sheet of pile yarn is bonded by roller to a layer of adhesive on a backing fabric. These carpets are characterised by their ribbed surface, in the valleys of which – on close inspection – it is possible to see the bonding bed.

4   Tufting process
In the tufting process the fibres are pushed through a backing layer, initially creating a looped pile layer.
a   Looped pile carpet (bouclé)
b   Cut pile carpet (velour) is created by cutting the loops

5   Weaving processes
a   Weaving with pile wires
In this process the fibres of the pile loop are interwoven with the fibres of the backing fabric.
b   Flat weaving
The flat weaving process creates two-dimensional fabrics without a layer of pile using the warp and weft system.

6   Needle felt production
Needle felt coverings consist of one or several layers of needle felt which are strengthened by needling, and sometimes by adding impregnation.

7   8   9

WOODEN FLOORING

Wood is one of the oldest floor coverings. With the many types of timber available and with different patterns, grades, treatments and installation methods, it is possible to influence the atmosphere of a room in different ways. What all wooden floors have in common is that they feel good underfoot when one walks on them. Since the thermal conductivity of wood is low, such floors are warm to the touch, have good impact sound insulation characteristics if appropriately installed, do not build up strong electrostatic charges and – in the case of hardwoods such as oak, wenge (Millettia laurentii), or walnut – are very abrasion resistant. Another aspect is that wooden floors age very well, with signs of wear not usually being perceived as detrimental. After installation, these floors have to be sanded down and treated with wax, oil or lacquer. Depending on the thickness of the flooring, this process can be repeated a number of times after many years of wear. Wooden floors can be installed in the form of floor boards, parquet or woodblock flooring. Laminates may be used as a low-cost alternative material; they do not consist of solid wood, but of compressed wood fibres with a decorative film attached.

BOARDED FLOORS
Boarded floors consist of planed wooden boards which may be fitted flush, or joined with a tongue-and-groove system. The boards are usually between 1 and 3 centimetres thick and can be up to 15 metres long; they can be nailed or screwed to a substructure of beams or bearers, either visibly or concealed, or they can be affixed to screed using adhesive. The bearers can be spaced between 50 and 80 centimetres apart. For the purpose of providing better sound insulation, they have to be placed on strips of mineral fibre or cork. To prevent the ingress of rising damp, it is possible to insert a PE sheet as a damp-proof membrane. The thickness of the boards and the beams or bearers must be designed to suit the expected loading. The narrower a board is, the less it will be prone to warping after installation. After installation, the boarded floor is sanded down and its surface is treated.

PARQUET
Parquet can be laid on any dry and level substrate. Generally, it is important to ensure that the supporting screed has fully cured and, if applicable, that the construction is suitable for underfloor heating. There are two main versions of parquet flooring: solid parquet flooring (strip parquet, wood mosaic and mosaic parquet finger blocks) and laminated parquet flooring (two- or three-layer laminates and panel parquet).
Solid parquet flooring: The 22 mm thick and approx. 50 cm long parquet strips are available in two versions.

In one version, the parquet strips have a groove running all around, into which end-grain tongues slot to connect the strips. In the other version, the parquet strips have a groove along one side and a tongue along the other. Usually, strip parquet is laid shear-resistant on screed, fully bonded with adhesive, but it can also be nailed onto a secondary supporting floor. A special form of strip parquet is 10 mm thick solid parquet, which consists of individual strips or strip panels. These are laid butt-jointed and glued directly on to screed. This was developed particularly for the refurbishment of existing buildings in order to avoid differences in level when new flooring was installed next to other floor finishes. Wood mosaic with a thickness of 8 mm consists of individual lamellae, which are combined in the factory to form a range of patterns. Finger block lamellae parquet consists of individual strips, 8 mm wide and approx. 16 cm long, which are joined together. Both of these types are installed by fully bonding to the substrate.

Laminated parquet flooring: Laminated parquet flooring, also referred to as prefabricated parquet (not to be confused with engineered wood flooring), consists of a 2 to 8 mm thick top layer backed by one or two layers of cheaper wood or wood-based material, which are bonded together and which are designed to prevent cupping or distortion. Usually the elements are given their final surface finish at the factory. These parquets come in a wide range of patterns, which are often combined to form larger units. A special form of laminated parquet comes in the form of parquet panels. In this parquet, thin wood elements are applied in complex patterns to backing boards which are installed as panels. Laminated parquet can be installed either fully floating, fixed with concealed nails, or fully bonded shear-resistant. When installed as a floating layer on loose insulation, the elements are connected with a bonded tongue-and-groove system, or a click-on system without adhesive. Alternatively, laminated parquet can be bonded shear-resistant on floating screed. ⟶ p. 56

WOOD BLOCK FLOORING
Wood block flooring consists either of individual blocks of wood that are laid individually next to each other with the end grain uppermost, or of pre-assembled elements. In both cases, they are fully bonded onto a levelled structural floor, or onto monolithic or floating screed. Suitable types of timber are primarily pine, larch, fir and oak. Wood block flooring is expensive to buy, but is extremely durable and is therefore also often installed in industrial buildings.

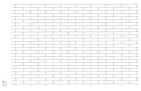

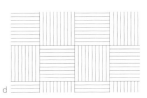
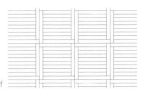

1   Examples of parquet flooring
By selecting a specific layout pattern and direction it is possible to visually enlarge, contract, elongate or shorten a room.
a   Ship's deck
b   Half bond, brick
c   Herringbone
d   Basket weave
e   Dutch
f   Cassette

Timber floor installation methods

2 Fully bonded on screed

3 Installed floating on a separating layer

4 Nailed or screwed to bearers or wood-based panels

a Structural floor
b Felt strip
c Bearer
d Cavity filler
e Screed
f Parquet adhesive
g Separating layer
h Wooden plank or parquet

5 Wooden plank with tongue and groove

6 Strip parquet
a The parquet strips have a groove on all sides and are connected with end-grain tongues.
b Other versions of parquet strips have a groove on one side and a tongue on the other.

7 Parquet finger blocks consist of many 8 mm wide "fingers" which are bonded together on edge to form the parquet blocks.

8 Prefabricated parquet consists of industrially manufactured elements with several layers. Only the face layer consists of hardwood.

9 Hall A, Munich, 2013, Designliga designers. The wood paving with its rough finish contrasts with the gold-coloured fitments and is a reminder of the previous industrial use of the hall.

10 Apartment, Munich, 2012, Oliv Architects. In this inner city conversion of a residential development, the intention is to create a visual distinction between new and old. Large window areas and the pale boarded flooring give the feeling of a larger space.

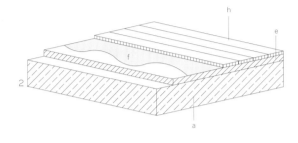

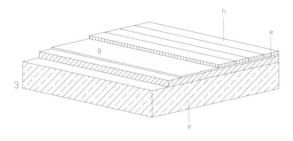

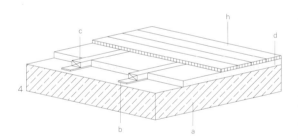

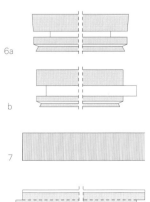

DETAILING OF EDGES AND JOINTS

All wood floorings are subject to expansion and contraction due to changes in room temperature and relative humidity.

These changes in the length and width are accommodated by a 10 to 20 mm wide expansion joint around the periphery of the room, which is covered by the skirting board or can be closed with cork strips. A slightly bevelled edge ensures that some movement can take place between elements without unsightly distortion of the edges. Expansion joints in the subfloor have to be replicated.

SURFACE TREATMENT

With the exception of laminated parquet, which is prefabricated and is usually supplied with surface treatment applied in the factory, the surfaces of wooden floors can be treated using a range of different methods. The objective of this treatment is to make the flooring resistant to dirt and moisture. Two main methods are used, depending on the anticipated use of the floor and on the maintenance requirements: oiling and waxing with natural materials, and sealing with water-based varnish. Sealing the floor closes any open pores and ensures maximum robustness. However, this also means that the flooring loses its natural texture and any wear on the varnish may leave unsightly traces. Floors treated with oil and/or wax retain their natural finish, but require regular subsequent oiling/waxing care. This can be done as part of the cleaning process. Various treatments exist to create an unusual appearance as a design feature, such as smoking or heat-treating the wood, or leaving the surface rough-sawn.

STONE AND CERAMIC FLOOR COVERINGS

Stone coverings are very durable and can therefore be used in many applications. They are ideal for heavily trafficked areas, such as entrance and retail areas, and in rooms that may be exposed to moisture, such as kitchens or bathrooms. A special aspect of stone flooring is that the same material is available with a range of surfaces that are specifically suited to particular situations and functional requirements. Avoiding a change of material makes it easier to design adjacent indoor and outdoor areas, or wet and dry areas, as a single, flowing space. As with all smooth flooring materials, it is important to ensure sufficient slip resistance; this can be achieved by roughening the surface, by the application of special coatings or coverings, and by mechanical anti-slip devices, sandblasting, or laser treatment. Depending on the intended purpose, it may be necessary to choose profiled tiles, which provide slip resistance even when there is a lot of water. ➔ Tab. 1, 2, p. 164 Stone flooring can be subdivided by source, binding agent and method of manufacture into several categories: natural stone, concrete slab, synthetic resin stone, asphalt tiles and ceramic tiles.

NATURAL STONE FLOORING
Among the types of stone suitable for use as a flooring material are granite, slate, travertine, marble and sandstone. The denser the material is, the better it is suited. The special character of natural stone flooring lies in the variation of strength and texture. It is very robust and therefore durable, and it ages well. Nowadays the material is usually industrially processed to obtain the desired format. Depending on the thickness and size, the material is referred to as paviours or slabs. Natural stone surfaces can be finished with a range of precisely controllable treatments, such as polishing, treating with acid, sandblasting or charring to achieve a certain effect or to suit different uses. ➔ p. 38 Natural stone can also be worked into units for other interior applications, for example as window sills, kitchen worktops or wall linings, thus creating a harmonious design effect.

ENGINEERED STONE FLOORING
In the manufacture of engineered stone, crushed natural stone is cast into different formats together with admixtures (if required) and synthetic resin (polyester resin or epoxy resin) as a binder. This makes it possible to produce not only floor slabs and tiles, but also specifically shaped components such as worktops with inset washbasins, or window sills.

RECONSTITUTED STONE FLOORING
Cast (or reconstituted) stone is produced with cement as the binding agent. It can be cast in many formats and with a range of different aggregates. Cast stone units are very hard-wearing and easy to maintain. They are also relatively cheap to produce. As flooring, they take the form of paving slabs, floor tiles or screed (terrazzo) ➔ p. 56, 60. Paving slabs can be produced in two different processes. In the single-layer process, the raw materials are cast into large blocks and these are then cut to obtain the desired thickness. Paviours produced in a two-layer process consist of a base concrete layer and a layer of facing concrete that is at least 4 mm thick. Paviours that will be ground again after installation on site must have a facing layer of at least 8 mm. One variant is an exposed aggregate finish. This is created by lining the mould with a retarding agent, which penetrates the upper few millimetres. After curing, the cement/sand matrix is washed away down to this depth with a water jet to expose the decorative aggregate.

ASPHALT TILES
Asphalt tiles consist of a mixture of limestone with bitumen as the binder. They can be used as hardwearing floors in heavily trafficked applications.
These tiles are slip-resistant, resilient, warm to the touch and, depending on composition, not susceptible to electrostatic charging. They are primarily used in commercial applications. The black/grey colour of the tiles results from the materials used in production, but it is also possible to add pigment for a range of surface colours.

CERAMIC TILES
Ceramic tiles are produced by firing clay material that is mixed with various aggregates. Their properties, appearance, quality and surface are largely affected by the raw materials, glazes and textures used in production. Ceramic tiles are subdivided into earthenware, stoneware and porcelain stoneware.
Earthenware (e.g. terracotta) consists of fine-grained, crystalline porous 'bodies' that may absorb up to 10% of water and are therefore mostly not suitable in exterior applications. Stoneware tiles (e.g. quarry tiles) are fired at higher temperatures so that their pores are largely closed. This means that potential water absorption is less than 3 percent. For this reason, stoneware tiles are frost-proof and can be used in external applications. Porcelain stoneware absorbs less than 0.5 percent of water. The tiles are extremely durable owing to the fine components and the high firing temperature. ➔ Tab. 4-6, p. 165

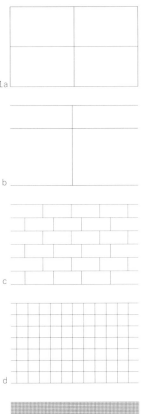

1 Stone and ceramic floor coverings are produced using a range of different methods, resulting in different formats. Depending on the type of material, the selection of the format determines the joint pattern and hence the effect on the room. It therefore makes sense to produce a layout drawing to check the effect of the floor design. Both the room design and any sanitary fittings have to be coordinated with the desired tile and joint patterns.
a   Natural stone
b   Synthetic resin stone
    Concrete slabs
c   Stoneware tiles
d   Porcelain stoneware tiles
e   Glass mosaic

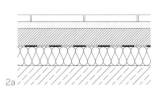

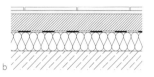

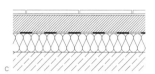

2a

2 Slab and tile installation methods
a   Mortar bed installation
This is the oldest and most conventional installation method, which today is primarily used for laying thicker natural stone slabs. The mortar is cement-bonded and applied wet in thicknesses of between 15 and 30 mm.

b

b   Medium-thick adhesive bed installation
This method is mostly used for large-format tiles on an uneven substrate. The adhesive bad is normally between 5 and 15 mm thick.

c

c   Adhesive bed installation
Nowadays, this is the most common method and is mostly used for tiles and thin slabs. The adhesive bed is less than 5 mm thick.

3

4

5

6

3 Separating membrane on problematic substrate

4 Laying natural stone slabs in a mortar bed

5 Laying tiles and thin slabs in a thin adhesive bed

6 Grouting

LAYING AND GROUTING

Stone and ceramic flooring materials can be laid either in thick mortar beds or thin tile adhesive beds, depending on the material, its thickness and the substrate. Substrates have to be prepared for the installation by applying a bonding coat and sometimes also a levelling coat. The thick mortar bed is usually used on uneven substrates, or when the tiles to be laid are uneven in thickness; it is therefore particularly suitable for natural stone. The substrate is prepared with a bonding coat upon which the mortar bed is applied with a thickness of up to 30 mm. This then receives the tiles.

When tiles are laid on a level and smooth surface, a thin bed of tile adhesive is applied first. A toothed spatula is used to apply the adhesive to the substrate. In this process, it is not possible to compensate for any but very minor unevenness. In the case of difficult substrates (for example when the structural floor consists of different materials, the irregularity or technical properties of which could affect the flooring finish), the face layer should be separated from the substrate by a levelling course or separating membranes.

JOINTS

After the installation, the tiles have to cure for a while before grouting is applied to the joints. It is important that the water content of the mortar/adhesive can properly dry out. Floor finishes laid in a thick mortar bed have to dry out for 7 days or longer, whereas tiles installed using a thin adhesive bed can usually be grouted after 1 to 3 days. Grouting the joints has the effect of sealing the surface and of evening out tolerances in the material. The usual width of interior tiling joints is 2 to 3 mm. Permissible dimensional tolerances increase with the size of tile; for this reason, larger tiles require joints of between 5 and 10 mm. Two different types of material are used for grouting: hydraulically curing joint mortar based on cement (proprietary joint mortar), and epoxy resin grout material which is resistant to chemicals and is largely unaffected by dampness. Joints with adjoining building components at edge strips, or over joints in the screed, as well as the mandatory joints at walls should be between 5 and 10 mm wide and sealed with elastomeric joint sealant. → p. 54

SKIRTING DETAILS

The primary considerations in the design of the transition between floor and wall are functional ones. Having said that, the problem stimulates designers to produce new design solutions again and again. In his architecture, Carlo Scarpa has defined the dummy joint as a transitional element that can make the floor look like a bridge, a carpet, or a platform and gives special importance to the joint between floor and wall. The base of the wall can also be made into a more sculptural element, as is shown in the house Vila Nova de Famalicao by Alvaro Siza. Siza has made use of the wooden skirting board element by extending it to form plinths, window and door reveals and even the handrail of a gallery. ➘ 1

FUNCTION AND CONSTRUCTION
The design of the transition between floor and wall has to address both construction details and technical issues: normally the floor covering must be separated from the wall by an expansion joint. One of the reasons is sound insulation, i.e. to prevent footfall sound from being transferred into the wall. Another reason is to allow for the expansion and contraction of the floor finishes. With timber floors in particular, an adequate gap must be provided between the flooring and the wall. This gap can also be closed by inserting a resilient material flush with the surface. In addition to the above aspects, which relate to building physics and visual appearance, skirting boards protect the wall from knocks and soiling resulting, for example, from floor cleaning work.

The construction of plinths in wet areas needs special consideration, since it is not possible to separate the floor from the wall by an open joint. It is rather important to prevent any moisture penetrating the wall. In areas with a modest degree of moisture, this may be achieved by filling the joint with an elastic joint sealant. In wetter areas, a skirting or plinth can be formed using specially shaped skirting tiles or profiles, which create a better transition to the wall. ➘ 3c Such skirting details are imperative in areas exposed to much use of water, for example in commercial kitchens.

DESIGN
The above functional aspects often lead to constructions that detract from the harmonious appearance of a room. It is therefore important to consider this detail at the design stage. The desire for a flush transition between floor and wall has led to special solutions, for example in the form of profiles that can be installed flush with the plaster of the wall. ➘ 3b It must be said, however, that the installation of such an element requires extreme precision in the interior fit-out work from an early stage. In view of the fact that the walls are usually plastered before the screed is laid, the profiles have to be placed exactly at the planned level, in anticipation of the finished flooring. An example of this being done successfully is in a home by Alvaro Siza's practice, where the skirting profile is an integral part of the floor, wall and fitments.

1   Residence in Vila Nova de Famalicao, 2000, Álvaro Siza. The skirting is of the same material as the floor and therefore creates a homogeneous transition between floor, wall and fitted furniture.

2   Residence Z, Frankfurt, 2012, Bayer & Strobel Architects. Here the change of material between floor and wall has been emphasised by a continuous joint.

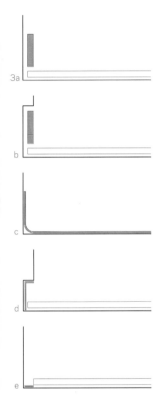

3a

b

c

d

e

3 Skirting design options
a Surface-mounted
b Flush
c Concave curved
d Dummy joint in the wall
e Dummy joint in the floor

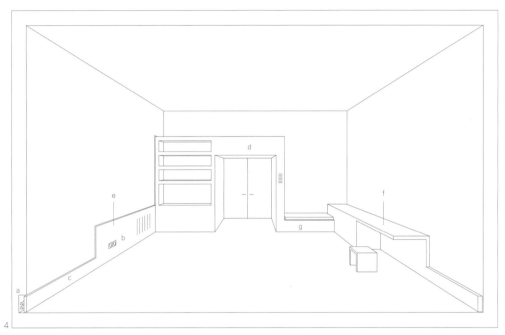

4

4 Skirting as transition and
space-forming element
a Used for installation
b Integration of services
c Flush
d Transition with door frame
e Wall panelling
f Continued as fitted furniture
g Podium

5 Surface-mounted skirting board
with parquet

a Separating layer
b Screed
c Edge strip

6 Skirting integrated into the wall

7 Concave curve skirting
d Plaster
e Floor finish
f Wooden skirting board fixed with
screws
g Aluminium profile in two parts,
can be used as cable duct

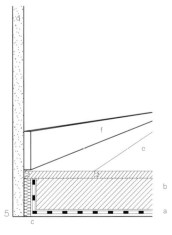

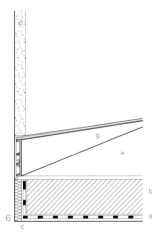

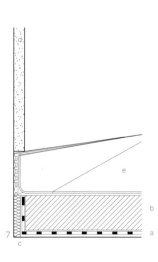

FURNISHING | ZONING
WALLS AND WALL SYSTEMS

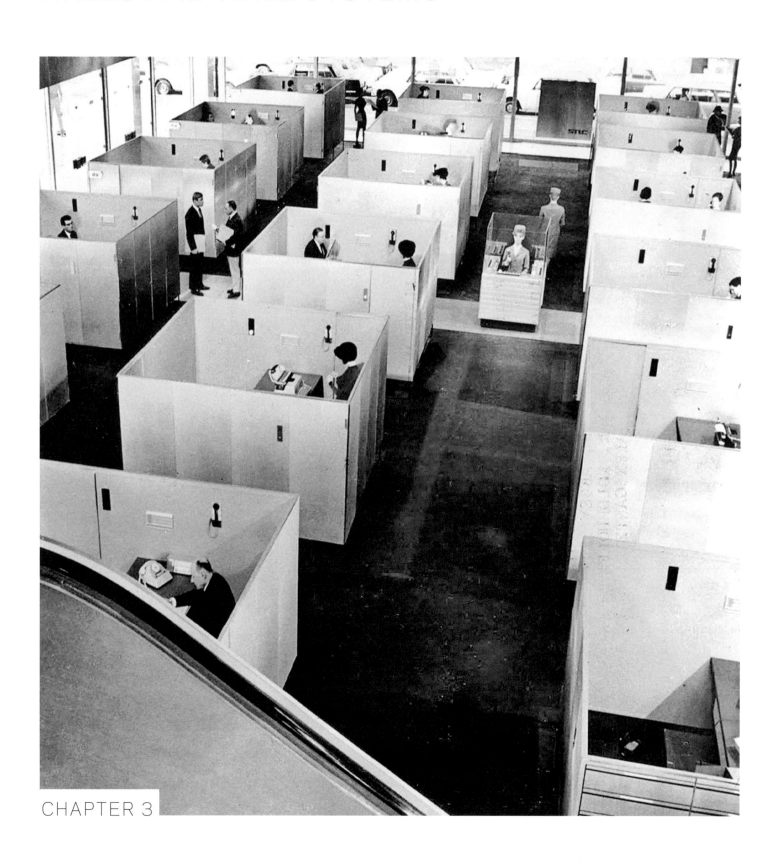

WALLS – SEPARATING AND CONNECTING

SPATIAL EFFECT AND MATERIAL

The shape and atmosphere of a room is largely influenced by the design of the walls. Walls direct where we look and our movements – they define or modify the space available to us. In addition to their formative character, importance is attached to their spatial effect and material. Connected to these are functional aspects, such as the flexibility of a room and its technical requirements (for example sound insulation, which affects the well-being of users – i.e. is a room loud or quiet?). The material of a wall, its thickness and surface properties affect our sense of space to a high degree. In combination with the colouring, these are the main factors that influence our perception of a room. The height of a wall is an important factor in relation to its spatial effect. A full-height wall creates a clear separation between rooms or functional areas. If the wall stops short of the ceiling, the larger space can be experienced. It follows that a lower wall not so much separates spaces, as creates separate functional areas within a space. A typical example is the zoning of a room into cooking, dining and sitting areas by walls of various heights, often in the form of furniture.

FLEXIBILITY

In the design of buildings, time and life-cycles play an important role. This is closely related to the issue of the flexibility and adaptability of the layout. The choice of materials and construction of the walls determine the degree of flexibility.

Which rooms serve a clearly defined use and which are more open? This leads to the question as to which walls could be loadbearing and which would be better as a demountable construction. It follows that questions relating to adaptability, the duration of use and the associated expense should be answered with reference to the type of room and its use. Other parameters for deciding the design of a wall are its size and weight, and the budget and construction time.

REQUIREMENTS

The requirements for non-loadbearing partition walls are defined in DIN 4103 and DIN 18183. On the following pages the focus is primarily on the technical requirements of non-loadbearing walls; the design considerations apply in equal measure to non-loadbearing and loadbearing walls. ⟶ SCALE, vol. 3, Support | Materialise Non-loadbearing partition walls function as room dividers, but as supports for the structural loads of the building. They are not stable in themselves, but need the connection to adjoining building components for their stability. In addition to their own weight and small attached loads (shelves, pictures), they have to be able to withstand impact loads and transfer these to adjoining components. The sound insulation requirements for a wall can vary greatly. They usually depend on the use of the adjoining room, and on whether this room is part of the same residential unit or of a neighbouring unit. In addition to the principle method of construction (e.g. solid or lightweight) it is the composition in cross section and the connection to adjoining walls, floors and ceilings that are important.

CLASSIFICATION

A distinction is made between permanently installed (single or multiple skin), removable and movable partitions (sliding and folding walls). In addition, furniture and curtains can be used as partitions or room dividers.

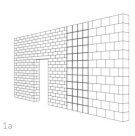 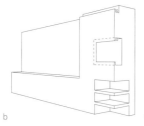 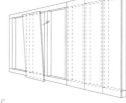 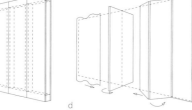

1a   b   c   d

1 Non-loadbearing partition walls can be distinguished by their construction methods:

a Permanently built solid walls
- brick masonry wall
- solid gypsum blocks
- aerated concrete blocks
- glass bricks

b Permanent lightweight partition walls
- lightweight partition walls with a timber substructure
- lightweight partition walls (e.g. timber boarding, plasterboard) with a metal stud substructure

c Removable partition walls
- panel walls
- monoblock walls
- glazed partition walls
- partition walls formed by fitments

d Movable partition walls
- sliding and folding walls
- curtains

2 Effect and relationship in space

a   Room-high wall with standard access door; clear separation between two units

b   A room-high door as a connection element produces a generous opening between the two rooms.

c   High level glazing and glass door. The wall becomes less solid; wall, floor and ceiling transition is more fluid.

d   All-glass wall, maximum visual connection between rooms while still providing separation

e   Furniture as separating element and storage, potentially usable from both sides; flexible because the item can be removed

f   Freestanding furniture creates zones in a room

g   Movable wall elements achieve both maximum connection and separation.

h   Sliding and side-hung doors are fixed in their room-separating function and both have specific sound protection characteristics.

i   Temporary visual separation without sound protection properties – folding wall, curtain, lightweight flexible partition element

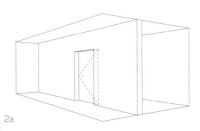
2a

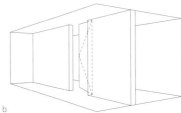
b

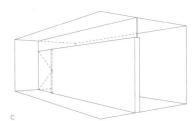
c

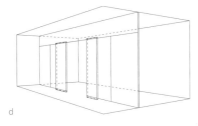
d

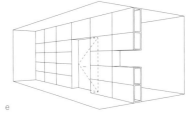
e

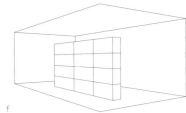
f

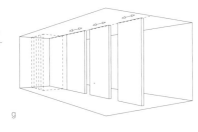
g

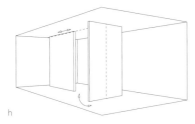
h

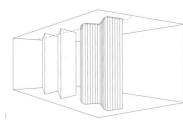
i

3 ADA office building, Hamburg, 2007, J. Mayer H. The minimalist partition wall system offers maximum transparency while providing good sound insulation for the required privacy. The curves of the facade are continued in the curved profiles of the all-glass system.

4 Apartment Nagi, Kanagawa, 2009, UUfie Architects. The curtains on two curtain rails close in the opposite direction and provide zoning into public and private areas; there is no acoustic separation.

3

4

SOLID PARTITION WALLS

Single-skin partition walls are solid constructions which are permanently constructed in a building for the subdivision of rooms. They must not be used for bracing a building or transferring structural loads, but they do support their own weight and have to be strong enough to carry attached loads, such as shelves, and to withstand any impact loads. Commonly used materials are clay bricks, lime-and-sand bricks, aerated concrete blocks, lightweight concrete blocks, gypsum planks and glass bricks. The choice of material depends on the existing shell construction, the ability of the structural system to support loads and the sound insulation requirements. Since these walls are not very thick, their weight per unit area is too little to provide adequate sound insulation. However, these values can be improved by adding an attenuating layer on the face of the wall.

Even very simple brick walls with a wall thickness of 11.5 centimetres comply with fire resistance class F30; when plastered on both sides, they can achieve class F90. Compared to hollow wall constructions, it is more difficult to fit installations into such a wall, which therefore have to be carefully designed by the services engineer and architect. Wiring and pipework may be installed on the surface of such walls, or may have to be recessed into chased grooves; in gypsum plank walls these grooves may be cut by a router.

CONNECTIONS

Partition walls obtain their necessary strength and bracing from connections to adjoining loadbearing building components. The connections can either be rigid or allow for some movement. A partition wall that has been constructed on a floor that is subject to deflection may tend to form a crack ➔1 where it connects to the adjoining rigid building component and may therefore need a flexible connection. Horizontal cracks in the lower courses of brick walls can be prevented by inserting metal reinforcement mesh. Where a smooth transition is wanted at the joint with the ceiling or another wall – if no suspended ceiling is used – the detailing has to be very exact in order to achieve a neat finish. ➔4, 5

BRICK-BUILT WALLS

Solid partition walls are usually built to a thickness of 11.5 centimetres, often using small-format masonry units such as clay or lime-and-sand bricks. ➔3a Large-format blocks, which are available in formats up to 50×100 centimetres, are more economical as they are quicker to lay. The dimensions of these types of wall can normally be determined in a simplified procedure by reference to a table. The installation of partition wall can be made more efficient by using prefabricated full-height elements made of aerated concrete. ➔3b

GYPSUM BLOCK PARTITION WALLS

Gypsum block partition walls are placed on a base layer of mortar and built up with the blocks in an overlapping bond; they are then skimmed and can be finished with wallpaper or a paint coat. The connecting joint with adjoining building components must be flexible. Where more substantial movement is expected due to the deflection of a floor, the connecting joint requires the insertion of a metal profile to accommodate this movement. Where gypsum blocks are used in wet rooms, they require additional impregnation. ➔3c

GLASS BRICK WALLS

Glass bricks are hollow glass units consisting of two pressed glass layers connected to each other. Glass bricks come in a variety of colours, different transparencies, sizes and profiles. They are transparent and very robust. ➔3d

1   Formation of cracks in non-loadbearing partition walls due to excessive deflection of the floor

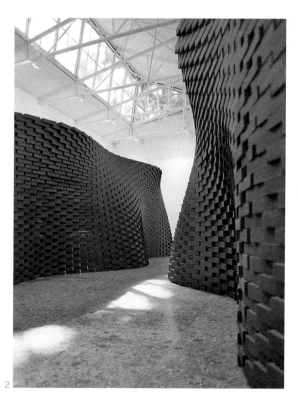

2   Structural Oscillations, Venice, 2007–2008, installation at the 11th Architecture Biennale in Venice, Gramazio & Kohler, Architecture and Digital Fabrication, ETH Zurich
The sculptural deformation of the wall defines the design of the surfaces. The almost textile character creates an effective contrast to the material of the bricks.

3 Types of solid, non-loadbearing partition wall
a Bricks/small-format masonry units
b Aerated concrete elements
c Gypsum blocks
d Glass brick wall

4 Wall connection
a Rigid wall connection, recessed, joint filled with mortar
b Rigid wall connection with flat steel ties
c Recessed wall connection allowing movement, joint filled with insulating material

5 Joint between wall and ceiling/floor above
a Rigid connection with mortar joint
b Joint allowing movement and filled with caulking strip and sealant to allow for deflection; the wall is held on three sides.
c Connection with steel angle, allowing movement

6 Office, Frankfurt, 2009, Oliv Architects. The translucence of the glass brick wall provides light to the circulation zones and visually unifies the space.

7 Wake room, Ingelheim, 2013, Bayer & Strobel Architects. The material of the natural stone wall of the inner courtyard continues inside and influences the perception of the room.

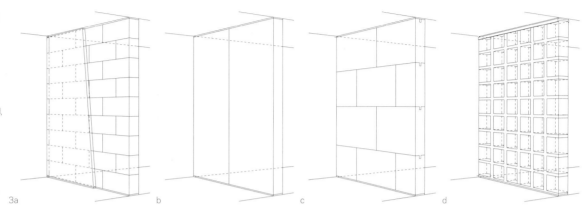

3a b c d

 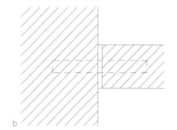 

4a b c

  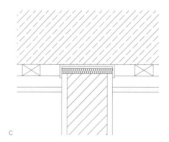

5a b c

6 7

STUD PARTITION SYSTEMS

Stud partitions differ from single-skin solid walls in their construction and weight. Being lightweight, these walls do not have to be located above each other and it is possible to lay out different storeys in different zoning arrangements. Since they are constructed without a significant amount of water, they are also referred to as drywall constructions.

Stud partition walls can be dismantled with little effort, which is an advantage for a flexible and adaptable layout. However, where room structures need to be changed more frequently, it is preferable to use industrially pre-fabricated movable wall systems. → p. 88

The physical and functional properties of stud partitions can be modified to suit a wide variety of requirements by varying the composition and construction of the various layers. Furthermore, it is easy to integrate services installations.

CONSTRUCTION

The basic structure of a stud partition consists of timber or metal studs which are fitted in situ as a skeleton construction. This is then usually lined on both sides with one or several layers of board material such as plasterboard or gypsum fibre board. It is also possible to use other materials such as chipboard, profiled timber boarding or fibre-cement board. Depending on requirements, it is possible to fill the cavity between the studs with insulation material. → 2b

The term 'veneered wall' refers to the construction of a facing layer of wall, which is attached but not bonded to the main part; veneered walls may be fitted to create a space for installations, or to improve acoustic or thermal insulation. → 2a

Stud partitions may also be used to build ducting that encases vertical installations passing through several floors. Here too it is important to take into account the fire safety and acoustic insulation requirements. Fire stops are inserted at the points where the ducts pass through floors/ceilings and inside walls. In order to sound-proof these ducts, pipes are encased in pipe insulation material and mineral fibre insulation is fitted inside the duct or inside the walls. → 2c

SUBSTRUCTURE

The system with metal studs and plasterboard lining to DIN 18183 is the most common construction method for partition walls. The profiles consist of galvanised steel and include CW profiles for the vertical elements and UW profiles for the horizontal connections to floor and ceiling. The spacing of the studs depends on the available formats of the boarding; a common dimension is 62.5 cm. → 1

Studs constructed of timber are less common. In accordance with DIN 4103-4 they can be produced from solid timber, laminated timber, or plywood. As a rule, their cross-sections measure between 30/60 mm and 40/80 mm, depending on the situation, the height of the wall and the type of lining.

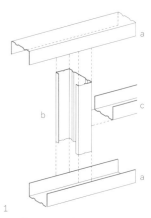

1 Substructure for plasterboard walls
a UW profile (connection or edge profile); the horizontal profile is fixed to floor and ceiling to provide a fixing for the vertical studs.
b CW profile (C stud profile for walls); vertical stud elements in stud walls; for greater rigidity the studs have a more complex profile.
c UA profile (bracing profile); this profile is installed horizontally and consists of thicker metal sheeting compared to UW profiles; required for door frames etc.

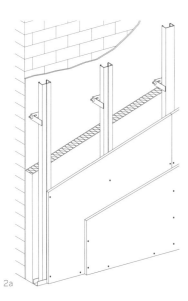
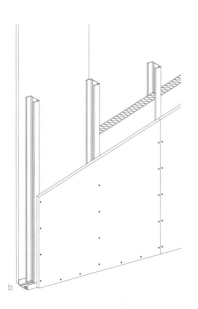
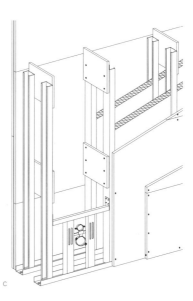

2 Types of stud partition
a Dry lining
b Metal stud partition, single board layer
c Double-stud wall with double board layer, with installation element for sanitary fittings

3 Creating different zones with stud partitions and installation walls

With the help of installation walls, the pipe installation for sanitary fittings and ducts can be concealed. It is possible to build stud partitions with integrated shelving recesses or built-in cabinets. In that case, it is important to take the whole room into consideration and consider the connections and transitions to floor and walls. At the transition between wall and ceiling, it is possible to insert a dummy joint which can also accommodate concealed lighting to provide indirect illumination; by constructing the floor appropriately a shower area can be provided, the tray of which is flush with the floor level.

a Installation wall
b Wall recess for shelving
c Shaft casing
d Bathtub panel with shelving on the side
e Freestanding wall
f Shower tray flush with floor level
g Suspended ceiling
h Recessed joint on all sides
i Recessed light fittings

4 A metal stud wall being installed

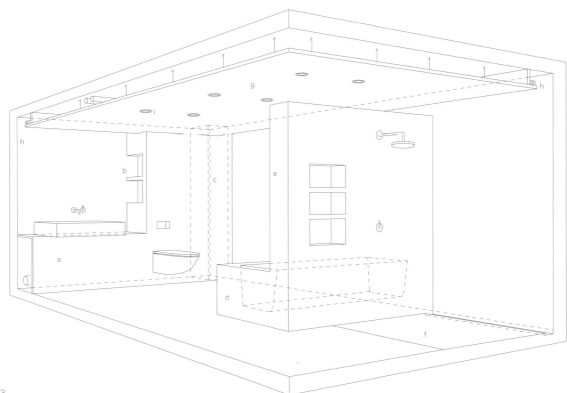

3

4

LINING

The type of lining applied to stud partitions has an impact on the appearance of the wall. Normally the lining is finished without visible joints. An exception is lining with profiled timber boards. All board material should be attached in a bond pattern with vertical joints always on a stud profile. Using full-height boards where board in such a format is available is an advantage since this means that horizontal joints can be avoided. The joints between boards are skimmed over with a filler in order to create a homogeneous surface. Scrim or other joint reinforcement tape is used to prevent the cracking of these joints. The surface quality is classified in four quality standards: Q1 (no specific requirement regarding appearance), Q2 (standard skim finish to DIN 18181), Q3 (increased requirement) and Q4 (maximum requirement, satisfying inspection under lateral lighting). Linings consisting of wood-based material are usually tongue-and-grooved. In order to avoid cracking, it is possible to strengthen the joints with adhesive. In spite of careful installation, the occurrence of cracks cannot be precluded, particularly at the corners and junctions between wall and floor or ceiling.

There are different kinds of plasterboard which are designed to meet specific applications and requirements. Standard plasterboard is available with no specific additional properties. Greenboard, which is impregnated plasterboard, is available for installation in rooms with higher humidity levels. There is also a type of plasterboard with increased fire resistance, as well as plasterboard that combines both these characteristics. Depending on the type of substructure, it is possible to achieve fire resistance class F120. Other more specific types of plasterboard are manufactured to fulfil increased sound insulation requirements or greater surface hardness requirements. ➔ Tab. 1–3, p. 166

NOISE CONTROL

Compared to solid walls, stud partitions – even though they may be thinner – can achieve better soundproofing values despite their lower weight per unit area. Sound-proofing requirements in partition walls are fulfilled by a number of different measures. Firstly, special sound insulation boards with a higher weight per unit area can be used and secondly, mineral wool can be inserted in the cavity between the studs to increase the sound insulation properties. It is also important for soundproofing that the components are acoustically disconnected. The metal studs have a wavy profile which attenuates vibrations. There are also thicker profiles, which are designed especially for sound insulation. In double-stud or installation walls, the construction makes it easier to achieve acoustic decoupling. Furthermore, the distance between the two linings is greater, which also has a positive effect on the sound insulation properties of the wall.

In addition to the acoustic properties of the wall itself, it is important to consider the sound transmission via adjoining building components. For this reason, the details of connections to floor, ceiling and other walls must be carefully designed. For example, where service installations prevent a direct connection between the top of a partition wall and the structural floor above, it is necessary to fill the gap with insulation material, or to make a joint between the wall and any suspended ceiling. ➔ p. 46

FIRE SAFETY

DIN 4102 defines the classification of walls into F30, F60 and F90 fire resistance classes. In addition to classification of the materials used in stud partitions (studs, lining, insulation material), partitions themselves are classified into four groups (A, B, AB and K).

Class A defines walls consisting of non-combustible material (gypsum) and class B covers walls with combustible materials (wood-based boarding). Walls of class AB consist primarily of non-combustible material, whereas class K refers to walls with non-combustible material on the surface, but with combustible material inside. ➔ p. 168

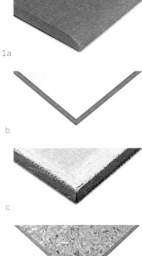

1a

b

c

d

1 Selection of board material for lining the substructure. Different materials are used depending on requirements.

a Plasterboard
Plasterboard consists of a gypsum core which is lined at both sides and at the edges with a layer of cardboard. There are different plasterboards for various applications.

b Gypsum fibreboard
This board consists of a mixture of cellulose fibres, gypsum and various additives. The fibres give the board material its tensile strength. These boards are stronger and have a better tensile strength than plasterboard.

c Fibre cement board
Fibre cement board consists of a mixture of cellulose or plastic fibres, cement and water. They are not combustible and, in contrast to untreated gypsum slabs, are resistant to water and the weather.

d Wood-based board
Wood-based board is produced in a range of types and with various properties. Common materials are: three- or five-layer plywood, Multiplex board, chipboard and OSB board.

2 Standard jointing details of a
drywall partition with a single layer
of plasterboard, scale 1:5
a Ceiling joint
b Floor joint
c Vertical joint with partition
d Corner joint

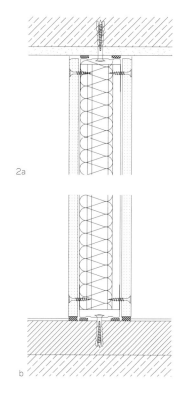

2a

b

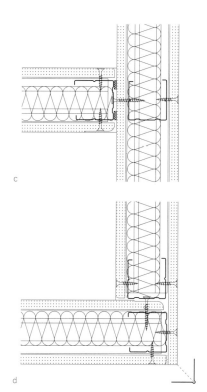

c

d

3 Acoustic and fire safety properties of drywall partitions compared
to solid wall constructions, scale
1:20

a Single stud partition wall, single
layer of gypsum fibreboard/
plasterboard

b Single stud partition wall, double
layer of gypsum fibreboard/
plasterboard

c Double stud partition, double
layer of gypsum fibreboard/
plasterboard

d Installation wall, double layer of
gypsum fibreboard/plasterboard

e Solid wall of clay bricks/sand-
lime bricks, 11.5 cm, plastered

f Solid wall of clay bricks/
sand-lime bricks, 24 cm, plastered

3	Construction	Thickness of component in mm	Weight per area in kg/m²	Sound insulation (R) in dB	Fire safety class	Thermal insulation (U-value) in W/m²/K
a		75-125	35-45	40-54	F30 - A	0.4-0.66
b		75-125	35-45	40-54	F30 - A	0.38-0.61
c		175-275	65-80	59-65	F90 A F 120 - A	0.21-0.47
d		195-220	65-80	52	F90 A	0.60
e		145	160-240	42-47	F90 A F 120 - A	1.71
f		270	260-500	48-55	F 180 - A BW	1.11

REMOVABLE PARTITION WALLS

Office buildings, hospitals, research institutes ➘3 and many other types of building frequently have to be adapted to changing patterns of use. Solid walls and walls with more than one skin are not very suitable for this purpose. Their removal and construction is expensive and, as a rule, the material cannot be re-used. This has led to the development of a number of different wall systems that are industrially prefabricated and installed on site, and which can be removed and re-installed using the same individual elements. These systems can roughly be divided into three types: monoblock walls, panel walls and removable wall elements.

The grid of a wall system should always be coordinated with the floor and ceiling construction, the column system and the facade grid of a building. When designing a new building, all parts are arranged such that they fit together in order to achieve maximum flexibility. There are three different types of grids: axial grids, banded grids and a combination of the two. ➘4 With flexible wall systems, the planning should always take sound insulation and fire safety into account. When the room layout is changed, it is important to ensure that no disadvantages or non-permissible situations are created. The junctions between walls, floors and ceilings must be decoupled by appropriate soundproofing measures.

The pattern of joints between elements should be considered as part of the interior design in the light of aesthetic criteria – a matter that does not arise with monolithic walls.

PANEL WALL

Panel walls consist of a number of panels, which are fitted on site in a modular system. Adjustable-height studs are installed on a flexible grid in floor and ceiling profiles. The studs have longitudinal slots in the direction of the wall. The gaps between the studs are filled with insulation material and wall panels are mounted on both sides. ➘1a

MONOBLOCK WALL

Monoblock walls are delivered to the building site as completely prefabricated wall elements (framing, fill material and linings). These elements are installed using push-fit connections and are fixed to floor, wall and ceiling rails. ➘1b

CUPBOARD WALL

A cupboard wall is a special form of partition wall, which combines the functions of room division and storage. ➘1c

In contrast to other non-loadbearing walls, the surfaces of these systems come with a final surface treatment and do not have to be skimmed, painted or lined. The systems available offer a wide variety in terms of the design of their elements. Different surface finishes and constructions are offered for various sound insulation and fire safety requirements; in addition there are glazed elements for transparency, various forms of door, and special elements incorporating shelves and media equipment. However, the thickness of the walls, details and joining principles of any given system remain the same. In this way it is possible to combine elements for different requirements.

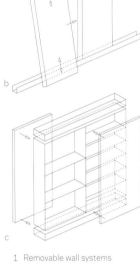

1 Removable wall systems
a Panel wall
b Monoblock wall
c Fitted cupboard wall

2 R+V Versicherung, Wiesbaden, 2010, wma wöhr mieslinger architects. The system of transparent prefabricated wall elements offers full views of the individual offices. The frames of the non-transparent elements also act as frames for the adjoining glass panes, which are therefore independent of the load-bearing structure of the building.

3 Centre for Chemical Biology, Konstanz University, 2013, Heinle, Wischer and Partners. The laboratory cubicles can be flexibly modified within the predefined grid, independently of the services installations. The wall panels also contain technical and work-related elements.

2

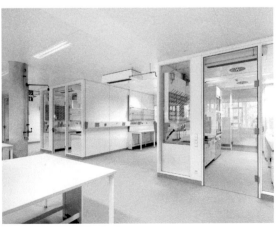

3

4 Construction elements of a panel wall
a Separating strip
b Ceiling and floor profiles
c Studs, also possible with slots or circular perforations in the face for fixing fitted elements (e.g. shelves) and for installations
d Insulation
e Holding strip
f Wall panel, steel sheet or board material
g Shelving, bracket
h Electrical socket

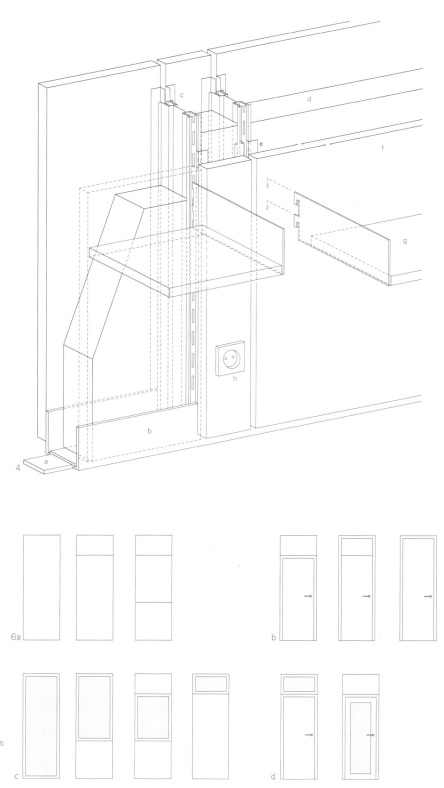

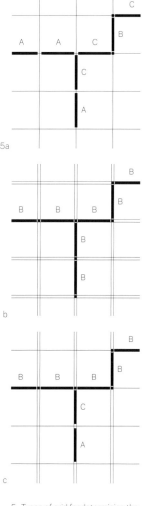

5 Types of grid for determining the dimensions of elements of movable partition walls
a Single-line grid
b Double-line grid
c Combined single and double-line grid

6 Examples of partition wall elements
a Non-transparent elements
b Non-transparent door elements
c Glazed elements
d Glazed door elements

GLAZED PARTITION WALLS

The use of glass is appropriate wherever rooms need to be visually connected, yet remain as separate spaces, or where it is required that daylight should reach internal room zones. Glazed partition walls allow better communication between adjoining areas, while providing some acoustic separation; they also have the effect of making spaces look more generous and more open. The extent of the openings in a partition wall and the transparency of the glass used determine the intensity of the connection between rooms. For example, in an office building with offices on either side of a central corridor, a clerestory fenestration band can supply daylight to the corridor and hence visually extend the space, and at night it can show the rooms in which the light is still on. ↘ **2, p. 76**
Glass partition walls can be installed permanently, or demountable, ↘ **p. 84** or in movable form as all-glass, sliding or folding doors ↘ **p. 90** or they may be designed as movable wall elements ↘ **p. 88**.

PRINCIPLES OF CONSTRUCTION
Glass partitions are available as frame systems ↘ **2**, as mullion-and-transom constructions ↘ **3** – either in wood or metal – or as all-glass designs ↘ **4**.
Glass is a brittle material, which cannot absorb any load from adjoining building components. For this reason, it must always be installed without leaving it subject to stress or external loads. The requirements for glazed partitions are different from those for glass facades. For example, partitions do not have to be designed to transfer wind load. Nevertheless they have to be able to withstand impact and, depending on requirements, must have

good sound insulation and fire safety properties. When designing glazed partitions for interiors, the size of glass panes is not so much limited by manufacturing constraints as by those of transport and installation. What limits the size of glass panes during transportation to the building site, as well as during their installation and subsequent use, is the practicality of handling them.

TYPES OF GLASS AND SPECIAL GLASS
In interior applications, it is usual to install toughened glass or laminated safety glass; for example, when damage or injury has to be prevented in the case of shattered glass, and when the protective function has to be maintained although the glass is partially destroyed. Depending on the sound insulation and fire safety requirements, it is also possible to use laminated glass with several layers.
The spatial effect and transparency can be controlled by the choice of glass. It is possible to colour glass during the manufacturing process and to texture its surface. Furthermore, the effect of the glass can be modified by coatings, by etching or sandblasting the surface and by inserting or attaching foils where, for example, privacy is required. If controllable transparency is needed, it is possible to use glazed partitions with integrated or surface-mounted blinds. A very expensive control method is the use of 'intelligent' glass. In this system, liquid crystals in the gap between two glass panes change the transparency of the assembly to an opaque state when subjected to an electric charge.

1   School building at Leutschenbach, Zurich, 2008, Christian Kerez. Translucent profiled structural glazing is used to provide visual and acoustic separation of classrooms instead of solid walls, thus allowing daylight to penetrate deep into the building.

2   System-based frame wall Feco
Forum, Karlsruhe
Prefabricated room-height frames
are assembled on site. The glazing
is fitted centrally using glazing bars.
The frames of the full-height glass
partition wall rest on the floor
covering, thus allowing for flexible
design.

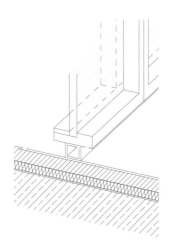

3   Mullion and transom wall Scala
office building, Stuttgart
This skeleton-type system consists
of slender vertical mullions with
transoms at floor and ceiling level,
as well as horizontal cross mem-
bers. Usually the glass panels are
held by glazing bars or, as in the
example shown, the frame is placed
on the substructure and fixed at
intervals.

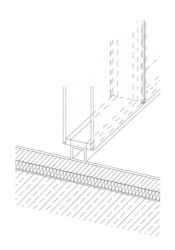

4   All-glass partition wall system
Adidas Laces, Herzogenaurach,
2011, kadawittfeldarchitektur.
The glass panels are held by a
profile on the floor and another on
the ceiling. The upper profile must
have sufficient depth to allow the
panel to be lifted in and be fixed
with pads. This system does not
require vertical uprights; if necessary the glass panels are bonded
to each other or connected via a
permanently elastic joint.

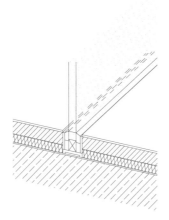

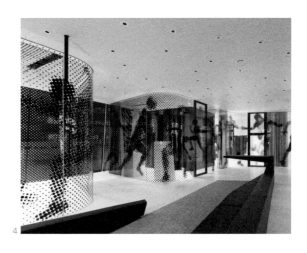

MOVABLE WALL ELEMENTS

Movable wall elements provide an advantage wherever users have to respond to changing space requirements on a daily basis. Among the simplest forms are sliding or revolving doors. ➙ **SCALE, vol. 1, Open | Close** Movable wall elements are ideal where the requirements for flexibility, durability and – to a limited extent – sound insulation are more extensive. They are used in conference centres, schools and dance studios, for example, wherever rooms need to be divided or combined very quickly.

The walls consist of metal frames, which can be lined on both sides with a range of different materials and, depending on the acoustic requirements, are filled with sound insulation material. In addition, there are various special elements such as doors or all-glass panels. ➙ **2** These wall elements have a thickness of 80 to 150 mm, are between 600 and 1,250 mm wide and are available in heights of up to ten metres and over. In this way, it is possible to subdivide even very large rooms, for example gymnasiums.

Usually the elements are only held in place by a guide rail at the top. No rails are required on the floor; however, it may be appropriate to provide fixing points set into the floor at the final positions.

The rooms can only be divided along the runs of the guide rails. The wall elements are moved in the rails via a central one or two-point holder and movable rollers. Although the one-point holder has the advantage that it does not require a second guide rail in the park position, it is more difficult to handle and there is a greater risk of damage through jamming. Given that the guide rails have to be installed absolutely horizontally, the accuracy of the structural ceiling is very important; alternatively, the system must have a means of adjusting to compensate for unevenness.

In addition to systems with manual or semi-automatic mechanisms for moving the wall panels, there are systems with fully automatic movement mechanisms. When the elements are not in use, they are moved into the park position. The parking of the panels requires a storage area and it is important that this is taken into consideration at the design stage. For example, it would not be desirable to have the parked elements protrude into the room and thereby detract from the appearance; therefore the design should make provision for parking space in the form of recesses or within built-in furniture. ➙ **1**

1a

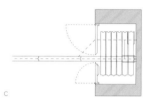
b

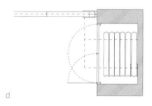
c

d

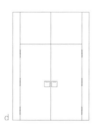

2a   b   c   d   e   f

1 Track layout and parking positions of movable wall elements
Elements are moved away from the track as follows: elements turned at 90° to the axis:
a Parked in parallel to the axis
b Parked in parallel to the axis behind a wall nib
c Parked at right angles to the axis, in a recess
d Parked at right angles to the axis in an offset recess

2 Different types of wall element
a Simple side-hung door
b Simple door that is part of the wall element, so-called wicket door
c Wall element
d Double door
e Glass element
f Wall connection with compression profile

3, 4 With the help of movable wall elements the seminar area can be subdivided into units of different sizes.

3

4

Movable wall element
The elements are fitted with a
clamping mechanism which holds
the wall firmly in position by press-
ing against floor and ceiling. The
mechanism is operated via a manual crank inserted from the side, or
an integrated motor. The elements
are only connected with each other
by a push-fit connection or via
magnets. They can be connected
to a permanent wall using a surface-mounted or recessed profile.
The last movable element has a
flexible edge on the side to make
the joint with the profile.

5 Isometric

6 Vertical section
Scale 1:5

7 Horizontal section
Scale 1:5
a Metal frame
b Face layer
c Joint profile
d Crank
e Clamping mechanism
f Ceiling track
g Carriage with rollers
h Side connection, tongue-and-
groove, rubber seal, magnetic strips

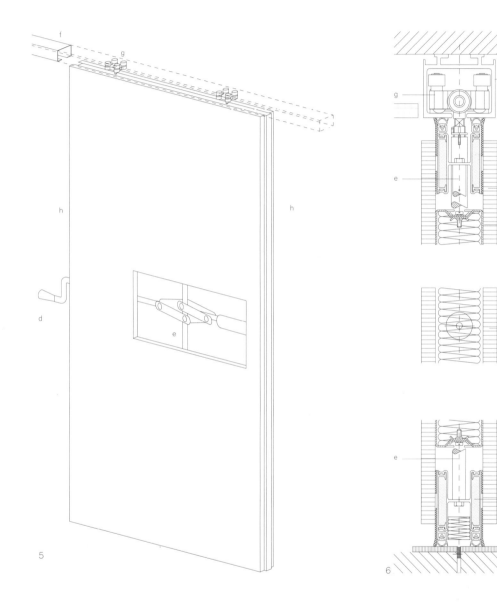

5

6

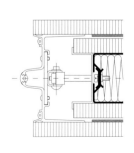
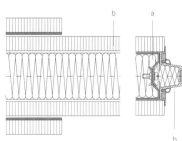
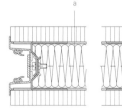

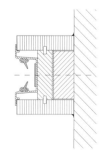

7

FOLDING WALLS

Folding walls, similar to folding doors, consist of hinged panels that can be retracted by pushing them along a guide rail. Usually the panels are made of metal and wood-based material. Glass is also frequently used, either in a window/door construction with a wooden or metal frame, or in the form of all-glass panels.

Depending on the size of the system, it is possible to design folding walls with a one or two-sided opening option. Larger systems should also include a panel that functions as a door.

A distinction is made between centre and off-centre suspended walls. It is important here that the space required for the movement of the wall is accommodated by any suspended ceiling. In centre-suspended folding walls, the suspension rollers are fitted at the centre of every other panel. This means that the elements in the open condition fold symmetrically around the axis of the running track. For this reason, the panel fitted next to the wall has only half of the normal width ⟋1. A floor rail is only required for wider types of this construction.

In the case of off-centre suspended folding walls, the suspension rollers are fitted at the edge of every other panel. This means that the panels project to one side of the rail, so this type of system can also be fitted in front of an opening. Owing to the asymmetrical load, it is necessary to guide the panels in a floor rail.

The grips for operating both these folding walls are always flush with the surface: they are either foldable handles or designed in the form of a recess.

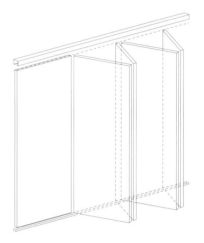

1 Isometric and layout of a centrally suspended folding wall opening to two sides

2 Isometric and layout of an off-centre suspended folding wall opening to two sides

3 Publisher's Hideaway, London, 2010 Alma-nac Collaborative Architecture. The private area in the gallery can be separated using an off-centre suspended folding wall.

4 Saint Laurentius Community Centre, 2010, Kaestle Ocker Roeder Architects. The foyer and multipurpose hall are linked via a movable, single-glazing partition wall consisting of 6 elements.

CURTAINS

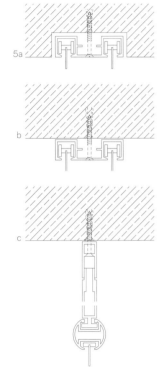

CURTAINS

In addition to their original purposes of blacking out, screening from view and reducing glare, curtains can also be used to create separate spaces. In that function they may be used as temporary dividers, or as an optical filter. Since curtains are easy to handle, such changes can be carried out with very little effort.

The choice of fabric very much depends on the respective requirements. The degree of transparency of the material influences the function of the curtain. Opaque curtains clearly have a stronger separating effect, whereas transparent materials between two areas only provide limited visual protection and allow a certain interaction between rooms. They are often used in situations where the separated area would not otherwise receive any direct daylight. The sensory feel of the fabric and the design of the curtain, i.e. whether it is folded or flat, affect the atmosphere of the room. When choosing the curtain material, it is also important to consider technical aspects such as fire safety, sound insulation and susceptibility to soiling.

Curtains can be suspended from single or multiple rails, which are either recessed in the ceiling or mounted on its surface; motorised drives are also available. Curtain rails can either be inserted into the structural ceiling during the casting process, fitted flush with the plaster finish, or installed as part of a suspended ceiling. Curtain rails with several tracks make it possible to move curtain segments in an overlapping fashion, which provides greater flexibility, particularly with longer curtain runs.

It is also possible to suspend curtains from rods and steel cables. These can be fitted to the wall with spacer brackets, while the former can also be fixed similarly to the ceiling. These versions are primarily suitable in situations where the curtain does not need to cover the full height of the room. ⟶ SCALE, vol. 1, Open | Close

6a   b   c

5 Track systems for various applications
a Integrated into the structure
b Surface-mounted on the ceiling
c Suspended from the ceiling

6 Fixing options for curtain systems

a The track is mounted directly on the ceiling or integrated within it
b The curtain track is suspended from the ceiling via a spacer, for example in very high rooms
c A track system is fixed to columns or existing walls or free-standing fitments

7 New Synagogue, Dresden, 2001, Wandel Hoefer Lorch + Hirsch. A metal mesh curtain forms the transparent enclosure to the room for worship.

8 Apartment Nagi, Kanagawa, 2009, UUfie Architects. Two-sided curtains and tracks are used for a temporary visual separation of zones.

PLASTERS AND COATINGS

The effect of walls and ceilings is determined by their colour and surface texture. → p. 40 Plasters and coatings offer an almost infinite range of surface finish options.

PLASTERS

Interior plaster, just like exterior render, is used to seal brickwork and produce a smooth and even surface. It has to meet certain general requirements, as well as specific ones. The general requirements include minimum hardness, adhesive properties, suitability for subsequent painting, wallpaper hanging, or the application of coatings, and the ability to regulate the climate by absorbing and releasing moisture. The specific requirements include those for fire safety, thermal and acoustic insulation, increased abrasion resistance and resistance to moisture. A distinction is made between plaster with mineral binders (mineral plaster) and plaster with organic binders (synthetic resin plaster).

Mineral plaster is defined in the DIN 18 550 standard and is subdivided into plaster groups PI to PV according to the type of binder. → Tab. 7, p. 165
Plasters can be applied in one coat, or in several layers, each of which should have a minimum thickness of 10 mm. When applying several layers of plaster, the strength of the plaster should be less than that of the substrate and the different layers should decrease in strength from the first to the last coat. The combined application of the various layers of plaster and any coatings is called a plaster system. The requirements vary according to the respective application and always apply to the whole plaster system. Internal plaster is usually based on either lime, or gypsum, or a lime/gypsum mix (plaster groups PI/PIV). A special form of mineral plaster is traditional stucco plaster, such as scagliola (a gypsum-bonded imitation marble) and stucco lustro (another form of imitation marble using lime plaster) which were once used in place of tiles, but are now more commonly applied as design features.

The use of clay as a plaster material is one of the oldest methods in construction. As a natural building material, clay has increased in popularity in recent years. Clay plaster is especially effective at regulating moisture. When applied in wet rooms, it requires separate protective measures, as the plaster is soluble in water.

The DIN 18 558 standard contains specifications for synthetic resin plaster, which is referred to as a coating of plaster-like appearance, since its thickness of less than 10 mm does not qualify it as a genuine plaster. → Tab. 7, p. 165 The coating materials contain organic binders in the form of emulsions or solutions and are supplied ready for application with a putty-like consistency. Synthetic resin plaster is usually applied as a finishing coat on mineral plaster, concrete, or boarding, particularly as the finishing coat of sandwich insulation systems. The surface of these plasters is resilient but tough, which means that they not only meet the general requirements, but also have increased abrasion resistance. For application in wet rooms, only coating materials of group P Org I are suitable. → 1

1 Classification of mineral plaster into plaster mortar groups to DIN 18 550:

P I – Lime plaster mortar
A mixture of sand and lime putty. Due to its high water-vapour permeability and the associated climate-regulating effect, lime plaster is used as an interior finish. However, it does not meet stricter abrasion requirements.

P II – Lime/cement plaster mortar
A mixture of sand, lime and cement. Lime/cement plaster mortar has the same climate-regulating properties as lime plaster but is more resistant to abrasion.

P III – Cement plaster mortar
A mixture of sand and cement, with or without the addition of lime hydrate. Cement-based plaster has lower water-vapour permeability and is therefore suitable for use in damp/humid conditions.

P IV – Gypsum plaster mortar
A mixture of gypsum and sand. Gypsum plaster has a strong climate-regulating effect and can be worked to a very smooth surface; however, it is water-soluble and therefore not really suitable in damp/humid conditions.

P V – Anhydrite plaster mortar
A mixture of sand and anhydrite. Anhydrite plaster mortar has similar properties to gypsum mortar but it is stronger; it is only suitable for interior application.

Classification of coating materials for synthetic resin plaster to DIN 18 558:

P Org 1 – synthetic resin plaster in interior and exterior applications
Polymer resins in the form of emulsions or solutions with added sand. This type of coating material is suitable in damp/humid rooms on plasters of groups P II and P III.

P Org 2 – synthetic resin plaster in interior applications
Polymer resins in the form of emulsions or solutions with added sand. This type of coating material is not suitable for application in damp/humid rooms.

2 Biedermann Museum, Donaueschingen, 2009, Gäbele & Raufer. Wall design with patina effect

3 House in Munich, 2009, Titus Bernhard Architects. Gold-coloured wall coating

4 Plaster profiles
a Plaster corner profile
b Plaster corner profile suitable
for a thin layer of synthetic resin
plaster
c Connection profile for the
formation of a dummy joint
d Dummy joint profile; the profile
of the adjoining fitting-out component engages in a groove

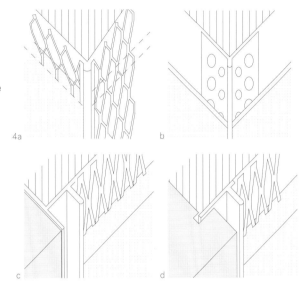

4a

b

c

d

There are different methods of applying plaster, which generate different surface textures and therefore have a strong impact on the visual effect of the plaster finish. Finishing methods include smooth-trowelling, smoothing with a wooden or sponge float, rough-casting or spraying plaster, scratching plaster and applying plaster by roller. ⟶ 5a-c As the plastering process involves much moisture and is generally very messy, the internal walls should be plastered before laying the screed, albeit (necessarily) after mounting the windows. In order to produce neat and accurate corners and connections to adjoining building elements, there is a wide range of plaster profiles, which are shaped to suit the various plaster materials, application methods and connection details. ⟶ 4 Especially the connections to doors, windows and fitted furniture, as well as at the base of the wall ⟶ p. 72 should be considered and specified early in the detail design stage.

COATINGS

The term coating refers to any surfacing material that is applied to the substrate by brushing, rolling or spraying. Coating materials are differentiated according to the type of binder into: distemper (glue base), paint based on either lime or a lime-and-white-cement mixture, and paint based on either silicate, emulsion, or silicone resin. Not all coatings can be applied to all substrates. Lime-based wall paint is a low-cost, water-resistant and vapour-permeable coating for application on substrates classed as groups P I, P II and P III. Wall paint based on a mixture of lime and white cement is also suitable for application in wet rooms.

Silicate-based paints are open-pored and hence highly vapour-permeable; they are suitable for application on all mineral substrates. Silicate-based paints come in a number of different specifications for a wide range of applications, for example on organic substrates such as emulsion paint or synthetic resin plaster.

Emulsion paint can be used to produce interior coatings with wet abrasion-resistance. They are suitable for almost any structurally sound substrate. Exceptions are the plasters of group P I and restoration plaster, owing to their limited water vapour permeability.

Silicone resin paints are water-resistant and water vapour-permeable. They have very good adhesion on all mineral and organic substrates, but are comparatively expensive.

DIN EN 13 300 classifies water-based coating materials for interior application by their intended purpose, the type of binder, the wet abrasion-resistance, the opacity, degree of gloss and grain size.

5 Examples of types of plaster and texture (a–c) as well as coatings (d–f)

a Polished plaster with float-finished structure, grain size 0–0.3 mm

b Natural clay plaster, floated and trowel-finished, grain size 0.8 mm

c Marble powder-based finishing plaster for high-quality polished plaster finishes

d Glossy gold-coloured coating based on acrylic resin with special metal pigments for special effects.

e Mineral coating based on lime finished with a patina effect achieved through a manual process

f Mineral coatings based on lime and marble powder; made to look like concrete with subsequent wax treatment

5a

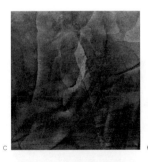

c

e

b

d

f

LININGS AND CLADDINGS

The visual impression of a room can be significantly modified by applying lining or cladding to a wall. Rooms are perceived differently in their proportion according to the direction, grain texture and structure of fitting-out elements, quite apart from the different visual, acoustic and tactile aspects. Where a material is applied directly to the plaster surface, such as wallpaper, it is called a 'lining'. Thicker materials which are attached to a wall on a substructure are referred to as 'cladding'. Lining is much easier to remove again and as this material is relatively thin, it can also be covered, e.g. papered over. Cladding is considerably more involved in its construction. As a rule, wall cladding is combined with the installation of services or built-ins.

LININGS

In accordance with DIN EN 233 and 234, wall linings (wallpapers) are subdivided into finished linings and linings for subsequent treatment. DIN EN 235 subdivides finished wall linings into paper, plastic, fleece, textile, velour, metal effect and natural material types and provides the respective information on their properties and application.

Owing to the wide distribution of digital printing, wallpaper has become a popular choice for creating a personalised interior finish in recent years. An important prerequisite for a perfect finish is the quality of the substrate and its suitability for the respective type of wallpaper.

There are a number of approaches to help with the removal of wallpaper; some wallpapers can be fully removed as they are coated on the back, which allows them to be removed without residue. In wallpapers that can be removed dry, the facing layer separates from the backing layer, which is thus left behind and can be used as lining for the new wallpaper. Paintable wallpapers with inseparable layers are removed by perforating them and soaking them with lye.

WALL CLADDINGS

Walls can be covered with cladding for a variety of reasons. Where special acoustic requirements have to be met, for example, a room may be clad with acoustically effective wall panels. ➔ p. 46 In addition, cladding can conceal services installations without the need to make slots or recesses in the wall. Wall cladding panels can be removed with relative ease, either to inspect the space behind or to replace some of the panels. The substructure for cladding may consist of base and counter battens and has to be fitted in a way that compensates for any unevenness of the existing wall, allows installations to be installed horizontally and vertically, permits insulation, if any, to be inserted and fixed, and facilitates air circulation . The detailed design and selection of materials should always be considered in connection with the adjoining building components. Typical materials used for wall cladding are wood, wood-based materials, plastics, sheet metal, ceramics, leather and fabric.

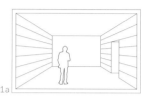
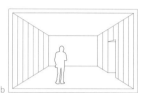
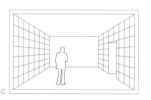

1   Visual effect
The texture and direction of claddings have an effect on the visual perception of the size of a room. For example, a room with a linear horizontal pattern ➔ a appears longer than a room with vertical elements ➔ b. A room with a small-format division of panels ➔ c appears larger than a room with large panel formats.

2   5 Jahreszeiten restaurant, Marburg: the textile wall covering functions purely on a graphic level. The images represent a play on the use and atmosphere of the room.

3   VIP wing, Munich, 2011, Erich Gassmann, Tina Aßmann. The textile wall lining in green velvet lends a particularly tactile atmosphere to the conference room and also has an acoustic effect.

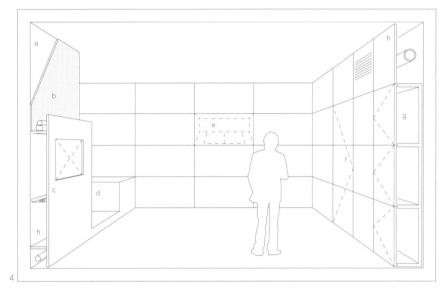

4

TEXTILE LININGS

Textile linings are often used as an acoustically effective wall lining, or as a background for the exhibits in museums and galleries. The acoustic effect can be increased by fitting additional insulation; while certain materials offer greater degrees of translucency or transparency, for use in combination with backlighting, for example. The substructure usually consists of timber framing, which can be covered with one or several layers, depending on requirements. Depending on the width of the fabric or membrane, it is possible to cover large areas without seams. A more expensive version consists of individually lined panels that are fitted to a metal substructure using clips or magnetic holders. On the other hand, this method makes it possible to replace individual panels, should they sustain damage or soiling. There are now also systems with a spring mechanism that automatically adjusts the tension of the lining fabric.

4 Lining and cladding
a Plaster
b Lining (wallpaper)
c Half-height cladding, optionally with backlighting
d Platform with seating continuing on from the cladding
e Integration of window/display cabinet/screen
f Door flush with surface finish
g Fitted furniture in wall recess
h Services installation

5 Kolumba, Cologne, 2007, Peter Zumthor. The reading room of the diocesan museum has been clad with mahogany veneer to create a luxurious interior in contrast to the plain exhibition rooms.

6 Residence, Munich, 2010, Unterlandstättner Architects. The interior – with its textile-lined wall units – takes its cue from the historic context of the house dating from the 1930s.

7 Office building, Munich, 2011, Landau + Kindelbacher. The conference area in the centre of the building has been finished with sculptural surfaces in a mineral-based material, in deliberate contrast to the other office areas. The horizontal pattern reinforces the dynamic geometry of the room.

5

6

7

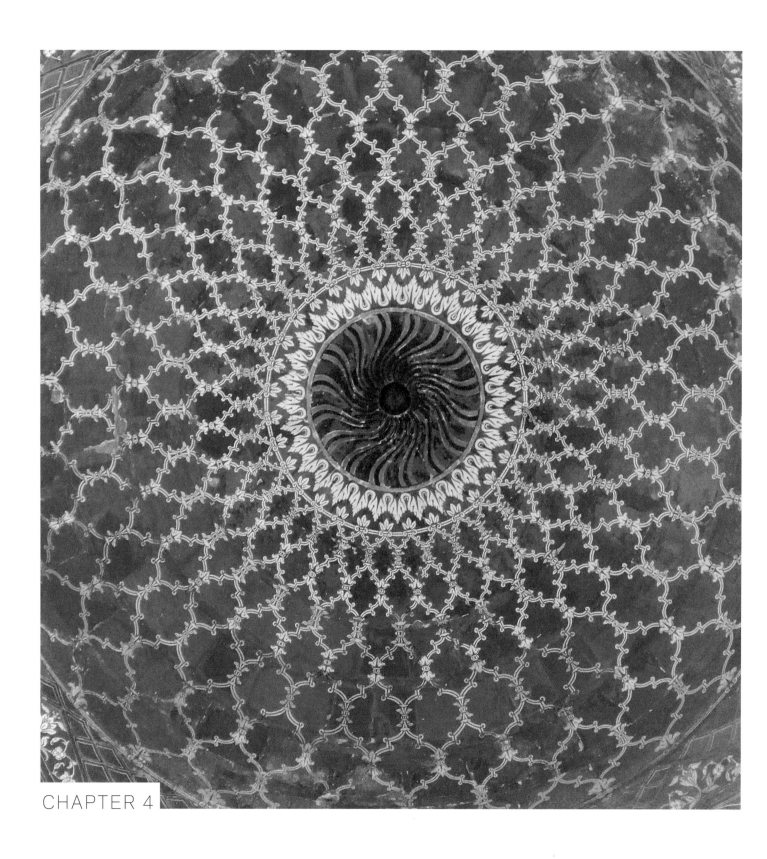

INTRODUCTION

As well as floors and walls, ceilings have a major impact on the atmosphere and effect of a room. The choice of material, grid pattern and colour of a ceiling significantly influences the proportion and appearance of a room. Light-coloured ceilings make a room appear higher and more airy, whereas dark wood cladding can convey a more cosy – but possibly also oppressive – effect. Depending on the colour of both ceiling and floor, it may also be possible to ensure that daylight penetrates deeper into the room, owing to its reflection from the floor/ceiling. Where there are joint patterns visible in the ceiling, either created by panelling or by the formwork (in the case of a fair-faced concrete ceiling), the size and format of the segments significantly affect the sense of proportion in the room. Thus the impression of the overall size of a room can be affected by the scale of the patterns, and the direction of any grid may be used to emphasise or counteract the sense of a room's length or width.

Other functions to be considered in the design of ceilings include lighting, ventilation, ducting, acoustics, fire safety, and thermal insulation. With the increasingly stricter requirements relating to services installations, the complexity and variety of ceiling constructions also increases. These requirements have a considerable effect on the ceiling design and therefore must be considered at an early stage. For this reason, it is common practice to produce reflected ceiling plans for ceilings with more complex designs or services installations; these show all types of installation and are used to adapt the ceiling design to the given parameters of the structural system and layout.

In the case of an exposed structural ceiling, its size and design are largely governed by technical requirements. This building element must perform its supporting function as well as visual and service functions. It is important that any services installations are well designed and carefully executed. These may be fitted within the structural ceiling itself, above it if there is space available in a raised floor, or exposed to view on its underside.

In the case of fair-faced concrete ceilings/floors, any installations have to be run through conduits inserted in the concrete. Light fittings can be inserted at a later stage into housings that have been included in the cast concrete. The position of such housings should be designed to fit in with the shuttering pattern. With nail-laminated decks, it is not possible to integrate conduits and installations within the deck. These items are therefore usually installed within the floor construction of the floor above. Electric cables are then dropped from that installation plane to the planned outlets. In public buildings requiring much technical infrastructure, pipes and cables are often installed visibly beneath the structural ceiling, where they are easily accessible for inspection and maintenance. If the installations and the structural ceiling need to be less noticeable, they can be painted black.
→ 2

In order to meet the various requirements for ceilings/floors, it is usually possible to separate primary and secondary functions.

1 Academy of Arts Berlin (Weißensee), auditorium, 2012, Baukanzlei Fiel Jennrich. The large-format timber panelling in the auditorium of the Academy of Arts, which dates from 1955/56 and is listed as an historic building, creates a very special atmosphere.

2 Restaurant, Cairo, 2010, .PSLAB. The services required for the room are integrated into the design concept. The black paint allows any detrimental detail to merge into the background. The black light fittings continue the theme and blend in with the overall image.

3 Fitments and transitions, designing jointing details
Technical requirements – such as the installation of services e.g. wiring and air conditioning – and building physics requirements relating to sound insulation and fire safety make the design of ceilings a complex task. This is particularly the case when functional elements such as shading devices or room dividers are to be integrated into a ceiling. The transition to adjoining building components is of special importance, as is the junction between wall and floor: junction details may be completely without a visible joint, or alternatively may have a dummy joint or a deliberately emphasised joint, as for example with integrated indirect light fittings. However, it is also possible to harmonise the transition to such an extent that floor, wall and ceiling become one continuous building component.

a   Structural ceiling
b   Ceiling lining
c   Suspended ceiling
d   Freeform element combining wall and ceiling
e   Recessed light fittings
f   Ventilation duct
g   Services lines
h   Inspection hatch
i   Ventilation outlet
j   Joint with hidden lighting

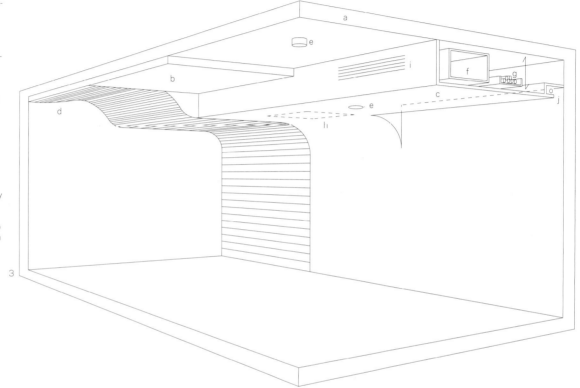

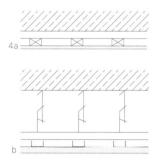

4   Differentiation between ceiling lining and suspended ceiling
⟶ DIN 18 168

a   Ceiling linings are in direct contact with the structural ceiling, either via a substructure or a levelling compound.

b   Suspended ceilings have an integral substructure in the form of profiles which are suspended from the structural ceiling.

Ceiling linings or suspended ceilings make it possible to achieve a degree of flexibility while accommodating the requirements of services installations and building preservation. This is advantageous for the maintenance and replacement of installations, which is important in view of the fact that the service life of technical installations is significantly shorter than that of the building.

Ceiling linings and suspended ceilings differ in their type of construction and in the function they fulfil.
A general distinction is made between rigid and lightweight construction. Lining finishes can be plaster (DIN 18550) or other linings that are directly attached to the loadbearing building component ⟶ 4a; alternatively it is possible to suspend ceilings either with a backing material for a plaster finish (DIN 4121) or to install a proprietary lightweight suspended ceiling ⟶ 4b.

Ceiling linings and plaster are primarily used to cover up inaccuracies and deviations that are part of the permissible tolerance in a structural ceiling. The technical advantages provided by these finishes are relatively limited. Depending on specification, they can improve the acoustics of a room or provide additional fire safety. In addition, it is possible that the void created by the substructure of a light, suspended ceiling can be used for electric installations and shallow inset light fittings.
The void created by suspended ceilings separates the loadbearing structure from the actual ceiling and provides space for the installation of technical infrastructure. This means that the interior fit-out – with all its requirements for ventilation, lighting, acoustics etc. – is largely independent of the structural system of the building.

Traditionally ceilings were built by craftsmen, sometimes to an elaborate standard – wood-panelled ceilings for example – which also exhibited regional cultural differences. The modern construction of ceiling linings and suspended ceilings is largely based on industrial methods. Lightweight prefabricated elements, which are fitted on site in a dry installation process, provide a high degree of flexibility. As with wall constructions consisting of several skins, these types of ceiling make it possible to comply with a wide range of functional and physical requirements, independently of the building shell. Owing to the low weight and short construction times, it is also possible to change the layout of rooms with relatively little effort.

The many different requirements are met by a corresponding variety of types of suspended ceiling. Designs include homogeneous board ceilings without joints, panelled ceilings based on a grid pattern (in particular slatted, tiled or bandraster suspended ceilings), and a variety of open suspended ceilings. These last can be built in a directional pattern (e.g. as a vertically slatted ceiling), or non-directional as a cassette, honeycomb, or grid ceiling.

The connection of both ceiling linings and suspended ceilings with the walls presents a challenge in terms both of appearance and of technical details. Flush connections often tend to result in cracking.
This can be counteracted by inserting a recessed joint. Such a recessed joint not only articulates the junction between wall and ceiling, but also provides an opportunity for design features such as indirect lighting. A traditional solution that calls attention to the transition between wall and ceiling is the fitting of various profiled battens; alternatively it is possible to fit coving which – with its concave shape – rather mediates between the two building elements.
Modern materials and production processes have helped to provide a greater variety of ceiling linings and suspended ceilings, ranging from individual elements and free forms through to the complete elimination of the boundary between wall and ceiling.

TYPES OF CEILING

Exposed ceilings
– with integrated services
– with surface-mounted services

Ceilings without joints
– plastered ceiling
– skimmed ceiling
– wire plaster ceiling
– boarded ceiling
– stretch ceiling

Segmented ceilings, closed
– slatted ceiling
– suspended tile ceiling
– suspended bandraster ceiling

Segmented ceilings, open
– vertical slatted ceiling
– cassette or honeycomb ceiling
– grid ceiling

1 Wake room, Aalen, 2009, Kaestle Ocker Roeder Architects. A new radial room shell is inserted into the existing listed building. It forms a kind of canopy for which woven willow has been chosen, which involves one of the oldest manual construction methods.

2 Opera House, Guangzhou, 2011, Zaha Hadid Architects. The interior of the main auditorium features a flowing structure of seamlessly joined sculptural fibreglass elements.

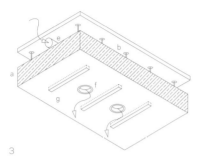
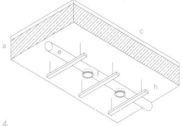
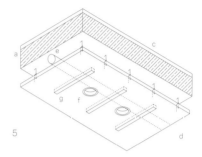

3

4

5

When designing a ceiling it is important to consider how services installations are integrated.
a Reinforced concrete structural ceiling
b Cavity floor
c Screed
d Suspended ceiling
e Ventilation duct
f Air outlet
g Integrated lighting
h Suspended lighting

3 Fair-faced ceiling with integrated installations: The wiring is installed in conduits and light fittings are mounted in light boxes. The layout of the shuttering should take the positioning of these items into account.

4 Fair-faced ceiling with exposed installations:
The installations are deliberately exposed below the structural ceiling and therefore have to be carefully planned and executed. They are directly accessible for the purpose of inspection. For design reasons, the entire ceiling and components are is frequently finished in black.

5 Ceiling suspended from the structural ceiling: In this construction, the primary and secondary functions are separated. A suspended ceiling provides a high degree of flexibility both for the integration of services and for the design of the actual ceiling.

6 Neue Galerie Kassel, 2011, Staab Architects. A modern daylight ceiling element in three parts has been installed flush in the upper ceiling in order to achieve an even spread of daylight in the foyer.

7 Credit Suisse, Zurich, 2013, Stücheli Architects. The mixed form involving the structural ceiling and flat ceiling lining integrates ventilation and other services with noise absorbing elements in a unique design.

6

7

TYPES OF CEILING

EXPOSED CEILINGS

Exposed structural ceilings
Fair-faced concrete ceilings
Ribbed slab ceilings
Nail-laminated ceilings

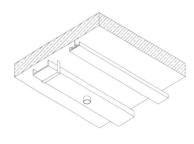

In the case of fair-faced structural ceilings, the position of integrated services has to be carefully designed. Any housings or conduits used for the services installation cannot be changed at a later date. If the services are surface-mounted, it is important to consider the visual effect on the entire space.

CEILINGS WITHOUT JOINTS

Plastered ceilings
Skimmed ceilings

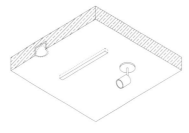

Plastering is probably the most common form of finishing ceilings. Plaster levels out any unevenness of the structural substrate. Concrete ceilings are often installed using prefabricated elements for reasons of cost efficiency. When this type of ceiling is correctly installed, it is often sufficient to fill the joints and transitions with a filler in order to achieve a smooth finish. It is also possible to sand the surface and finish it with a lacquer or stain.

Wire plaster ceilings
Lath and plaster ceilings
Boarded ceilings

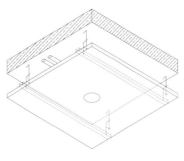

Any more serious defects in existing ceilings can be hidden by installing a boarded or reinforced plaster ceiling (in existing buildings, the reinforcement often consists of timber lath or reed). This also provides the opportunity to integrate pipes or other services in the cavity created. Common finishing materials are plasterboard with skim, gypsum fibre and mineral fibre boards.

Stretch ceilings

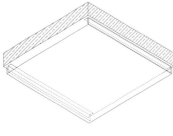

Stretch ceilings are primarily used in situations where a flat ceiling is required with a void above, without an expensive substructure. Common materials used are polymer foils, which can be opaque or translucent, and can also be perforated in order to improve the room acoustics. Where lighting elements are fitted above a translucent foil, it is possible to create large-format light ceilings.

SEGMENTED CEILINGS, CLOSED

Slatted ceilings

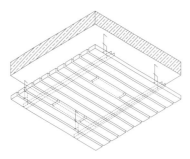

By installing linear strips it is possible to cover a relatively large ceiling using a relatively inexpensive substructure. It is common to use metal or plastic strip panels in a range of finishes. Solid wood or wood-based panels can be either butt-jointed or fitted as a tongue-and-groove lining.

Suspended tile ceilings

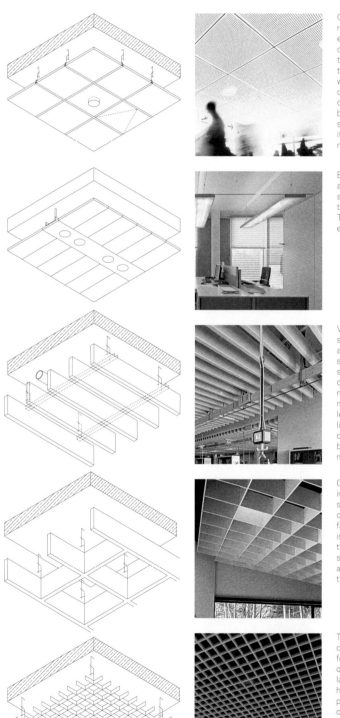

Originally, the term 'cassette ceiling' referred to a craftsman-built wooden ceiling with a distinct three-dimensional form. Nowadays the term also relates to modular systems consisting of a substructure with metal, gypsum or wood-based cassette tiles. This type of ceiling construction is widely used in office buildings and lends itself to the installation of services; furthermore, it is flexible and can easily be modified.

Suspended bandraster ceilings

Bandraster suspended ceilings are a mixed form, characterised by a substructure of broader profiles that can be used to install services. The spaces in between can be covered with slats or suspended tiles.

SEGMENTED CEILINGS, OPEN

Vertical slatted ceilings

Vertical slatted ceilings are installed as a second layer beneath an existing structural ceiling. Any services installed above can be seen. Depending on the angle of observation, the linear ceiling elements convey a rather open or more closed structure. This system lends itself to the integration of linear lighting elements. The slats can be made of solid wood, wood-based material, mineral fibre or metal.

Cassette ceilings
Honeycomb ceilings

Open cassette or honeycomb ceilings can be manufactured from the same materials as vertical slatted ceilings. Owing to the enlarged surface area and the materials used, it is possible to significantly improve the room acoustics. Services installations are visible from below and – owing to the open construction – are easy to service/inspect.

Grid ceilings

The pattern of grid ceilings (also called cell grid ceilings) is a small-format pattern, resulting in a quiet appearance. They consist of larger grid panels made of plastic, hardboard or metal, which are suspended from the structural ceiling or inserted into a substructure. Grid panels have limited acoustic properties, which is why they are often used in conjunction with sound absorbers installed above the ceiling.

CEILINGS WITHOUT JOINTS

Ceilings without joints are in widespread use, particularly in residential construction. A distinction has to be made between ceiling linings (primarily plaster) on one hand, which are applied to compensate for unevenness of the structural ceiling within tolerances and to improve the room acoustics, and suspended ceilings on the other hand, which also allow the installation of services in the void above. A special form is the so-called 'stretch' ceiling, which is frequently used in commercial applications, for example in sales rooms. The visual effect of ceilings without joints is to make a room appear larger and to provide a neutral backdrop.

PLASTERS
Plaster makes a firm connection with the substrate. In interior applications, it is usual to use gypsum or lime-cement based plaster, which has a regulating effect on the humidity in the room. With interior plaster, it is possible to produce very smooth surfaces. Textured surfaces may be required for visual reasons or for the improvement of the acoustics in a room. It is possible to integrate services in plaster finishes, although this requires careful consideration at the design stage. For that purpose, it is possible to cut slots or insert conduit at the plastering stage.

WIRE PLASTER CEILINGS
The wire plaster ceiling – in its historical form also known as a lath and plaster ceiling – consists of a plastered support structure, such as metal lath, wooden lath (slats) or reed mats, fixed to the underside of a timber floor or substructure. In its suspended form, a wire plaster ceiling provides a void for the installation of services. The construction is relatively expensive and access for servicing the installations is quite involved, as special openings need to be provided; for this reason these ceilings are now primarily used in refurbishments, having otherwise lost out to lightweight suspended ceilings.

BOARDED CEILINGS
The facing layer of boarded ceilings normally consists of plasterboard or gypsum fibreboard which, for acoustic reasons, may be perforated or include an insulation backing. The supporting structure can be constructed of timber or metal.
Boarded ceilings can either be suspended from the structural ceiling or fitted directly to it. Where ceiling board is fitted directly to the structural ceiling, it usually requires some form of battening, sometimes with counter-battens, as a substructure. The void created in this way can be used for the installation of services. The substructure should be spaced at intervals to suit the dimensions of the board so that the joints are supported. A common width of board material is 1200 mm, therefore a suitable spacing of battens is either 600 mm or 400 mm, depending on the thickness of the board. → 3

Different systems exist for constructing a suspended board ceiling. As in the case of ceiling linings, common materials for fixing a suspended ceiling are timber battens and counter-battens, as well as profiles of aluminium or galvanised steel. The construction can be suspended from elements such as slotted straps, clips and vernier hangers → 2c which themselves are fixed directly or via installation slats to the loadbearing building component. → 2 The ceiling board is screwed or nailed to the substructure and then the joints between boards, and the screw or nail heads, are skimmed over. The void above the board makes it easy to install services and light fittings; an appropriate number of access points should be provided for maintenance and their positions recorded in a reflected ceiling plan. → 4

The connection detail of the ceiling to the wall has an impact on the feel of a room. A connection without a visible joint creates a homogeneous appearance. In such cases, an elastic joint should be provided in order to avoid any cracking. The insertion of a recessed joint creates a succinctly defined ceiling field and can be used for the installation of indirect lighting. → 1, 5

STRETCH CEILINGS
Stretch ceilings are a special form of ceiling without joints; their construction method and low weight make them suitable for spans of up to ten metres. Several lengths of elastic polymer membrane, about two metres wide, are welded together into one sheet, which is fitted at the edges with special clips and beading; these are used to hold the sheet in tracks that are fitted to the walls and have the effect of framing the ceiling. When fully installed, the sheet is constantly under tension, which means that no additional substructure is necessary. Stretch ceilings are often used in combination with backlighting. In that case, translucent membranes are used to ensure that light is evenly diffused throughout the room.

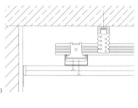
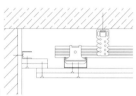
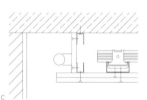

1   General detail options for the joint between wall and suspended ceiling
a   Butt connection without joint
b   Shadow joint
c   Enlarged joint or coving for the integration of lighting

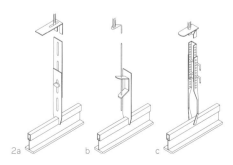

2   Different types of metal suspension hook for suspended ceilings
a   Slotted strap hanger
b   Clip hanger
c   Vernier hanger
→ 4a

3 Ceiling lining with battens and
counter-battens as wooden
substructure
a Fixing to structural ceiling
b Primary batten
c Counter-batten
d Board lining

4 Suspended ceiling with
substructure of galvanised metal
profiles, suspended from quick
suspension hangers
a Hanger
b Primary profile
c Counter profile
d Board lining

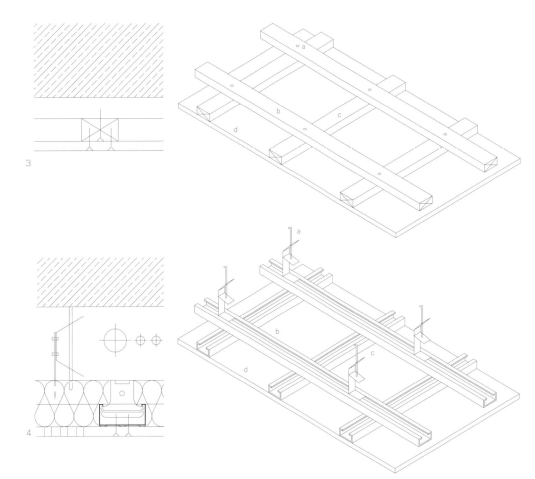

5 Canteen, Munich, 2013, Landau
+ Kindelbacher. Plasterboard ceiling, smooth and perforated, with
integrated services and a coving
with indirect lighting

6 Day nursery, Atterberry, 2011,
dirschl.federle Architects. The
ceiling lining consists of cement-
bonded wood-fibre panels.

SEGMENTED CEILINGS, CLOSED

Segmented ceilings are primarily used in public buildings such as offices, hospitals and sales rooms. The modular construction allows a high degree of flexibility, both in use and for servicing, upgrading or modification. Segmented ceilings with a closed facing layer also create a void which can be used for the installation of services. There is a wide variety of construction principles, which are optimised for various applications. A basic distinction is made between slatted, tiled and bandraster ceilings.

SLATTED CEILINGS

The term 'slatted ceiling' refers to a construction in which the facing consists of individual rectangular or longitudinal units, or 'slats' made of wood, metal or plastic, which are fixed to the substructure. Depending on the requirements, these slats come in different versions, for example with perforations in order to improve acoustic performance. They may be fixed with bracket, tie or clip systems, which are usually concealed. The space between the slats is often left open as a recessed joint which makes it possible – in spite of the closed appearance of the ceiling – for ventilation inlets and outlets to be situated above them; these joints can also compensate for and hide inaccuracies in the shell construction. Individual slats can be replaced with relative ease at any time; often light fittings are integrated using special panels which easily fit into the system. Owing to the strongly directional character of slatted ceilings, they can also be used either to emphasise or to counteract the perceived proportions of a room. → 2

Slatted ceilings are distinct from panel ceilings, which usually consist of purpose-made wooden boards or wood-based panels, mounted on a wooden substructure. The boards can be produced with butt, tongue-and-groove or overlapping joints.

SUSPENDED TILE CEILINGS

Suspended tile ceilings usually consist of square elements inserted into a suspended substructure. This means that they are easy to replace, as well as offering access to any technical infrastructure that may have been installed above. Suspended tile ceilings are often used as a low-cost suspended ceiling for improving the acoustics in rooms where many people congregate. The elements themselves usually consist of perforated gypsum, mineral fibre, or foam board. It is also possible to use metal, or wood-based materials. There are many different systems on the market, which have been designed for a range of different technical requirements. It is therefore no surprise that special elements for lighting and ventilation are available for the more popular systems. Normally the substructure consists of metal framing which – in the case of superimposed tiles – is visible in the gap between the tiles. Systems with more complex rebates on the tiles that are inserted into the substructure do not show the framing, but only reveal a narrow V-groove at the joint of the tiles. → 3

The term 'cassette ceiling' is used for constructions based on square, rectangular, or polygonal grids with a more sculptural effect, i.e. with the edges raised to create a three-dimensional shape. Although this type of construction has its roots in traditional craftsmanship, the principle is still applied today in modern versions. The frame of the cassette serves as substructure and design element at the same time; it is usually made of timber and can sometimes have very elaborate profiling. The material and colour of a cassette are usually the same as those of the cassette frame, but they may be different for aesthetic or technical reasons, e.g. for the purpose of improving the acoustic performance or for the integration of services. It is also conceivable for a textile lining to be used instead of metal, gypsum or wood-based materials. Owing to their distinct profiling, cassette ceilings are acoustically effective. They are prominent in their appearance and the grid pattern can be used to influence the feel of a room.

A special form of closed segmented ceiling is the pyramid ceiling. These ceilings use the advantage of modular construction for the installation of lighting and ventilation openings, as well as for generating an acoustically effective profile. The pyramidal elements may consist of wood-based materials, mineral fibre board or metal sheet, and are inserted into a metal substructure.

SUSPENDED BANDRASTER CEILINGS

This mixed form of closed segmented ceiling is characterised by a continuous longitudinal substructure, which is primarily designed for the installation of light fittings or fire-alarm systems and which can also be used in combination with lightweight partition walls. The 'bandraster' profiles support the ceiling elements between them, which may be in the form of slats or tiles. → 4

1a

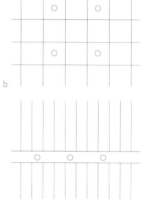
b

c

1 The basic structure of the reflected ceiling plan is determined by the dimensions of the type of grid. In turn it defines the position of walls and any services installations such as lighting and ventilation.
a Slatted ceiling
b Suspended tile ceiling
c Suspended bandraster ceiling

2 Slatted ceiling with the option
of inserting metal slats of different
widths into a bracket suspended
from the structural ceiling
a Various metal profiles
b Suspension system
c Cross runner

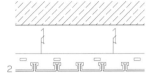

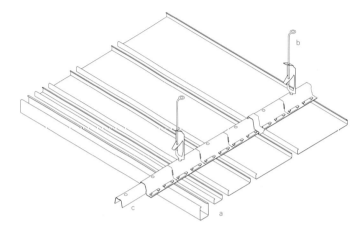

3 Suspended tile ceiling
a Cross section, system with
visible substructure
b Cross section, Z-system with
removable ceiling tiles and concealed substructure
c Hanger
d Main runner/tee bar
e Cross tee
f Ceiling tile

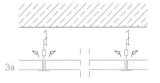

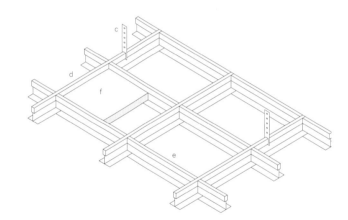

4 Bandraster ceiling with metal
panels
a Hanger
b Bandraster profile
c Connection element
d Wall connection element

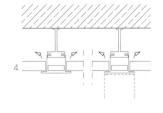

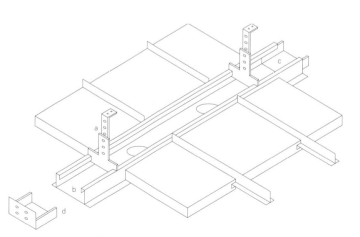

SEGMENTED CEILINGS, OPEN

Open segmented ceilings are used in rooms in which the services installed underneath the structural ceiling require a direct connection to the room beneath. These types of ceiling lend themselves well to the installation of complex systems such as ventilation, air conditioning, or sprinklers, which would be difficult to integrate and access in the case of a closed ceiling. Despite these services being visible, they are not obtrusive and the room imparts a sense of openness, which may be particularly important in rooms with a low ceiling height; although the ceiling appears open when one looks straight at it, the impression from a more indirect perspective is that it is closed. So in spite of its open structure, this type of construction forms a visually closed ceiling. By painting the structural ceiling and any services installations black, they merge more into the background and the ceiling itself seems more like a spatial boundary.

VERTICAL SLATTED CEILINGS

Vertical slatted ceilings consist of vertically arranged, parallel slats or form elements, which are suspended from a substructure. The void is used for the installation of services. Since vertical slatted ceilings are clearly directional, they are often used in order to influence the perception of a room's proportions. When these slats are installed across the direction of view, they have a shortening effect, whereas when they run parallel to it, they emphasise the depth of the space. Furthermore, they can be used to control the direction of light and for the installation of glare-free or indirect lighting. Vertical slatted ceilings are acoustically effective. A wide range of materials can be used for the slats (wood, metal, plastic or mineral-based materials); in addition, the surface of the material can be profiled or perforated in order to optimise the acoustic effect.

CASSETTE AND HONEYCOMB CEILINGS

Honeycomb and open cassette ceilings are constructed in a similar way to vertical slatted ceilings, using vertical elements, but these are arranged in such a way as to form enclosed subdivisions. In the case of a cassette ceiling, these are square or rectangular, while in a honeycomb ceiling they are polygonal. The surface area of such elements in the horizontal plane is small and therefore does not restrict air exchange or the ingress of light. Nevertheless, the vertical depth of the elements is sufficient to afford effective glare protection as well as effective sound absorption.

GRID CEILINGS

Grid ceilings usually consist of suspended grid elements that are made of plastic or metal. Grid ceilings function rather like a filter to create an open spatial boundary. Owing to the relatively small grid pattern, they convey the impression of a homogeneous, continuous ceiling. This visual effect makes it possible to place any services installations wherever they are needed; for example, the outlets of ventilation or air conditioning systems can be positioned wherever required. Correspondingly, the services can be accessed at any location, because any grid element can be removed.

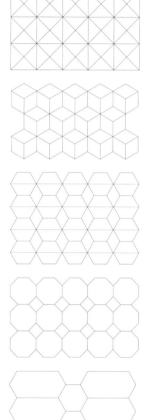

1

2

3

1 Schematic illustration of honeycomb ceiling grids ➔ 5

2 Office, Aachen, 2011, kadawittfeldarchitektur. The ceiling with vertical slats is ideally suited for the installation of linear lighting elements. When viewed from a position at right angles to the slats the impression is one of a flat ceiling.

3 Frankfurt Airport Centre, 2011, Menzel Kossowski. The layer of aluminium cylinders conceals the services installations and provides easy access for servicing; it also acts as a light filter.

4   Vertical slatted ceiling with
suspended wood slats
a   Hanger
b   Hanger profile with slots on both
sides
c   Wooden slat

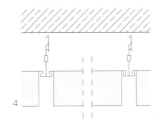

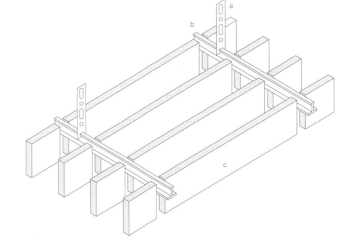

5   Open cassette ceiling,
rectangular honeycomb-type
ceiling
a   Hanger
b   Tee bars
c   Cross tees

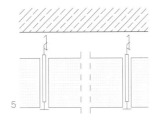

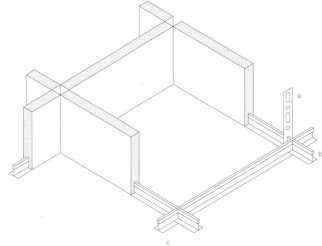

6   Light metal grid ceiling
a   Hanger
b   Metal grid

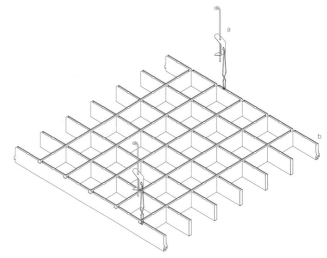

FURNISHING | ZONING
FURNITURE AND FIXTURES

FITTING, PLACING AND FURNISHING

The effect of rooms can be influenced by the inclusion of fixtures. These can become an integral part of the existing space, or they can divide it into zones by being placed in a certain position and used in a certain way. By means of their shape, construction, material and degree of contrast with the rest of the room, these elements – beyond their purely functional aspect – can change the perception of a room. Fixtures can either be assembled from prefabricated elements or be built individually. With the latter, it is possible to create a better match to the specific situation in a room, although of course the higher input of manual labour means that they are more expensive. Fitted furniture is often placed in existing recesses, but can also be freestanding in front of a wall. If it is placed projecting into the room, it will define a distinct area of the room.

In contrast to ordinary furniture, fixtures – as the name implies – cannot be moved. However, their advantage is that they can be individually designed for a certain function or an existing space, which can result in freestanding and specific solutions. The type of fitment depends on the requirements. When fitted in recesses, in corners, or under staircases, it is possible to create additional storage space. On the other hand, it is also possible to build a cupboard wall in front of an existing wall to create a walk-in wardrobe or other storage facility.

In offices and consultancy rooms, it is possible to conceal necessary storage facilities behind innocuous fronts without detracting from the desired effect of the room. In this way it is possible to integrate back office, storage and archiving areas that visually merge with the room.

In the home, it is possible to use fitted furniture as room dividers, which can be accessed either from one side only or from both sides. Such room dividers can incorporate a range of functional elements such as shelving for storage and even a table or bed, any of which can be activated by an intelligent fold-out mechanism.

As the basic unit both of prefabricated modules and of purpose-made fixtures, carcass elements are usually based on standard dimensions. This makes it easier to combine both kinds of product. Where such modules cannot be combined to match the dimensions of a room exactly, any remaining gap can be filled with smaller purpose-made units or, in the case of very small spaces, with covering elements e.g. pelmets or fascias.

These carcasses may come with holes pre-drilled at a standard spacing, which can be used for the insertion of items such as shelves and drawers, or for fitting ironmongery for doors and flaps. Sliding doors require special fittings, which are either recessed into the carcass or surface-mounted. Both doors and drawers can be opened either by means of recesses or handles, which are available in a wide range of designs.

The aesthetics of fitted furniture and their effect on the atmosphere of a room depend on the surface of the visible parts. These are commonly produced from warp-free, wood-based materials such as medium-density fibreboard (MDF) or chipboard, which are then finished with a coating, veneer or high-pressure laminate (HPL).

The choice of surface and colour decides whether a fitment blends in with the appearance of the room, forms a distinct element, or dominates the whole room. This applies in particular to shop fittings, in restaurants and exhibitions – in other words: where a certain atmosphere needs to be created. Such situations, in which the fitted furniture is also used as design element, sometimes give rise to complex geometries and unusual combinations of functions. For example, elements may serve as display areas, information points, media terminals, seating and storage facilities.

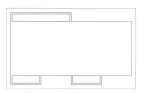

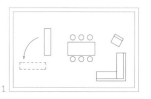

1   Three types of furniture can be distinguished:
a   Fitted furniture
b   Freestanding fitted furniture
c   Non-fitted furniture

2

2   Warborn apartment, V. N. de Gaia, 2009, Caiano Morgado Arquitectos Associados. The function and structure of the fitment overlap and serve several functions.

3 Fitted furniture
Fitted furniture is often placed in existing space created by the building fabric, e.g. in window recesses. In new buildings it should ideally be considered in the design for the structural shell. This ensures that it fits functionally and aesthetically into the overall design. Compared to freestanding furniture, changing the use is difficult since the function of the furniture is largely determined by the fact that it is fitted.

Freestanding fitted furniture
This can be used to create specific zones in a room; it can be accessible from several sides and can combine a range of functions.

Non-fitted furniture
With this type of furniture the room remains neutral in its function as the furniture can be moved at any time.

a Integration of openings
b Storage
c Shelving
d Integration of services
e Integration of a desk
f Sliding elements
g Open storage
h Freestanding furniture

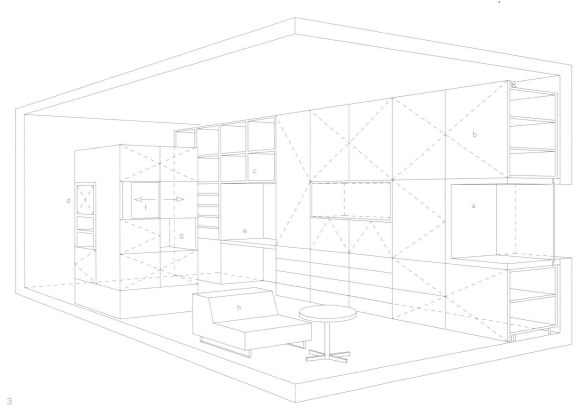

3

4 Haus am See, Berlin, 2010, Behles Jochimsen Architects. Fitted island furniture creates specific zones in the otherwise open space.

5 Office, Passau, 2012, Hiendl_Schineis Architekten-partnerschaft. The freestanding furniture can be moved to suit the required function and situation.

4

5

CONNECTIONS AND FIXING

As a rule, fitted furniture is made up of prefabricated modules that are made in standard sizes. Since production tolerances in furniture construction are significantly smaller than tolerances in building construction, it is necessary to tailor the furniture to fit the existing space in the building. Special connection details may be required at the sides, top and bottom and possibly the back.

CONNECTIONS

Where fitted furniture leaves a gap at the sides between the furniture and the walls, this gap needs to be filled. The same applies at the top between the furniture and the ceiling. A common solution is to fit profiles or battens – slightly recessed – at the end of the fitment; these are shaped to accommodate any discrepancy between the end of the furniture and the wall. If fixtures within a recess are intended to finish flush with the building fabric, a precise finish is required. Another option is to use the space between the fitment and the building fabric for backlighting, i.e. for the installation of indirect lighting. In the case of both freestanding fixtures and furniture fitted in front of a wall or in a recess, units are usually placed on adjustable feet, which can compensate for any unevenness in the floor finish and ensure that the furniture is steady. The void created between the carcass and the floor can be used for the installation of services. Visually, the space between the unit and the floor can be covered with a kick-board or similar type of profile. From the user's point of view, it is an advantage – particularly in kitchens – if these kick-boards are somewhat recessed from the front of the unit in order to leave room for the user's feet. If the surface finish of the units is delicate, it is advisable to finish the kick-board in a less susceptible colour or material, especially since it also serves the function of a skirting board. Where a flush version is desired, it is possible to insert a profile or continue the furniture fascia down to the floor. In the latter case, it is imperative to provide a dummy joint at floor level, especially if the fitment includes movable components.

SUSPENSION

Suspended cabinets can be fitted to the wall using matching wedge-shaped fitting profiles. The profile that is fixed to the wall is adjusted via oblong holes and is capable of supporting linear loads. An easier method is installation using specially designed suspension fittings which engage in rails or hooks fitted to the wall. These fittings are adjustable both vertically and horizontally, which means that precise installation is also possible on very uneven walls. In the case of heavy loads or deeper projections it is preferable to use support brackets.

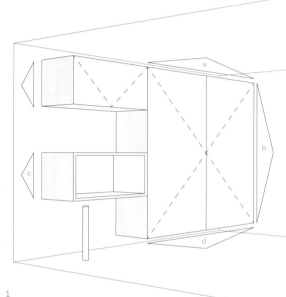

1

1 Both the front and visible sides of furniture must be taken into account. Furthermore, the designer has to decide how the carcass of the furniture connects to the adjoining building fabric. This requires attention to the different tolerances between the building and the furniture, and detailing of the fixing and installation.

a Ceiling connection
b Wall connection
c Suspension
d Floor connection

2 Office, Passau, 2013, Hiendl_Schineis Architektenpartnerschaft. Simple shelving elements in black-painted MDF are fitted into the recess of the existing building fabric using spacers.

3 Apartment, Stockholm, 2011, Guise. Freestanding furniture elements divide the room into zones.

2

3

4 Wall and ceiling connections
Furniture can be connected to the building fabric using a flush joint or a deliberate dummy joint. A special cover strip can be used to hide any discrepancies resulting from structural tolerances. It is also possible to provide a larger joint with light fittings.

a   Recessed cover panel
b   Flush cover panel
c   Dummy joint with light fittings

5 Floor connection
The adjustable feet of the furniture make it possible to accommodate any unevenness in the floor. The void created underneath the furniture can be used for services installations. A cover panel can be used to cover the open space. Where the furniture is used for working, the cover panel should be recessed to allow space for the feet.

a   Flush cover panel
b   Recessed cover panel
c   The panel can be covered by a longer door to create a flush front

6 Suspension
Wall-mounted cabinets should be fitted with special brackets that make it possible to align the cabinets horizontally.

a   Traditional method for mounting cabinets to the wall using two horizontal battens with matching slanting edges. The batten fitted to the wall is aligned horizontally using oblong holes before suspending the cabinet.
b   Cabinet mounting brackets with adjustment option in two directions. The bracket attached to the cabinet sides engages into a bracket or suspension rail on the wall.
c   In the case of greater loads or deeper cantilevers it may be necessary to place the cabinet on supporting brackets.

4a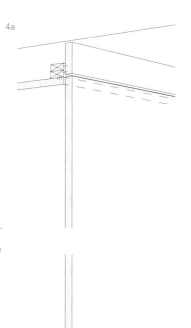

b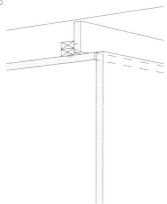

c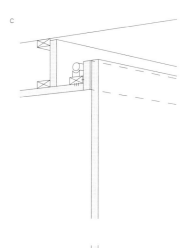

5a

b

c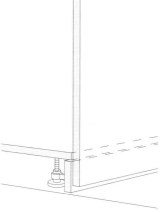

6a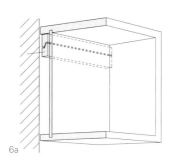

b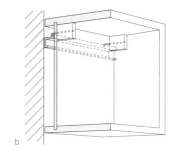

c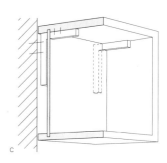

CARCASSES, SHELVES
AND DRAWERS

Furniture elements consist of several parts, which contribute in varying degrees to the stability and function of the unit. The basic element is the carcass, which consists of the sides, top, base and a back. The sides are often pre-drilled with holes at a standard spacing of 32 mm, which can be used for inserting shelves, drawers and other accessories, and also for attaching ironmongery. Furniture is fitted with doors in order to protect the contents from dirt and to create a visual screen while allowing access. The closing mechanism can take several forms, depending on the required function and available space; options are doors, flaps, sliding elements and drawers. The dimensions of the elements on the market have been standardised, which makes it possible to combine different systems and is also important – for example in kitchens – for the integration of white goods.

SYSTEMS AND JOINTING PRINCIPLES

In system furniture construction, a range of jointing principles are used for the elements described above.

A number of carcass units can be combined. They are bolted together using furniture connectors inserted in the pre-drilled holes in the sides of the units. Since this construction method does not require a substructure, it is suitable for creating a number of configurations in a simple way without being limited by system requirements. It must be borne in mind, however, that any changes to the overall assembly would require more work than usual and possibly its complete dismantling.

Systems in which the casing elements and shelves are suspended either directly from the wall behind, or from wall-mounted support rails, are very flexible and adaptable. 'Systemregal 606' by Dieter Rams provides an example of the various combination options offered by this construction method. However, when using this sys-

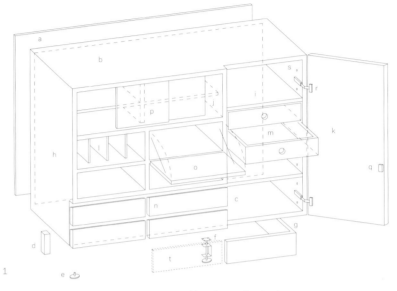

tem all forces have to be supported by the wall, which means that the wall construction itself must be strong enough or, conversely, that the loadbearing capacity of the furniture is limited accordingly.

Where the carcasses, shelves, drawers etc. are suspended from side elements, the forces are transferred to the floor via these. This system is more flexible and capable of supporting greater loads. The vertical elements are visually dominant to a degree that depends on the design.

Where an item of system furniture is assembled from vertical and horizontal structural parts, the latter are attached at both end to the side elements. Shelves and walls etc. can easily be fitted where a row of holes at 32 mm intervals has been provided.

1   Elements and designations
a   Back wall
b   Top
c   Base
d   Foot
e   Slider
f   Adjustable foot
g   Plinth/cover panel
h   Side panel
i   Adjustable shelf
j   Upright dividing panel
k   Door
l   Horizontal dividing panel
m   Inset drawer
n   Lay-on drawer
o   Flap
p   Sliding door
q   Furniture lock
r   Cup hinge
s   Holes for adjustable shelves
t   Cover panel

2   BM House, Ghent, 2011, de vylder vinck taillieu architects. Freestanding cupboard elements and fitments create distinct zones in the room, and at the same time provide the necessary storage with a minimal footprint without taking up precious space along the walls. The shell construction and the fitments are all part of the design.

3   Modular shelving 606 by Dieter Rams. Prefabricated shelves and other furniture elements are suspended from rails fitted on the wall.

4   Jointing principles of modular furniture

a   Individual boxes or entire cupboard elements are placed next to each other and joined using furniture-connection fittings.

b   Individual elements are suspended from a back wall or supporting rails. This means that no vertical elements are visible from the front.

c   Individual boxes or shelves are suspended from side panels or ladder frames.

d   The cabinet/shelving unit is made up of individual parts using connector fittings. Within the dimensions of the prefabricated units the system is very flexible, and can easily be modified to create a different layout.

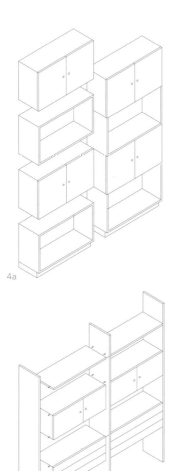

4a

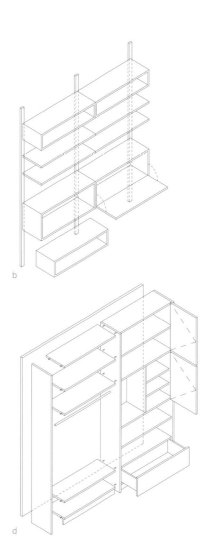

b

c

d

5   "Sleep and Dream" exhibition in the German Hygiene Museum, Dresden, 2007, Wandel Hoefer Lorch + Hirsch with the Technical University of Darmstadt. Exhibition system using vertical panels with display cabinets and exhibit mounts installed between the uprights

6   Apartment, Porto, 2011, Pedro Varela & Renata Pinho. Fitted storage wall made up of a range of vertical and horizontal elements, some with closed fronts

5

6

DOORS AND FITTINGS

Side-hung doors are fitted with hinges to the vertical side on which the door pivots. Therefore this type of door requires movement space to the front of the furniture. A distinction is made between left-hand and right-hand doors, the definition referring to the position of the hinges as seen from the exterior.

Double doors require a rebate at the closing joint; the primary opening leaf may be fitted with a lock or magnetic catch, while the secondary leaf may be fitted with a bolt. There are a number of ways in which doors can be hung, including flush-fitting, rebated or laid on. This determines the position and type of hinges to be used. The door hanging detail and number and type of hinges depend on aesthetic aspects as well as on the material, weight and dimensions of the planned door; normally the width of a door should not be greater than its height, with 650 mm being a common standard dimension.

FLUSH-FITTING DOORS

Flush-fitting doors fit in between the elements that make up the carcass, i.e. its side walls, top and base. As the door fronts fit flush with the front of the carcass, they need to fit very accurately, since any deviation in the joint is very visible. As a variation these doors may also be fitted slightly recessed or protruding from the carcass front.

REBATED DOORS

Rebating doors is the traditional craftsman's method of hanging doors. These doors are rebated on all four sides: the overlap covers the front edge of the carcass while the rebated part sits between the carcass elements. In this way, rebated doors are efficient at keeping out dust and dirt, but when closed they protrude from the front of the carcass.

LAY-ON DOORS

Lay-on doors do not have a rebate and they fully cover the front of the carcass, which greatly reduces any visible joints. The hinges are specially designed for this purpose and usually take the form of cup hinges, concealed on the inside.

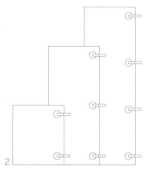

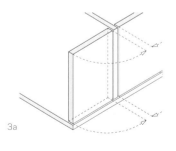
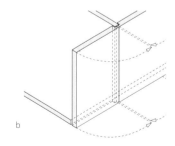
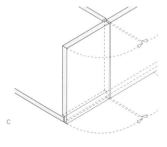

3a

b

c

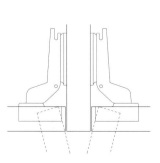
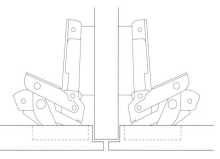
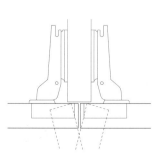

1 Opening angle of doors
The opening angle of doors can vary between 60 and 270° depending on the design of the hinges. A wide range of hinges exists to cater for different door hanging methods.

2 Guideline for the number of furniture hinges when using cup hinges: depending on the width, material and weight of a door, a 90 cm high door should be fitted with two, a door of up to 180 cm high with three, and a door of up to 240 cm high with four cup hinges.

3 Stop details
a Flush-fitting:
the door fits between the uprights, either flush or protruding or recessed within the cabinet, which means that the front of the carcass remains visible
b Rebated:
the rebate of the door lays on the front of the carcass, while the rebated part of the door is between the uprights
c Laid on:
the door closes on to the front of the carcass, fully covering it

4   Types of hinge
Depending on the way the door is
hung, the hinges may need to be
cropped.
a   Hinge with screw-in pins
b   Butt hinge
c   Piano hinge, available in long
lengths and are usually fitted along
the full height of the door
d   Pivot hinge
e   Recessed butt hinge
f   Cup hinge

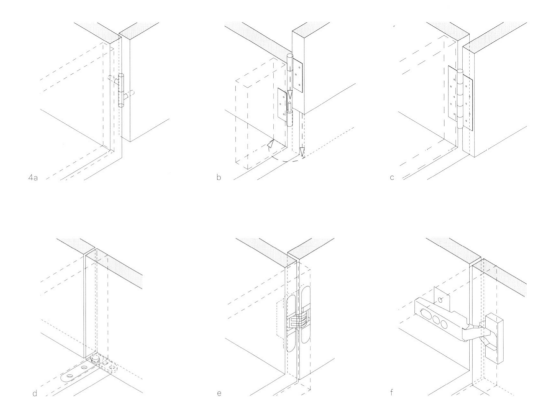

4a
b
c
d
e
f

5   Apartment, Munich, 2012,
Holzrausch. The monolithic effect
of the kitchen island unit is
reinforced by the side-hung door
wrapping around the edge.

6   Modular wardrobe system

5
6

FLAPS

Flaps can be used instead of doors and may be bottom-hung, top-hung, or lie in the horizontal plane. They are attached along a horizontal edge around which they turn. Depending on the hinge used, flaps can be flush-fitting or of a lay-on design. Rebated or mitre-cut versions are also possible.

BOTTOM-HUNG FLAPS

Bottom-hung flaps are usually used with cupboards and shelves. They are attached at the bottom edge and pivot downwards when opened; in the open position they can also be used as a surface. In the case of secretaires, the flap that hides the contents of the furniture when closed serves as the writing surface in its open position. The load imposed upon the flap in the open position is usually borne by brackets or stays fitted at the sides. Owing to the considerable forces that may be imposed on the open flap, however, it should not project by more than about 550 mm. To prevent flaps from falling open rapidly, it is possible to fit stays with mechanical or pneumatic brakes.

TOP-HUNG FLAPS

Top-hung flaps are primarily used for wall-hung cabinets in kitchens. They are attached along their top edge, around which they pivot, and are held open by mechanical or pneumatic holder devices, or by special hinges. In order to ensure that the flap can still be reached in the open position, its angle of opening is limited to approx. 80°, depending on the fitting. Up-and-over flaps are a special form of top-hung flap whereby the entire flap disappears into the top of the cabinet. When installing a top-hung flap it is important to consider not only the height of the handle for easy reaching, but also its height in the open position in order to prevent injuries to the head.

HORIZONTAL FLAPS

Horizontal flaps are used in chests and often in benches too. They provide a top cover to the piece of furniture; they open upwards and are fitted using either concealed or visible hinges. When open, these flaps are held in position by mechanical or pneumatic stays. The flap is kept closed by its own weight; a potential risk is that of trapping fingers and limbs when closing the flap. For this reason, it is preferable for these flaps to project beyond the part of the furniture that they cover, particularly so in the case of a seat.

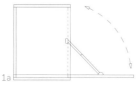

1 Bottom-hung flap, e.g. for storage and also in secretaires
a Flush-fitting, bottom-hung flap with stay
b Flush-fitting, bottom-hung flap with friction fitting

2 Top-hung flap, e.g. for wall-hung kitchen cabinets
a Hold-open stay with automatic hold mechanism which releases when lifted. Alternative: hold-open stay with friction fitting
b Parallel motion flap that moves in parallel to the front of the cabinet

3 Horizontal flap, e.g. for chest of drawers
a Hinged at the back, supported by pneumatic stay
b Hinged within the horizontal top, held by a mechanical stay

4 Kitchen detail, Munich, 2013, Holzrausch. For improved comfort during cooking, the bottom-hung flap activates lighting integrated in the cabinet

SLIDING ELEMENTS

5a

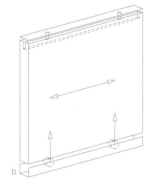

b

5 Operating mechanisms of sliding doors
a Sliding doors with bottom rails rest with their lower edge on gliders or rollers and, at the top edge, are held in vertical position with guide fittings
b Sliding doors are suspended from tracks at the top and have gliding or roller fittings at the top edge of the door which engage in the tracks. At the bottom, the sliding doors are guided by guide rails and secured against being dislodged

6 Lay-on and inset door systems
a Inset sliding doors running on parallel tracks
b Lay-on sliding door
c Combination of inset and lay-on systems

Sliding doors are opened by moving them sideways and in parallel to the front of the furniture, which means that only a little movement space is required in front of the furniture. A disadvantage is the fact that only part of the interior can be open at a time, since the other part is then covered by the door.

The guide rails for sliding doors may be fitted at the bottom or the top. Depending on the format, material and design requirements, single or multiple rails and doors can be installed either in front of the carcass or within it. Smoothness of operation depends on a combination of weight, leverage, the position of the handle and the design of the guide rails. Taking the above aspects into account, it may be necessary to use a range of different fittings in a piece of furniture in order to achieve the desired functionality and appearance.

POSITION OF DOORS

Sliding doors can be fitted and operated in different ways. Depending on the position in relation to the carcass, a distinction is made between lay-on and inside door systems; it is also possible to use both versions in combination. If the doors are operated within the carcass, the guide rails are fitted recessed in the base and top of the carcass. In order to improve operating characteristics and durability it is possible to use metal rails, which can either be inserted or surface-mounted. When the sliding

doors are fitted in front of the carcass, the guide rails are fitted to the face of the carcass elements. This means that a sliding element can fully cover the opening in the carcass at the top and bottom. Brakes and stops are used at the end of the guide rail in order to prevent the doors from over-running.

A disadvantage of sliding doors that consist of several panels is that these panels have to run in different planes, which means that they are set back from one another – a fact that is particularly noticeable in the closed position. To counteract this effect, special guide rails have been devised for two-part sliding doors, which bring both elements into the same plane when closed and thus lend the furniture a more unified appearance.

Also available are special forms that are based on the sliding-door principle, but which, from a geometrical point of view, incorporate other methods of opening. Folding sliding doors, for example, function in the same way as eccentrically suspended folding walls. → p. 90 In the open position, they reveal almost the entire width of the interior but, like side-hung doors, they require space for movement to the front of the furniture.

In the case of side-hung sliding doors, the open door panel is turned through 90° at the side of the opening: either towards the front or backwards into the carcass, which again means that extra space is required.

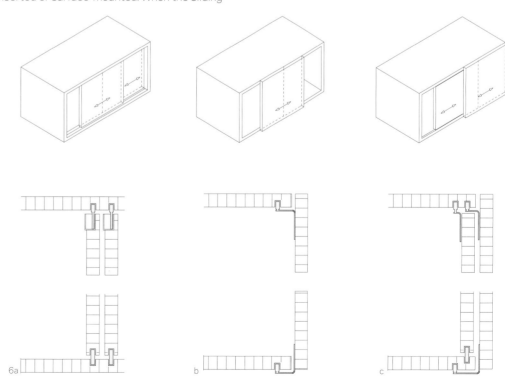

6a   b   c

DRAWERS AND PULL-OUTS

Drawers and pull-outs are used for the orderly storage of objects. They comprise the drawer box and the movement mechanism. The drawer box consists of the front or fascia panel with a handle, the back, sides and the base, which is usually inserted into recessed grooves.

CRAFT CONSTRUCTION METHOD

In this type of construction, the movement mechanism of the drawer is attached to the side. The drawer may either be resting on runners, be held laterally by contact rails and be secured at the top against tilting or falling out by holding rails, or it may have a groove recessed in its side into which the runner engages. Drawers suspended at the top run in slide rails that are attached to shelves or the underside of worktops and engage in the side panels of the drawers. If it is intended to pull out a shelf board instead of a drawer, the movement mechanism is fitted to the side walls of the carcass underneath the worktop. The mechanism is concealed by a panel at the front. ⟍ 3 In order to ensure good running and wear characteristics and prevent the drawer from jamming in the guide rails, the use of warp-free material, such as hardwood, is preferred in craft-built furniture. For similar reasons, the craft-based construction method is better suited to smaller formats; furthermore, the width of units should always be less than their depth.

INDUSTRIAL CONSTRUCTION METHOD

With industrial construction it is possible to produce much bigger drawer systems. These systems feature metal guide rails with sliding or ball bearings, which are either fitted underneath or on the sides of drawers and which – owing to their mechanical complexity – require a certain amount of space. They offer excellent running characteristics and good operating comfort, including features such as spring-cushioned automatic draw-in

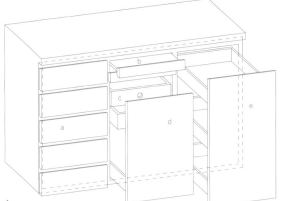

1 Pull-out types
a Lay-on drawer
b Pull-out shelf board
c Inset drawer
d Pull-out with high door front
e Pantry pull-out

mechanisms or pull-out stops, and can be very precisely adjusted. Depending on the design, they can carry high loads and are available with partial, full or over-extension, with the latter providing complete access to the drawer and its contents. The configuration of the running rails determines the degree of accessibility to the drawer.

PULL-OUT TYPES

Various designs of pull-out are used in furniture construction. In addition to the straightforward drawer with direct access, pull-outs are available which consist of the mechanism with a front panel and a number of internal drawers hidden behind that panel. In this way it is possible – for example in kitchens – to design base unit fronts without any horizontal subdivision. However, access to the drawers is somewhat restricted owing to the large front panel. A pull-out with a front panel that covers the full height of a tall cabinet is called a pantry pull-out. In this construction, the internal compartments are attached to the front panel and are only accessible from the side.

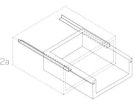
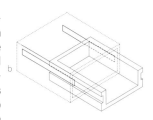
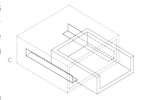

2 Drawer slides
a Suspended
b Side-mounted
c Underneath

3 Kitchen, Munich, 2011, Holzrausch. Large pull-out with concealed inset drawers

4 Staircase study house, Hamburg, 2012, Gerd Streng. Drawers fitted as part of a seating area

5 Apartment, Munich, Holzrausch. Pantry pull-out as part of a wardrobe unit

HANDLES

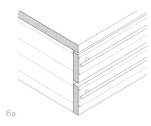

6a

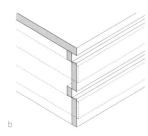

b

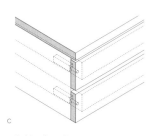

c

6 Handle options
a Handle bar as separate
component
b Handle bar in the form of a
dummy joint
c Push-to-open fitting

All of the elements described above need handles or mechanisms for opening and closing. Doors, flaps, fixtures and flexible room elements have to be fitted with devices that facilitate opening, pulling out, sliding and folding up or down. These devices are not only functionally necessary, but they can also add interesting design accents in terms of form, material and surface texture. Handles may be made of wood, plastic, glass, rubber, metal, leather, porcelain, stone etc. and may be surface-mounted or recessed, or they may consist of a moulded handle groove or strip.

PRACTICAL DESIGN ASPECTS

When designing free-standing or fitted furniture, it is necessary to consider not only the types of handle, but also their position. The number and positioning of handles depends on the size, weight and type of the elements to be opened, and on their direction of movement.

INTEGRATED SOLUTIONS

In considering the design of furniture as a whole, the designer may opt for solutions that avoid handles or knobs as added elements and incorporate the required function in the furniture element itself.

For example, a moulded handle groove or strip at the top or side of a front fulfils the same purpose without drawing attention away from the element itself. Handles can also be unobtrusively incorporated in dummy joints, in which case it is important to ensure that the joint is wide enough for ergonomic operation. In push-to-open systems, a slight push on the front of the drawer causes the

drawer to open; this can be combined with self-closing or soft-closing mechanisms for additional user comfort, but it means that the surface of the front has to be sufficiently robust for this type of use.

FUNCTIONAL ASPECTS

Suitability for use is one of the key tenets of designing. Accordingly, the choice of handle should be appropriate for the planned use and load. A heavy glazed sliding door can be opened more easily with a strong handle strip or a recessed handle groove that give a good purchase than with a small furniture knob. Items of furniture exposed to regular wear and daily operation must be designed with adequate strength and fittings. For example, it would be appropriate to fit functional handles to drawers and flaps of fitted furniture which is in constant use, whereas the opening device of a flap on a glass display unit should be less conspicuous and perhaps less accessible.

As a general principle, handles and opening devices should be designed and sized for their purpose, ensuring that any injury hazard – such as may be caused by trapping or by collision with other elements – is avoided. It is also important to consider the risk of surface-mounted handles causing obstruction or damage to adjacent components when the respective door or flap is opened. Another relevant design aspect is the age of the user, which has an impact on the size and position of an opening mechanism. For example, recessed handles at the lower edge of the unit may not be suitable for older or disabled people, whereas it may be advisable to conceal the opening elements of nursery furniture.

7 Bathroom, Munich, 2011,
Landau + Kindelbacher. Handle bar
in the form of a dummy joint of a
drawer

8 Wardrobe, Munich, 2010,
Unterlandstättner Architects.
Textile covering of a wardrobe
unit with recessed grips

9 Kitchen studio, Munich, 2011,
Holzrausch. Handle incorporated in
the design of a cabinet door, part of
the surface texture of the furniture

7

8

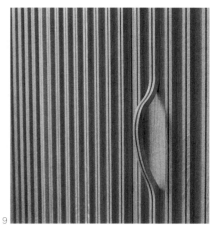

9

INTEGRATING TECHNOLOGY

Electronic media and computer-controlled processes dominate more and more areas of our life, be it in the home, at work, at public events, or in leisure activities. The technology that is shaping our daily lives also has a direct effect on the home and its functions. Fitted furniture provides an obvious opportunity for integrating technical equipment and controls in an inconspicuous way. For example, the control unit of a network system for the control of heating, ventilation and lighting in a home may be inserted recessed in the front of a fitted cabinet, as could be switches and sockets. The wiring has to be considered at an early stage during the design. It is usual to install wiring in the plinth area or behind the back panel. It is imperative to provide access possibilities, both for inspection purposes and for the installation of equipment and light fittings, and to integrate them in the design. Owing to the fact that electronic equipment generates heat when in operation, it is important to ensure good ventilation.

RECEPTION AND SALES

Counters such as are used in the receptions of medical centres and hotels, as well as in shops, have one side that faces the visitor and one that serves as a work area for staff. As a rule, the visitor side conceals the technical infrastructure such as PCs, monitors, cash registers or control elements for lighting, ventilation and access, which are housed at the back. In retail design, these counters often include a display area, which is open to view from the front and top, and which can be accessed on the sales side e.g. via lockable pull-outs.

DISPLAY CABINETS

In museums, fitted units are used to accommodate a number of different functions at the same time. These go beyond the classic presentation of exhibits in display cabinets and enter the realm of audio-visual media and graphic information, which means that the fitted unit may not only be a vehicle for conveying information, but becomes an exhibit in itself. Display cabinets themselves are used to present two or three-dimensional exhibits in a protected manner. These units need to be designed for optimal presentation, while taking conservation and security needs into consideration. The display of exhibits in museums always represents a compromise in terms of security and conservation . Display units may be protected against unauthorised access by fitting locks, or possibly concealed security bolts to their panes or domes. The materials used for the construction of display cabinets should be certified with respect to their emission properties.

The lighting in display cabinets should be dimmable and glare-free so that the light intensity can be adjusted to within the maximum permitted for any particular exhibit under conservation aspects. In recent years, LED lighting has become popular because it generates less heat; however, the lamps used should be tested with respect to their colour rendering and UV radiation.

Display cabinets should be designed to be dust-free. Depending on the type of exhibit, it may be desirable to allow for a controlled exchange of air. Sensitive exhibits – notably paper – require a very constant climate. In climate-controlled display cabinets, the relative humidity is usually controlled by silica gel inserted in the base.

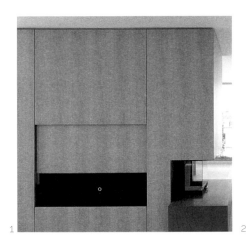

1 Apartment, Munich, 2011, Holzrausch. Integration of a flat-screen television within wall cladding. When the unit is not in use, it can be concealed behind a vertical sliding element which fits flush with the adjoining surfaces.

2 Weißraum practice, Munich, 2010, Ippolito Fleitz Group. Indirect lighting in the plinth area of a reception counter

3 Future Hotel Showcase, 2008, LAVA, Laboratory for Visionary Architecture. Lighting recessed in the joint of wall cladding slanted at different angles.

4 Documentation and meeting centre of the SS Special Camp/ Hinzert Concentration Camp/ Memorial, 2005, Wandel Hoefer Lorch + Hirsch. The documentation and meeting centre with its stark Corten steel structure is located in the rugged landscape of the Hunsrück mountain range. The site was used as an SS 'special camp' and as a concentration camp during the period of National Socialist rule. The triangulated structure of the external envelope is continued on the inside of the building. All exhibition media such as display cabinets, screens, audio stations and lighting are integrated in the wall and ceiling. The graphic displays, which are directly applied to the wooden triangular elements, continue throughout the interior wall surfaces – including the large window area, where an image of the concentration camp as it once was is superimposed on today's landscape.

a Display cabinet lighting
b Opaque acrylic glass used to diffuse light
c Toughened safety glass of display cabinet; upper section removable
d Holder for exhibit
e Back wall of display cabinet, veneered
f Display cabinet substructure, mounted to cross bar
g Wall panel, veneered
h Hardwood plinth panel, veneered

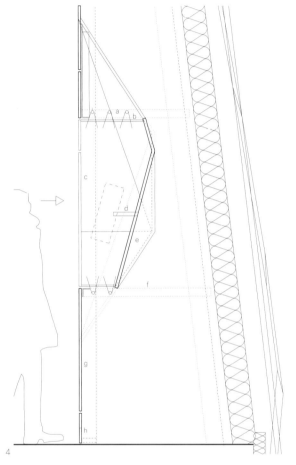

4

MEDIA TECHNOLOGY

Media equipment and entertainment electronics are now a ubiquitous feature of almost all spheres of life. Flat screens can often be integrated in furniture to save space, either behind a cut-out in the furniture front, which conceals the frame of the screen, or behind a flap or sliding element, which only reveals the unit when opened. Likewise, network-based audio/video players can easily be concealed in furniture, since it is not necessary to change storage media and the equipment only needs to be accessed for inspection purposes. In museums it is becoming popular to use radio frequency identification (RFID) chips, which can be used to start interactive applications, for example, as soon as the visitor approaches an exhibit. Likewise, it is possible to integrate loudspeakers in furniture, although it must be borne in mind that such furniture it not normally optimised in terms of resonance and sound reproduction.

LIGHTING

Light fittings are also frequently integrated in fitted furniture. These may be downlighters in the top of a built-in cupboard, or projecting light fittings such as the swanneck lights used in libraries. The top and side connections of fixtures, as well as the plinth area, are suitable for the installation of indirect light fittings. In this situation, LED light fittings are particularly suitable as they require less space and emit less heat.

An integrated design approach offers the opportunity to provide well designed solutions for dealing with the growing amount of technology in our daily lives in order to combine the benefit of this equipment with the aesthetic appeal of an interior.

5 Documentation and meeting centre of the SS Special Camp/ Hinzert Concentration Camp/ Memorial, 2005, Wandel Hoefer Lorch + Hirsch

a The flush-mounted display cabinets fit in with the geometry of the wall structure.
b A secondary display level with graphic elements and display boxes can be accessed via pull-outs.
c The graphics display involves the entire surface in the storytelling. The media stations and veneered lighting elements form integral parts of the surface.

5a   b   c

FURNISHING | ZONING
CASE STUDIES

CHAPTER 6

ALMEDINA BOOKSHOPS, PORTO/LISBON, PORTUGAL
AIRES MATEUS, PORTO

A number of bookshops were created in Lisbon and Porto for the Portuguese bookseller, Almedina. All interior fit-outs follow the same design concept, which ignores the existing building fabric, with the walls of the structural shell painted black similar to the interior around a stage set. White fitted elements are then placed in this context, which redefine the space with their inner shells. These basic archetypal elements are used to create individual zones, which provide a structure to the bookshops and define subject-specific areas.

The interior design elements are extremely simple and minimalist in their construction. The fitments are attached to a substructure of steel tubes. These are installed first and define the respective areas before the units are attached to them. Overhead elements are suspended from the ceiling and light fittings are concealed and integrated in the top shelves. All visible loadbearing or service elements such as existing ceilings, walls, installations and trunking are painted black and thereby merge into the background.

The interior design comes to life through its juxtaposition of opposites. The contrast between black and white, the light focused on the insides of the new fitments and the creation of a perspective effect generate rooms with an almost unreal, yet highly recognisable image. At the same time the design creates easily grasped, minimalist, distinct rooms for contemplation, where customers can focus on the medium of the book. The theme of free-standing fitments has been implemented in a succinct manner while creating a distinct atmosphere.

Abstracted layout and section through the bookshop

View of bookshop as built

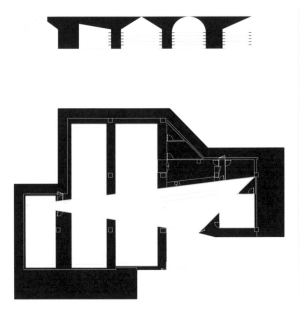

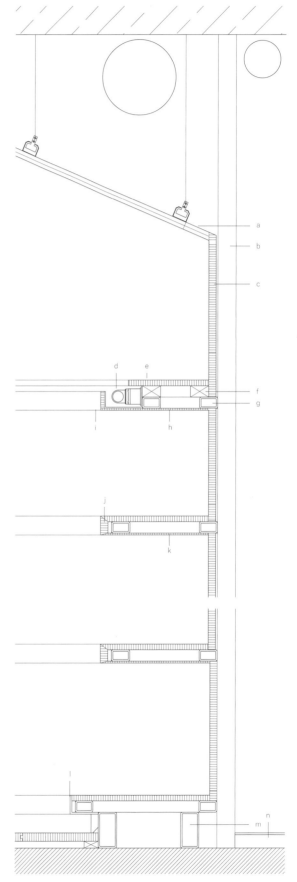

Detail section, scale 1:10

a Plasterboard ceiling, white
b 50 × 50 mm metal profiles, fixed to the structural ceiling
c Wood fibre board (MDF), screwed to metal profiles, finished in white paint
d Fluorescent lighting
e Wood fibre board (MDF), screwed to timber battens, finished in white paint
f Timber battens
g 50 × 30 mm metal profile, soldered
h Wood fibre board (MDF), screwed to the ceiling panels, finished in white paint
i 3 mm ribbed cladding
j Cover strip mitre-cut from wood fibre board (MDF), screwed to the profile, finished in white paint
k Wood fibre board (MDF), screwed to timber battens, finished in white paint
l 5 mm cover strip
m 100 × 50 mm metal profile, soldered
n Polyurethane floor covering, black, MBT Conipur 255A

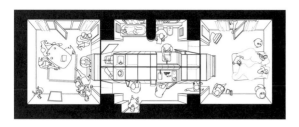

Perspective from above

CLASSIC LOFT XS, BERLIN, GERMANY
BEHLES & JOCHIMSEN, BERLIN

The converted apartment is located in the penthouse storey of the "Haus des Kindes", a building designed by Hermann Henselmann at Strausberger Platz in Berlin.
The two-room apartment was largely stripped out. What remained were the loadbearing walls, which also determine the basic layout. The space was divided into three rooms of equal size by including a former connecting corridor. The key interior design feature is a block of multifunctional furniture in the middle room, which was built along the main axis of the layout. It has both a separating and connecting effect and takes care of all service functions.
Through the installation of this block, the previously linear layout of the apartment was changed into a circular functional arrangement: the middle room now consists of a small reception area with a kitchen on one side and a bathroom on the other side, both of which also serve to connect the two outer rooms. These rooms can be separated off by doors which lie within the reveals of the cross-wall openings and give access to the interior of the block of furniture.
The multi-functionality of this furniture is highlighted by the colour scheme. While the high-gloss pink on the outside of the monolith resonates quietly with the rooms, the contrasting matt dark red of all the inside spaces announces transformation.
Whereas the washbasin and kitchen area are in full view, all storage and all the services installations of the apartment are hidden behind a seemingly endless multiplicity of flaps, doors and drawers. Folding sliding doors are used for wardrobes, top-hung flaps close off storage compartments, pantry pull-outs hold kitchen and bathroom utensils, and conventional side-hung doors conceal the washing machine and dryer.
The focus of the conversion is on one central element in which all functional elements are concentrated, thus leaving the historic rooms almost untouched.

The fitted furniture element connects the three rooms. If required, the rooms can be separated by closing the doors fitted in the reveals of the wall openings.

All non-loadbearing walls have been removed and the size of the openings in the loadbearing walls increased. The central fitment allows a new layout organisation.
Scale 1:100

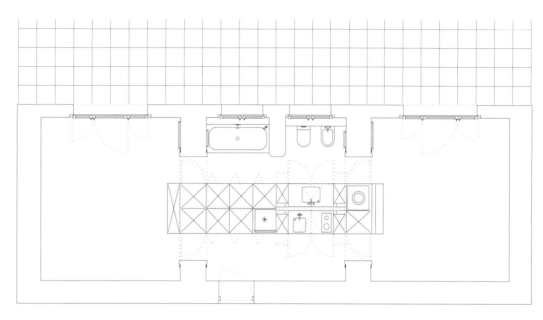

When closed, the element conveys a sense of tranquillity with its even, vertical joint pattern. The cross section reveals the many functions included.
Scale 1:100

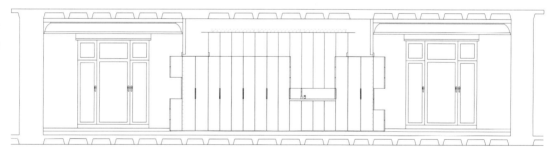

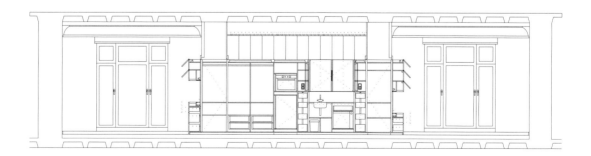

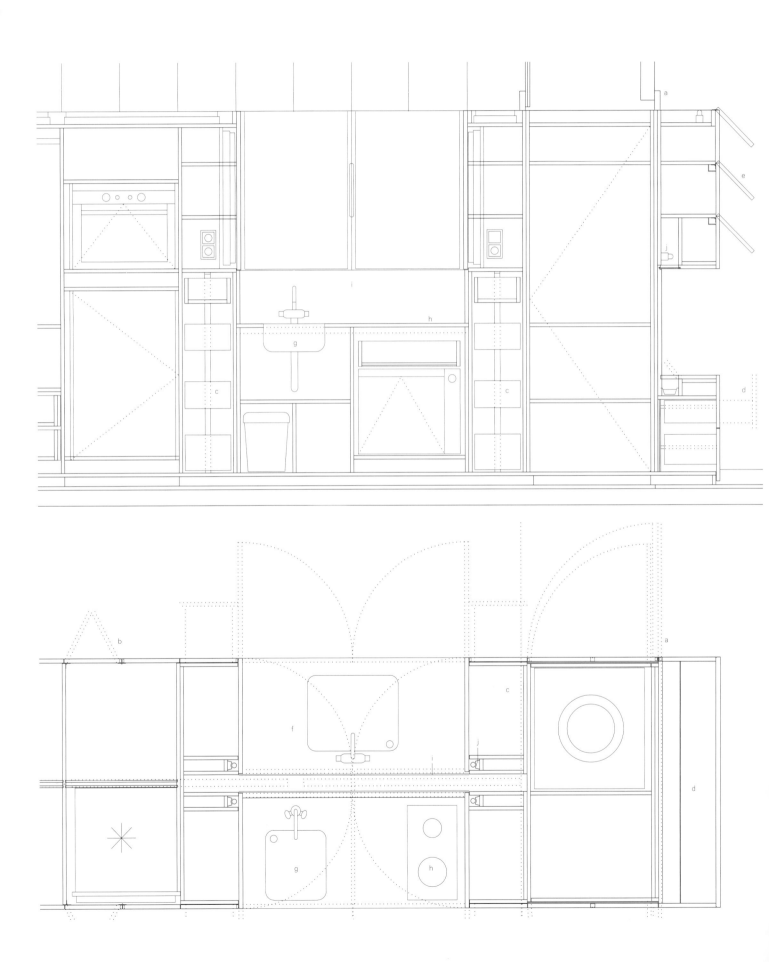

Section and layout, scale 1:20
a   Double door: the outer leaf closes off the room and has a mirror, the inner leaf closes the cupboard.
b   Folding sliding door in front of cupboard door
c   Pantry pull-out
d   Drawer
e   Storage cubicle with top-hung flap
f   Washstand
g   Sink
h   Hob
i   Glass wall, frosted
j   Fluorescent light fitting

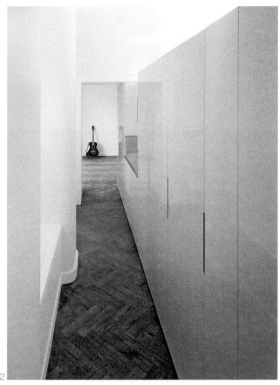

By concentrating all functions in one element it was possible to leave the original form of the rooms visible.
The contrast in the inside and outside colouring underscores the functional diversity, which is also indicated by the numerous doors and drawers.

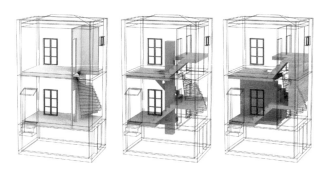

Development studies

UN MEUBLE HABITÉ, CHATOU, FRANCE
H2O ARCHITECTES, PARIS

A small building in the family's back yard, which had been neglected over the years, was upgraded to provide accommodation for the son. The idea was to provide independence for the various living areas – only meals were to be taken together by the family.

The building only measures twelve square metres and, in view of its height of over six metres, a vertical arrangement of functions seemed logical. A walk-in piece of furniture organises the functional sequence in a split-level arrangement. Each level is assigned a specific domestic sphere. Taking into account teenager's potential for development, the spaces offer a mixture of areas that are fully determined and areas that are open to adaptation. While the existing building provides the outer envelope, the interior fitment blurs the boundary between room-dividing components and furniture. This means that walls can be used for storage purposes and staircases as seats. The material has been selected to reflect this combination of functionality and structure. The interior structure is entirely built of silver birch plywood, thus creating a clear contrast with the building envelope and strengthening the inserted character of the fitment. The jointing of the material and details such as cupboard doors and handle holes are of a simple design and optimised to make best use of the space – as was the whole project.

The functions are arranged in sequence on several split levels. Each level is assigned a specific living zone.

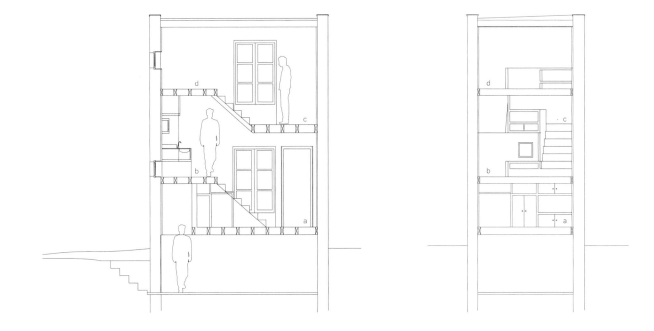

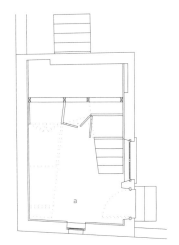

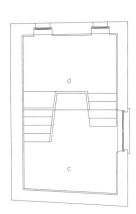

Longitudinal section
Cross section
Layouts
Scale 1:100

a   Lounge level
b   Washing level
c   Work level
d   Sleep level

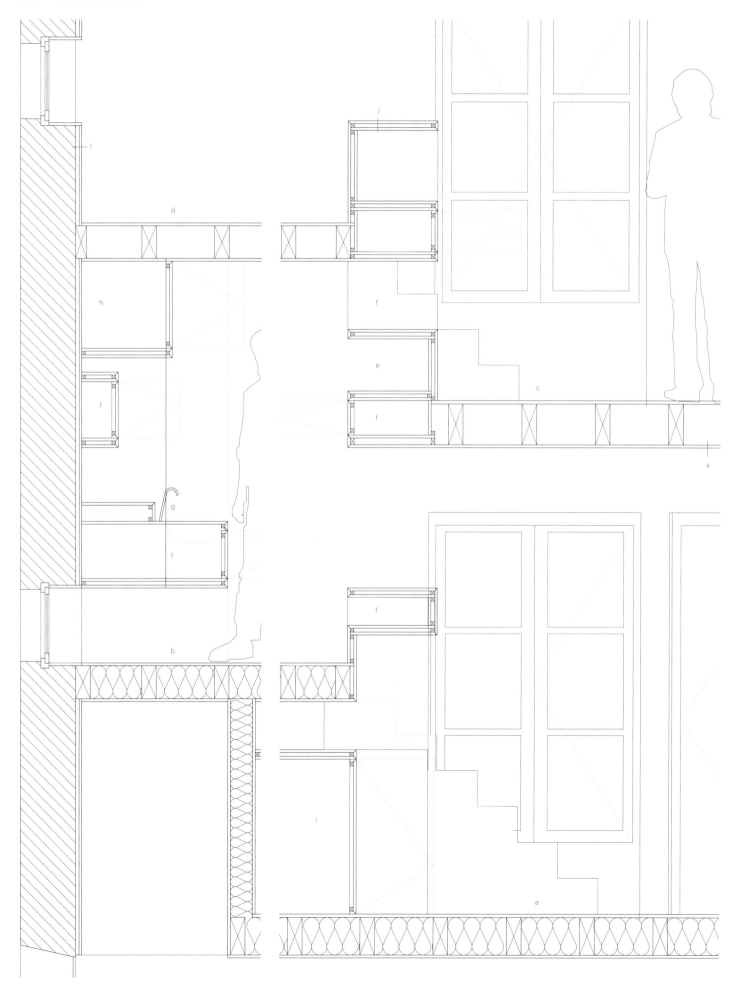

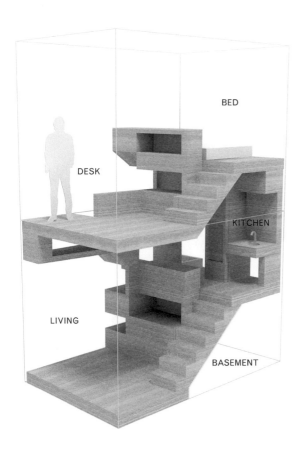

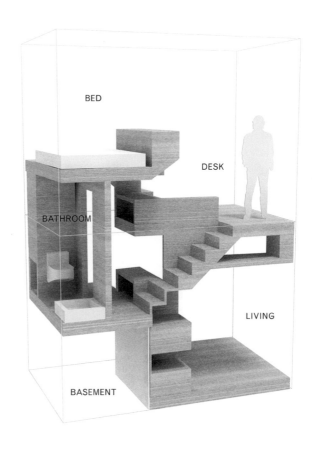

The coherence of the material allows the close correspondence between the functions and the construction to become apparent.

a   Lounge level
b   Washing level
c   Work level
d   Sleep level
e   Niche
f   Storage
g   Washbasin
h   Microwave
i   Wardrobe
j   Furniture construction layers:
–   silver birch plywood 14 mm
–   construction batten
–   silver birch plywood
    mitre-cut at joint
k   Floor construction – 200 mm:
–   silver birch plywood 14 mm
–   joists
–   silver birch plywood
l   Construction of wall lining
–   silver birch plywood
–   insulation layer
–   existing wall

FAMILY RESIDENCE,
ENGELBERG, SWITZERLAND
ANDREAS FUHRIMANN, GABRIELLE HÄCHLER
ARCHITECTS, ZURICH

————————

This new family home was built in a historic village in central Switzerland, the traditional core of which has been extended with contemporary housing. The form of the new building and the materials and traditional construction methods used create a link between the two poles of traditional and contemporary architecture.

The house has been placed on a concrete base and features a concrete core, which serves as the loadbearing structure and around which the polygonal timber building has been erected as a prefabricated panel construction. The concrete base includes a deep projection to accommodate the topographic situation – specifically, in order to create usable floor space on the steep terrain. The fair-faced concrete core of the building forms its backbone, basement and a retaining wall which brace the otherwise timber structure against soil pressure. The visual effect of the interior is largely influenced by the concrete structure, as loadbearing element, and the wooden building envelope. This is highlighted by exposing both these materials and their haptic qualities. The loadbearing structure and interior fit-out go hand in hand. While the loadbearing structure has been formed in untreated fair-faced concrete without any finishing treatment, so as to resemble the raw nature of the surrounding rock formations – and which is expressed in the sculptural effect of the stairwell – the floor, walls and ceilings of the private areas contrast with their large-format plywood panels in light silver fir.

The centre of the building is the two-storey living room. The solid, full-height fireplace, which extends into a seat and storage area, emphasises the sacral feel of the room. The library is presented as a store of knowledge in a wooden container. Somewhat separated from the main living room and other communal areas, and raised by two steps, is a cosy den area where the height of the room is reduced to just 2.26 metres. The distinction of rooms with different heights and of materials to reflect different room functions can be seen as an interpretation of Adolf Loos''Raumplan' concept. The accurate finishing of the details of the different materials is further highlighted by the careful selection of angles and jointing methods.

The new building blends well into the Alpine landscape with respect to its size and use of typical local materials. But instead of the usual dark shingles covering a lightly cantilevering roof, the architects opted for a flat metal roof without overhang and sawn weatherboarding, in order to emphasise the shape of the house.

The sculptural effect of the two-storey living room is created by the incoming daylight from above and the contrast in material between the fair-faced concrete and the flat surfaces of silver fir board.

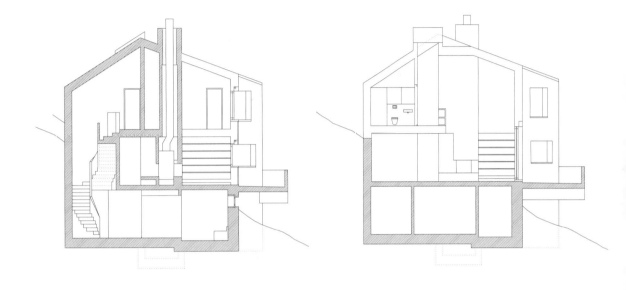

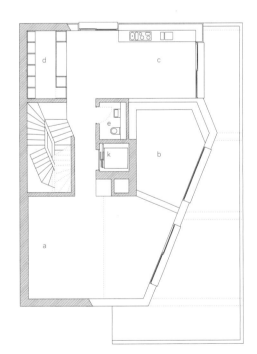

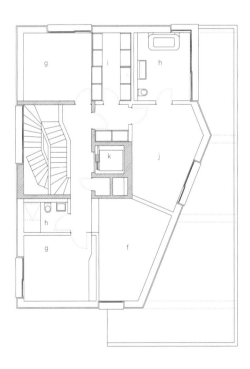

Cross sections, scale 1:200
Layout of ground floor,
upper floor, scale 1:200

a Living room
b Library
c Kitchen
d Pantry
e WC
f Void
g Guest room
h Bathroom
i Dressing room
j Bedroom
k Lift

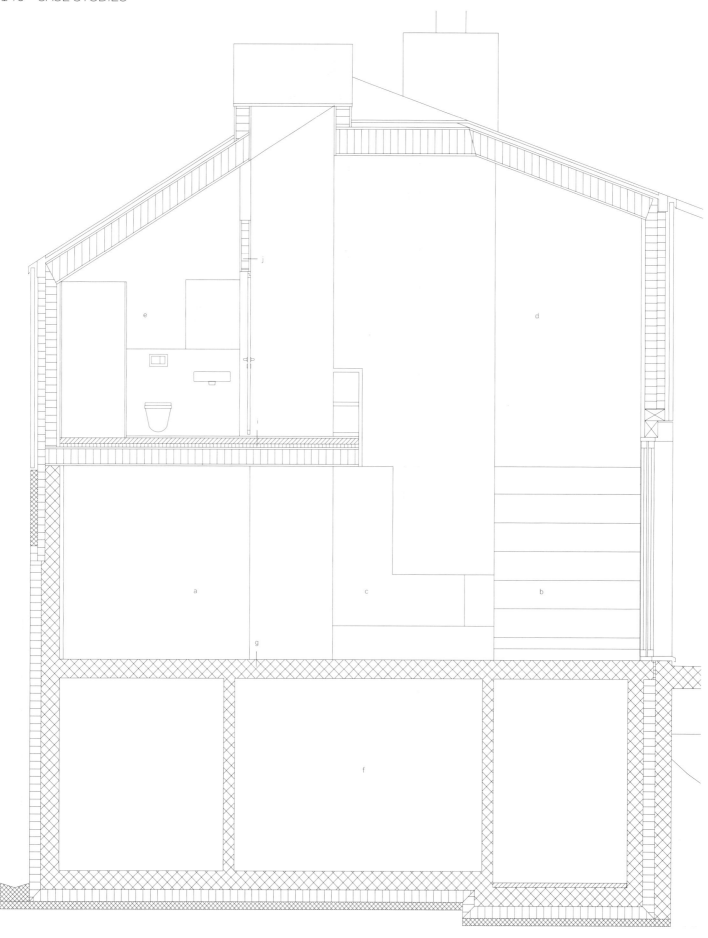

The focal point of the two-storey living room is the solid full-height fireplace, which extends to form a seating and storage area.

The transition between the solid loadbearing structure and the plywood boarded interior is visible, yet seamless. Accurate joints characterise the interface between the concrete (ground or left as cast) and the timber cladding (natural or painted).

Cross section, scale 1:50
Sectional elevation, detail fireplace/library, scale 1:20

a Living room
b Library
c Fireplace
d Void
e Bathroom
f Wellness

g Concrete slab
250 mm concrete, ground

h Timber flooring on concrete slab above ground floor
25 mm plywood board
80 mm screed
with underfloor heating
40 mm impact sound insulation
25 mm plywood board
130 mm cavity
250 mm concrete

i Timber ceiling
25 mm plywood board
80 mm screed with underfloor heating
45 mm impact sound insulation
25 mm plywood board
200 mm timber joists
25 mm plywood board

j Construction layers of timber partition
25 mm plywood board
100 mm timber stud with internal insulation core
25 mm plywood board

k Timber fitments in library
The floor of this introverted space was raised to reduce the room height to 2.26 metres.
25 mm shelf made of plywood, fixed to the lining on the concrete wall
360 mm internal dimension of shelves

l Fireplace
The open solid fireplace in the two-storey space is extended on one side to form a seating and storage area.

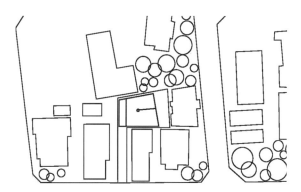

TREEHOUSE, TOKYO, JAPAN
MOUNT FUJI ARCHITECTS STUDIO, TOKYO

———————

This house for a young couple is located in a residential district of northern Tokyo. The site is completely enclosed by neighbouring buildings and is slightly elevated, with the ground rising gently from the entrance to the opposite boundary.

In addition to accommodating this topographical situation, the aim was to create a space with as much daylight as possible, while retaining privacy.

In search of a geometric structure that can accommodate these requirements, the architects relied on a polar coordinate system. Each point in the system is related to the central fixed point, depending on its distance and angle.

The resulting rule is simple. A number of frames are placed around a fixed point with a spacing angle of 11.25° between them, with each frame being 55 millimetres higher than the previous one. All together, the 32 frames that make up the entire 360° create a tree-like structure. Owing to the gradual change in height, a 1.70 metre-high gallery space is created where the lowest frame meets the highest.

Starting from the central support, the main interior space is divided into four different zones. These follow the gradient of the terrain and accommodate different functional areas; they are also distinct regarding their geometry, orientation and fenestration. In its radial sequence of rooms, the height gradually increases – an image that reflects the growth of a tree.

The selected geometric principle can be sensed in all zones and also defines the geometry of the openings and interior elements. By inserting horizontal shelving between the different frames on the external wall, the entire structure becomes a full-height book and storage wall. The loadbearing structure and the spatial concept of the house are identical.

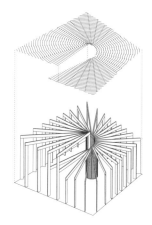

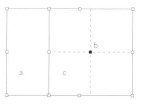

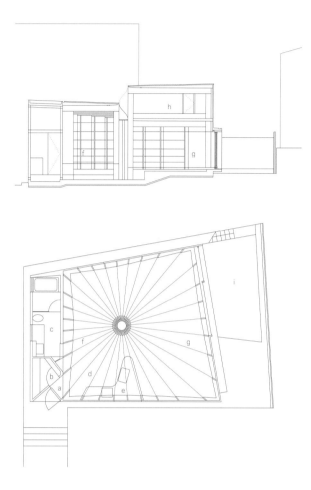

Axonometric drawing of structure
The loadbearing structure and the room concept of the house are identical.
The arched structure consists of veneered plywood frames with a thickness of 51 mm which are placed at 11.25 degrees to each other, turning around a central axis with a 55 mm change of height between each.

The geometry of the house has been derived from the geometry of the site and superimposed with a polar coordinate system.

Traditional Japanese dwelling
(layout diagram and interior)
a   Water area
b   Central support
c   Living area

Cross section, layout level 1
Scale 1:100
a   Entrance
b   Storage space
c   Bathroom
d   Entrance area
e   Kitchen
f   Living room 2
g   Living room 1
h   Bedroom
i   Terrace

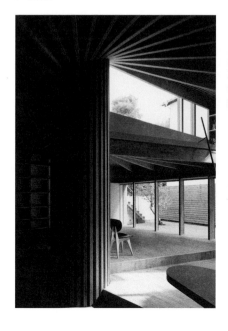

HOUSE ON THE ALB,
WALDSTETTEN-WISSGOLDINGEN
KAESTLE OCKER ROEDER ARCHITEKTEN,
STUTTGART

An unassuming building on sloping terrain, hardly visible from the street, opens up to the valley landscape. The large open space on the ground floor is used for sitting, dining and cooking. On the upper floor, which is the entrance level, are the bedrooms of the four-person family. The wish to have separate bathrooms for parents and children has resulted in a flexible solution, creating two separate wash/WC areas which are linked via a shared bathtub and shower area. Movable cupboard elements close off or open up the respective spaces, offering maximum storage space and, at the same time, the freedom of alternative access. In the wash areas, the flooring consists of oak parquet, whereas the walls and floor in the central wet area have been finished with polyurethane coating.

All fitted elements are made of MDF and finished in white, high-gloss paint. The fitted furniture comprises various sizes of compartment with drawers and side-hung doors to cater for a wide range of storage requirements. A number of mirrors (some of them integrated into the cupboard doors) create interesting visual relationships and make the landscape part of the bathing experience.

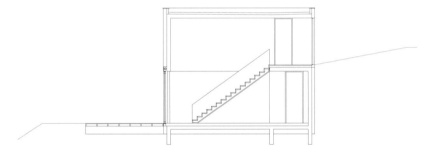

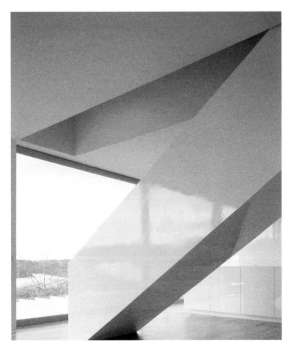

Living area with staircase to the upper floor

Cross section
Layout of entrance level
Scale 1:200

a   Parents' bedroom
b   Parents' bathroom
c   Shared sanitary area
d   Children's bathroom
e   Children's bedrooms
f   Corridor with fitted wardrobe
g   Entrance
h   Garage

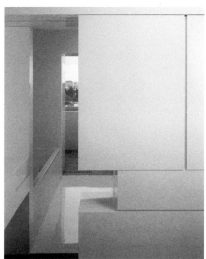

Multi-functional bathroom

View from the children's bathroom through the shared sanitary area to the parents' bathroom. The movable wardrobe unit can be seen in the foreground on the right.

The movable wardrobe element with the opening partly closed.

Layouts and section, scale 1:50

a   Parents' bathroom
b   Shared sanitary area
c   bathroom

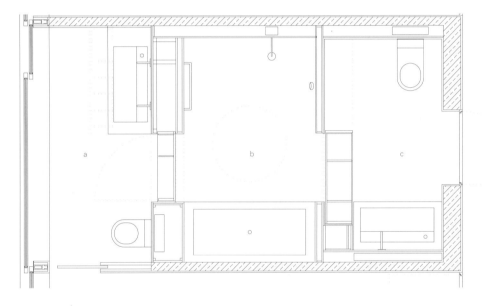
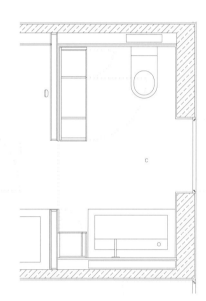

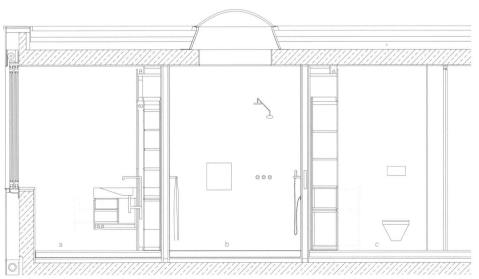

Layout, scale 1:20
a   Movable wardrobe element
b   Concealed handle
c   Drawer element
d   Integrated lighting

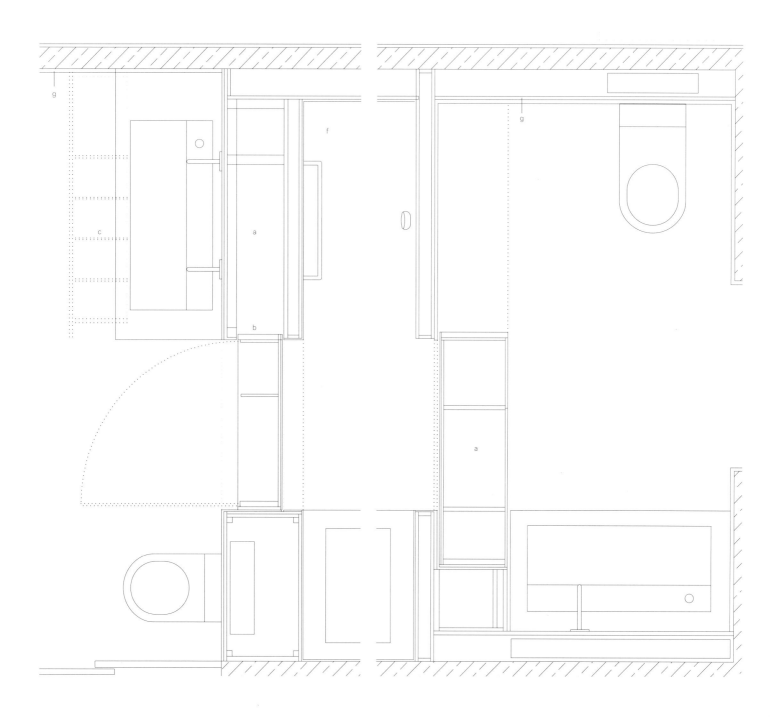

Detail of washstand in parent's bathroom

Section, scale 1:20
a   Movable wardrobe element
b   Concealed handle
c   Drawer element
d   Integrated lighting
e   Solid oak parquet

f   Polyurethane coating in the shower area (floor and wall)
g   2-coat lime plaster with fine floated finish and mineral paint coat (walls of parents' and children's bathrooms)

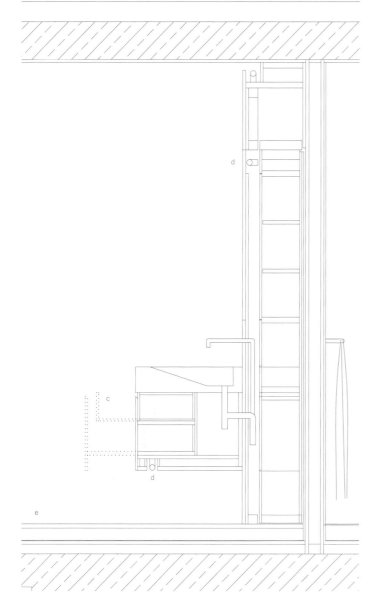

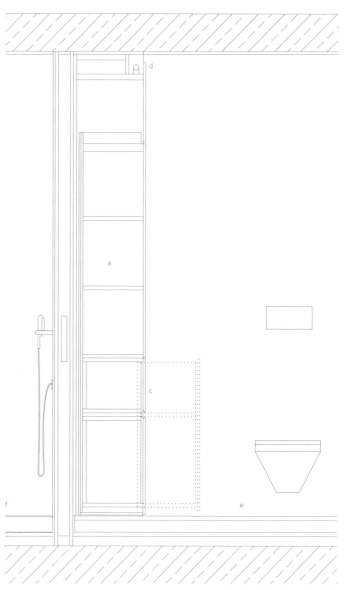

FIAT LUX, TOWNHOUSE, BRUSSELS, BELGIUM
LABEL ARCHITECTURE, BRUSSELS

———————

The existing, classic division of rooms in this four-storey townhouse had to be redesigned for a family with children. The low budget and the fact that only the interior of the house could be changed meant that a creative approach was needed for the existing building. The room layout is defined by a shared living area and space for family and communication, but also by private areas with equivalent spatial qualities, and storage space.

Zones are created with the help of the central functional area, which contains both the circulation space and secondary functions such as sanitary and storage facilities. This area forms a distinct core zone, which is emphasised by the change in material and which links the functional facilities with the living spaces.

The vertical connection is made via a perforated metal staircase, placed within a stairwell that is finished in white from top to bottom. In stark contrast to the white stairwell are the black rooms on each floor, which have been assigned to the various functions. This zone, which is defined by specific processes, creates a flowing inter-

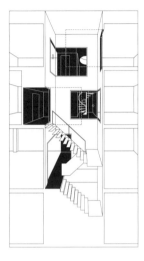

mediate space as a result of the imperceptible transition from floor to wall and ceiling. Its visual and haptic definition by means of material, surface finish and colour distinctly identifies and separates this typical secondary zone and directs attention to the adjoining living areas. These can therefore be used flexibly without any concession to functional requirements.

The stairwell – which extends over three floors – receives diffuse, filtered daylight via an illuminated ceiling. The separating elements between the habitable rooms consist of full-height glazing or mirrored elements. Depending on the viewpoint, this creates a play on perception, an optical illusion of extended space, or the impression of a secondary light source. On each floor, the functional areas are either set back or extended to suit the respective functional requirements. The resulting play of vistas, views and glimpses – horizontally throughout the depth of the building and vertically via the white space – reinforces the illusion of rooms merging into infinity.

The futuristic impression while passing through the space is reminiscent of a time-warp leading to another world. An intentional irritation, which cannot unfold its effect without the contrast with the existing building. A play with the obvious – achieving the maximum effect.

Sectional perspective showing space concept
The staircase space becomes the central element of the house, visually integrating functionality and design.

The exterior elevation of the traditional narrow townhouse in Brussels was not altered during the conversion.

The zoning within the building was achieved by using contrasting materials and colours.

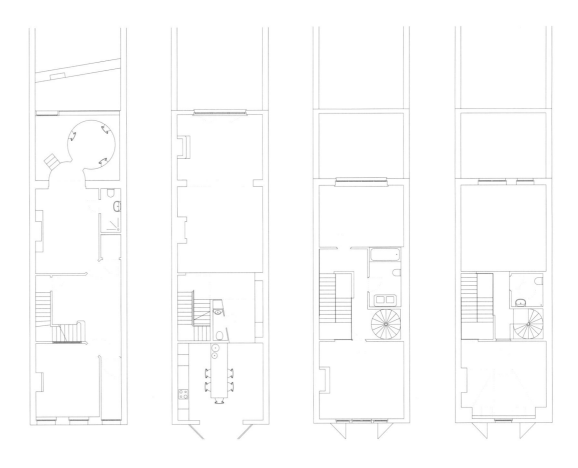

Layout of ground floor,
piano nobile, upper floors
scale 1:200
Communication and less-domestic
areas in the lower floors, with the
upper floors accommodating communal and personal rooms of an
increasingly private nature.

The functional core works as an intermediary between the floor levels
and room functions. Instead of a
small-format arrangement of wall
surfaces, openings and cupboard
elements, an homogeneous effect
has been created through the
choice of colour and material, which
eliminates the boundaries between
floor, wall and ceiling. The neutral
basic structure makes it possible to
use the adjoining rooms flexibly
given their materials and surfaces.

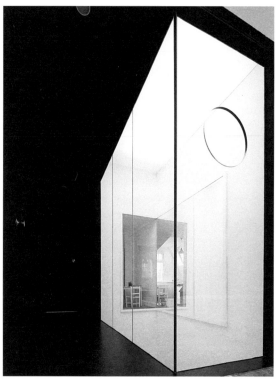

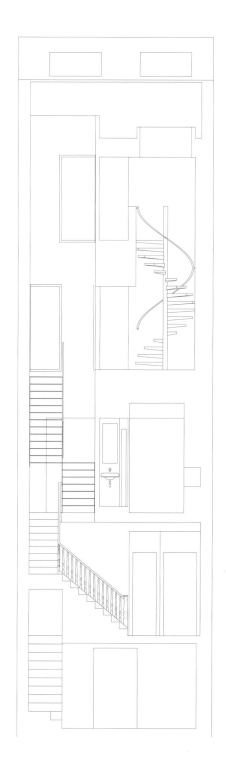

Light ceiling
The previously fully enclosed stairwell now has the benefit of natural
daylight. The installation of an additional rooflight together with a
horizontal fabric membrane provides even distribution of filtered
light without shadows and unwel-
come light effects. At night-time,
this even lighting effect is achieved
with a series of fluorescent lamps.
The upper part of the space is
suffused with light, dissolving its
contours.

Black wall lining
The surfaces in all circulation areas
are lined with 18 mm thick plywood
panels – a rather simple material,
which conveys a more elegant
impression as a result of being
stained black with lustre finish. The
resulting atmosphere liberates the
space from its functional character.

Glazing, mirrors, doors, openings
The insertion of the new staircase
disconnects the central functional
zone from the loadbearing structure. Openings can be arranged
straddling several storeys.
The glazed and mirror surfaces
change the spatial effect and con-
duct the filtered daylight into the
adjoining rooms either directly or
via reflection. New openings allow
direct communication beyond the
functional area.

Section, scale 1:100

Detailed section, scale 1:10
a Light ceiling
b Steel U profile 50 × 30 × 3 mm
c Mirror
d Two 8 mm glass panes
e Plywood panels, 18 mm thick,
stained black
f Plaster

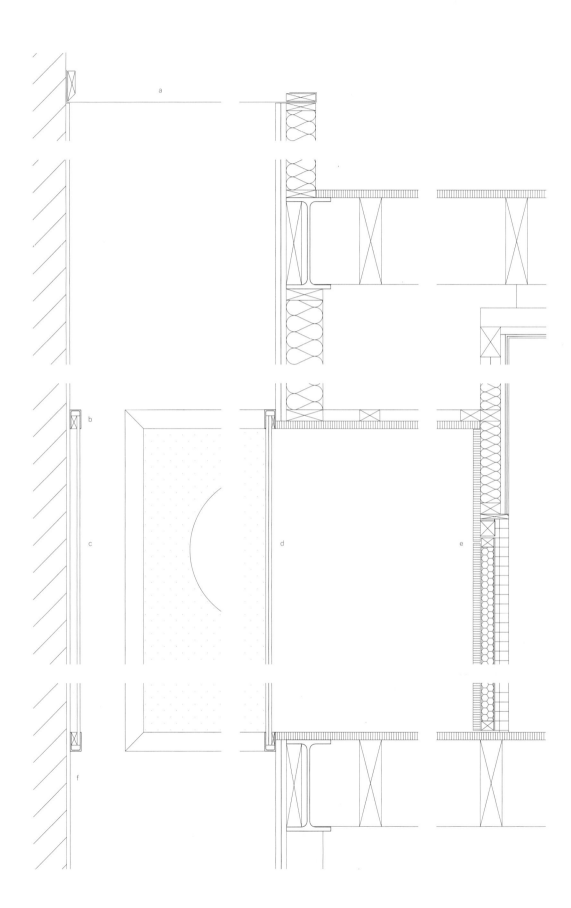

KIRSCHGARTEN GRAMMAR SCHOOL REFECTORY, BASEL, SWITZERLAND
HHF ARCHITECTS, BASEL

An open colonnade between two school buildings was converted to form a canteen and cafeteria in response to the increased demand for lunchtime catering. Since the building is protected by a listed building order, only minimum intervention was permitted in the existing building structure and it had to be possible to remove all new work at a later date. The work included the integration of all catering equipment, storage facilities, power and water supply, ventilation, acoustic and fire safety measures, as well as the weatherproof enclosure of the facade, including solar screening. The existing difference in the levels between the colonnade and the school yard was integrated and the seating to be created along the facade increased the quality of the space in front of the refectory. The previous function of the colonnade, which connects the two school buildings, explains the structural difficulties encountered in the upgrade. The largely unprotected filigree exterior elements did not allow the support of additional loads. Therefore the new structure needed to include structural elements as well as thermal and sound insulation and the existing difference in level had to be made up. As a result, the new structure fits neatly but separately into the existing open space, making only minimal contact with the listed building substance. The orientation towards the exterior space is evident from the inclusion of the seating steps, the interior cladding and the roof projection – including the integrated solar screening – with the only solid element being the thin profiles of the glass facade which serves as the thermal separation. Zoning of the room was achieved by timber bands consisting of individual plywood panels with graded colouring, which reflect the grid of the existing structure and its uprights. An offset in the exterior wall creates a niche for the lobby and kitchen. The vertical grid is modified by the irregular arrangement of the bands, involving different widths, colours and finishes. Acoustically effective elements and light fittings can be integrated almost invisibly in the self-supporting cladding. In addition to the central dining and buffet area, narrower social areas are created in the side wings, fitted with seating that appears to grow out of the timber bands. The colour scheme of the walls consists of light grey/beige shades, thus contrasting the lightness of the new building structure with the specifically designed solid wooden furniture.

Photograph at dusk following the conversion

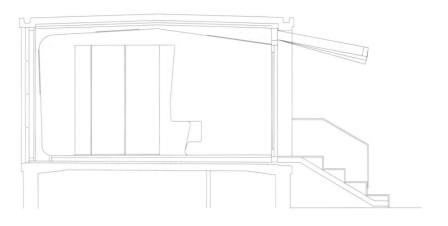

Sectional sketch and layout,
not to scale

Interior of refectory
The existing building fabric is lined
with three different panel formats
which absorb noise, accommodate
the lighting and meet the functional requirements for a gastronomy
area with kitchen for heating/
warming food.

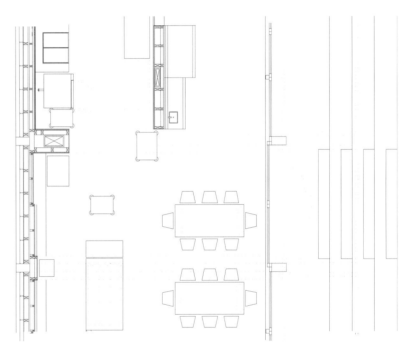

Refectory layout plan,
not to scale

Colonnade before the conversion
Architect: Hans Bernoulli

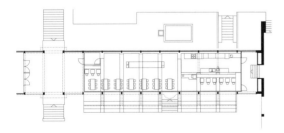

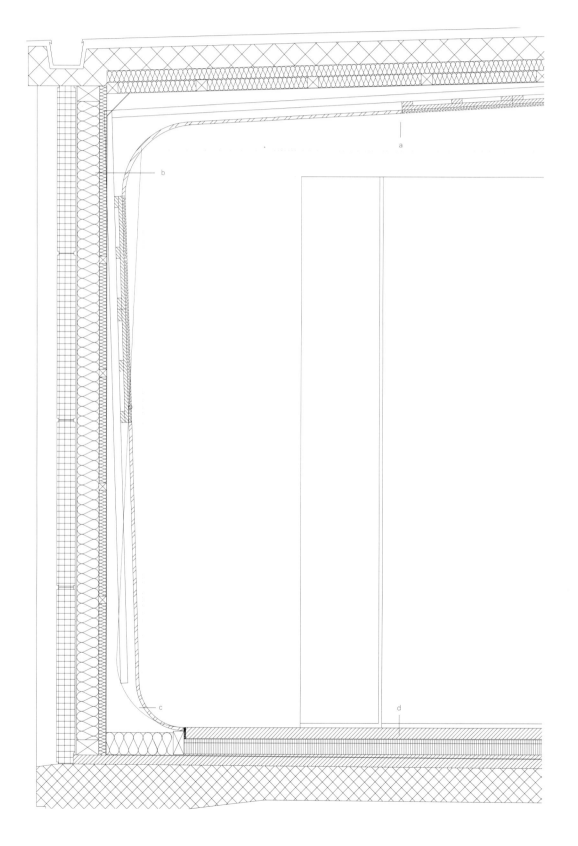

Detailed sections, scale 1:10
Floor, wall, ceiling
Working counter
Seating

a   Ceiling construction:
-   2 × 6 cm insulation between
    crosswise installed ceiling joists
-   vapour barrier
-   cavity for installations
-   timber cladding/acoustics
    element, finished in coloured
    spray paint

b   Wall construction:
-   acoustic element, finished in
    coloured spray paint, 16 mm
    MDF cladding, finished in
    coloured spray paint
-   conical grid of fixing battens
-   vapour barrier
-   4 × 4 cm counter-battens, with
    insulation infill
-   12 × 6 cm studs, with insulation
    infill, no fixing at back of studs
-   separating membrane
-   existing concrete element, listed
    as part of historic building

c   Wall-to-floor joint
Concave transition with internal
radius = 245 mm,
painted polyurethane

d   Floor construction of refectory:
-   ready-mixed anhydrite screed,
    6 cm, with white pigment,
    ground finish, underfloor heating
-   separating layer
-   insulation 20 mm, 60 mm
-   separating layer
-   packing layer on existing slope

Glass sliding door in aluminium
frame, electric controls with floor
switch

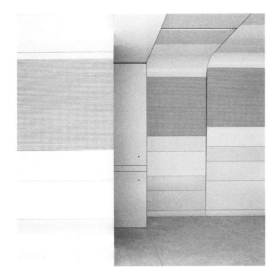

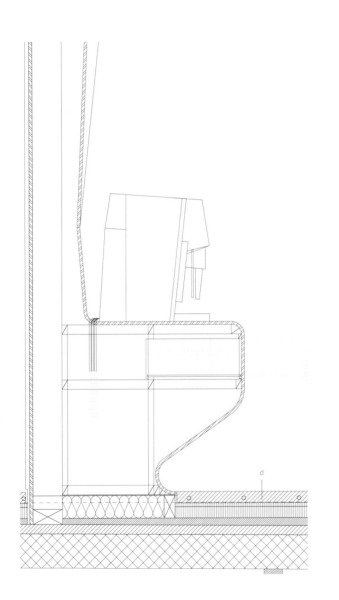

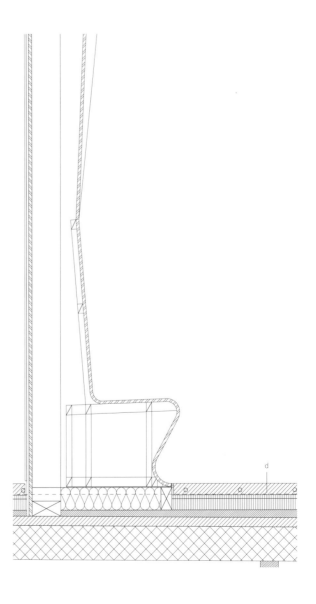

FURNISHING | ZONING
APPENDIX

PLACES OF WORK
TABLES AND INFORMATION

	Cellular office	Shared office	Combination office	Open-plan office
No. of people	1	2-3	1-2**	≥8
Size of room [m²]	≥10.4	21.6-29.2*	8.9-29.2**	≥100
Width of room [m]	≥2.60	≥5.40	2.70-5.40**	variable
Depth of room [m]	4.00-5.40	4.00-5.40*	3.30-4.60	≥13.50
Clear room height [m]	≥2.50	≥2.50	≥2.50	≥3.00
Dimensions of desk [m]	≥1.60 × 0.80			
Movement area at work place [m²]	≥1.50 Minimum depth for work place assigned to one person: 1.00 m Minimum depth for work place not in regular use: 0.80 m			
Access	Corridor	Corridor	Combination zone	Integrated
Ventilation	Normally natural	Normally natural	Normally natural	Mechanical
Lighting	Normally natural	Normally natural	Natural, artificial in the combination zone	Primarily artificial
Services installations	Duct under window/ underfloor	Duct under window/ underfloor	Duct under window Duct under floor Cavity floor Raised floor	Duct under floor Cavity floor Raised floor

* depends on number of people, **per cellular office

1

1 General office requirements: Grids and dimensions, air changes and lighting.
All data are guidelines only. A range of factors, requirements and constraints to be considered during the design have not been taken into account, ⟶ p. 30

2 Workplace field of vision
The requirements for computer-based workplaces specified in the DIN standard and Health and Safety at Work Directive are based on the human eye. In addition to the lighting conditions – various work activities require different lighting intensities ⟶ 3 – and the age of the person ⟶ 4, the horizontal and vertical field of vision ⟶ 2 plays a role in the design of workplaces.

a Maximum field of vision
b Preferred field of vision
c Optimum field of vision

3 Effect of lighting (lx) on visual performance (in %) depending on the intensity of the activity.

4 Visual acuity over time (dioptre) related to age (years).

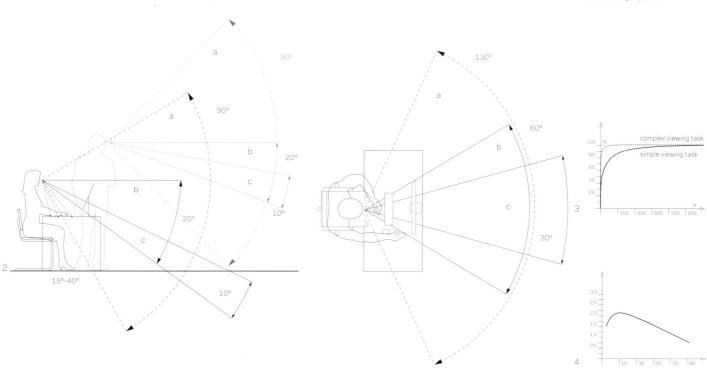

2

3

4

LIGHTING
TABLES AND INFORMATION

5 Colour temperature
The colour temperature of a light source is measured in kelvin and describes the temperature to which a black object (black-body radiation) would have to be heated in order to produce the same colour impression as the light source. The higher the value, the colder the colour impression.

6 Colour rendering index
The colour rendering index CRI describes the quality of the colour rendering of a light source compared to a reference light source of equal colour temperature. The maximum achievable value is 100. However, the colour rendering index is not a percentage value. Negative values are therefore also possible.

7 Nominal illumination intensity
DIN 5035 and the Health and Safety at Work Directive define minimum values for illumination intensity in interiors.

Colour of light	Colour temperature [K]	Effect	Use
Warm white (ww)	<3300	comfortable	Homes
Neutral white (nw)	3300–5300	neutral	Schools Public spaces
Daylight white (dw)	>5.300	cool	Offices Studios Museums

5

	Colour rendering index CRI
Incandescent lamp	≤100
Fluorescent lamp (warm white)	50–90
Fluorescent lamp (neutral white)	70–84
Fluorescent lamp (cold white)	85–100
LED, white	80–95
Halogen metal vapour lamp	80–85

6

Use	Nominal illumination intensity E_n in lx	Viewing task requirement depending on activity	Colour rendering grade, quality
Offices	500	medium to high	2A good
Offices, with access to daylight (next to window)	300	medium to high	2A good
Open-plan offices	750–1,000*	medium	2A good
Reception spaces	100	moderate	2A good
Meeting rooms	300	medium	1B very good
Circulation areas	100	low	2B adequate
Staff rooms	100	low	2B adequate
Kitchenettes	200	moderate	2B adequate
Workshop/ production	200–2,000**	moderate to very high	1A optimal
Theatre	300	medium	1B very good
Concert hall	300	medium	1B very good
Exhibition rooms	300	medium	1A optimal
Retail areas	300	medium	2A good
Sacral spaces	200	moderate	1B very good
Auditoriums	500	medium	2A good
Classrooms	300–500	medium	2A good
Sports halls	200–400	moderate to medium	1B very good
Restaurants	200	moderate	1B very good
Commercial kitchens	500	medium	2B adequate
Hospital ward	100	low	1B very good
Operating theatre	10,000	exceptional	1A optimal
Laboratory	500	medium	1B very good
Storage rooms	50	very low	4 poor
Living room/ bedroom	50–300	very low to medium	–
Kitchen/bathroom	300–1000	medium to high	–
Summer day, overcast	10,000***		
Summer day, sunny	20,000***		
Winter day, overcast	3,500***		
Candle light	1***		

* depends on the degree of reflection in the environment
** depends on the activity and degree of detail involved in the production
*** for comparison

7

SOUND INSULATION
TABLES AND INFORMATION

Use/component	Weighted sound reduction index R'w [dB]		Weighted standard impact sound level L'n, w [dB]	
	Minimum requirement	Increased requirement	Minimum requirement	Increased requirement
DETACHED, SEMI-DETACHED AND TERRACED HOUSES				
Ceilings, intermediate floors	–	–	48	38
Staircases, landings and ceilings beneath corridors	–	–	53	46
Party walls	57	67	–	
APARTMENTS				
Separating floors and staircases >2 units	54	55	53	46
Floors above cellars, main corridors, stairwells beneath living rooms	52	55	53	46
Ceilings/floors beneath corridors	–	–	53	46
Floors beneath bathrooms and WCs	54	55	53	46
Staircases and landings	–	–	58	46
Staircases and landings within apartments	–	–	53	46
Walls between apartments	53	55	–	–
Stairwell walls and walls next to main corridors	52	55	–	–
Walls next to exterior access passages	55	55	–	–
Doors from main corridors and stairwells to apartment corridors	27	37	–	–
Doors from main corridors and stairwells to living rooms	37	37	–	–
Walls between noisy and quiet rooms with different functions within a residential unit	40	47	–	–
OFFICES AND OFFICE BUILDINGS				
Intermediate floors, staircases, floors above corridors and stairwell walls	52	55	53	46
Walls between rooms with standard office activity	37	42	–	–
Walls between corridors and rooms with standard office activity	37	42	–	–
Doors between rooms with standard office activity or corridors and similar	27	32	–	–
Walls between rooms with standard office activity and rooms for concentrated/confidential activity	45	52	–	–
Walls between corridors and rooms for concentrated/confidential activity	45	52	–	–
Doors between rooms for concentrated/confidential activity or corridors and similar	37	–	–	

1   Sound insulation to DIN 4109
The weighted sound reduction index R'_w refers to the requirement for airborne sound insulation of a built-in building component, i.e. taking into account sound transmission via adjoining components. The weighted standard impact sound level L'_w refers to the requirement for impact sound insulation of a built-in building component, i.e. taking into account impact sound transmission via adjoining components.
While the sound reduction index should be as large as possible, the impact sound level should be as small as possible.

2   Sound propagation in rooms separated by removable partition walls:
a   horizontal sound propagation
b   vertical sound propagation
c   open joint between wall and ceiling
d   sound-conducting ceiling lining material
e   uninsulated void of suspended ceiling
f   unfavourable floor coverings
g   continuous floating screed

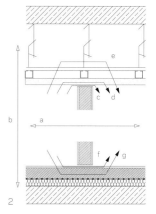

1

2

SOUND LIMITS
TABLES AND INFORMATION

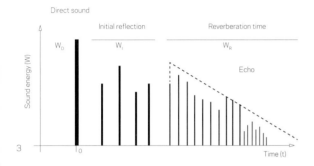

3 Schematic illustration of sound energy and reverberation time

4 Sound limits
Interiors must conform to sound pressure and reverberation time limits, depending on their respective functions. While the sound pressure level defines the recommended maximum sound level in a room, the reverberation time refers to the acoustic properties of a room. It is defined by the time taken for the sound level to reduce by 60 dB after cessation of the sound emission, and it has a very important effect on how speech can be heard in a room. The parameters are the size of the room and its geometry, the degree of sound absorption of the materials used and the number of people present in the room.

5 Sound absorption coefficient α
The sound absorption coefficient describes the degree to which the sound impacting on a component or a material is absorbed. A sound absorption coefficient of $\alpha = 0$ means that the sound is fully reflected, whereas a value of $\alpha = 1.0$ means that it is fully absorbed. The reverberation time of a material varies with the frequency of the sound. For this reason the sound absorption coefficient of a material should always be considered in combination with the frequency of the sound it is exposed to.

Use	Sound pressure level [dB]	Reverberation time [s]
Cellular or shared offices / Cellular room in combination offices	40	0.5
Open-plan office	45	0.5
Meeting room, conference room	35	1
Theatre	30	1
Concert hall	25	2
Cinema	35	1
Museum	40	1.5
Sacral space	35	3
Auditorium	35	1
Reading room	35	1
Classroom	40	1
Swimming pool	50	2
Gymnasium	45	1.5
Restaurants	40–55	1
Hospital wards, daytime	35	1
Hospital wards, night-time	30	1
Medical consultation room	40	2
Living room	35	0.5
Bedroom	30	0.5

Material/surface	125 Hz	250 Hz	500 Hz	1000 Hz	2000 Hz	4000 Hz
Screed, tiles, stone coverings	0.01	0.01	0.15	0.02	0.02	0.02
Parquet on screed	0.04	0.04	0.07	0.06	0.06	0.07
Wood flooring on timber beams	0.15	0.11	0.10	0.07	0.06	0.07
Textile floor finish on screed	0.02	0.06	0.14	0.37	0.60	0.65
Textile floor finish with foam backing	0.08	0.24	0.57	0.69	0.71	0.73
Linoleum, PVC on screed	0.02	0.03	0.03	0.03	0.03	0.02
Concrete, unfinished	0.36	0.44	0.31	0.29	0.39	0.25
Concrete with paint coating	0.10	0.05	0.06	0.07	0.09	0.08
Brickwork	0.03	0.03	0.03	0.04	0.05	0.07
Brickwork with paint coating	0.01	0.01	0.02	0.02	0.02	0.03
Plaster, textured (wall/ceiling)	0.02	0.03	0.04	0.05	0.04	0.03
Plaster, smooth (wall/ceiling)	0.01	0.02	0.02	0.03	0.04	0.05
Tiles	0.01	0.01	0.01	0.01	0.02	0.02
Plasterboard (wall/ceiling)	0.29	0.10	0.05	0.04	0.07	0.09
Wood panels (wall/ceiling)	0.28	0.22	0.17	0.09	0.10	0.11
Wood cladding	0.15	0.10	0.10	0.07	0.06	0.07
Glazing, windows	0.35	0.25	0.18	0.12	0.07	0.04
Curtain, 340 g/m² fabric	0.03	0.04	0.11	0.17	0.24	0.35
Curtain, 610 g/m² fabric	0.14	0.35	0.55	0.72	0.70	0.65
Padding with textile covering	0.49	0.66	0.80	0.88	0.82	0.70

FLOOR CONSTRUCTION AND FINISHES
TABLES AND INFORMATION

Component	Distance between measured points [m]				
	0.10	1.00	4.00	10.00	15.00
	Depth limit [mm]				
Surfaces of floors not ready to receive finishes, base concrete and structural floors	10	15	20	25	30
As above, but with stricter requirements, e.g. for the installation of floating screed, monolithic screed, industrial floors, tile finishes, or as finished surface for less demanding functions	5	8	12	15	20
Surfaces of floors ready to receive finishes e.g. screed as finished flooring or as base for floor coverings, tiling, coverings attached with adhesive on levelled surface	2	4	10	12	15
As above, but with stricter requirements	1	3	9	12	15
Walls without finishes and undersides of structural ceilings	5	10	15	25	30
Walls with finishes and undersides of ceilings (e.g. plaster linings or suspended ceilings)	3	5	10	20	25
As above, but with stricter requirements	2	3	8	15	20

1

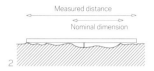

1 Evenness tolerances
DIN 18202 *Tolerances in buildings* specifies the evenness tolerances for the execution of buildings and building components.

2 The unevenness is measured using a procedure with a measuring board and measuring wedge. The limits for the differences in depth vary in accordance with the distance between measuring points.

3 Screed
Classification by binding agent and requirements and properties in acc. with DIN 18560-2 and DIN EN 13813.

Type of screed	Abbreviation	Binding agent	Curing time (without additives)	Ready for coverings (without additive)	Flexural strength class to DIN EN 13813	Compressibility of insulation layer under vertically imposed loads			
						c ≤ 5 mm		c ≤ 3 mm	
						Distributed load ≤ 2 kN/m³	Distributed load ≤ 3 kN/m² Point load ≤ 2 kN	Distributed load ≤ 4 kN/m² Point load ≤ 3 kN	Distributed load ≤ 5 kN/m² Point load ≤ 4 kN
						Nominal screed thickness [mm]			
Cement screed	CT	Cement	14 days	≥ 26 days	F 4	≥ 45	≥ 65	≥ 70	≥ 75
					F 5	≥ 40	≥ 55	≥ 60	≥ 65
Calcium sulphate screed (anhydrite screed)	CA	Calcium sulphate	3 days	≥ 24 days	F 4	≥ 45	≥ 65	≥ 70	≥ 75
					F 5	≥ 40	≥ 55	≥ 60	≥ 65
					F 7	≥ 35	≥ 50	≥ 55	≥ 60
Ready-mixed calcium sulphate screed	CAF				F 4	≥ 35	≥ 50	≥ 60	≥ 65
					F 5	≥ 30	≥ 45	≥ 50	≥ 55
					F 7	≥ 30	≥ 40	≥ 45	≥ 50
Mastic asphalt	AS	Bitumen	12 hours	≥ 1 day	IC 10	≥ 25	≥ 30	≥ 30	≥ 35
Synthetic resin screed	SR	Synthetic reaction resin	8-12 hours	≥ 3 days	F 7	≥ 35	≥ 50	≥ 55	≥ 60
					F 10	≥ 30	≥ 40	≥ 45	≥ 50
Magnesite screed	MA	Caustic magnesia, magnesium chloride	2 days	≥ 21 days	F 4	≥ 45	≥ 65	≥ 70	≥ 75
					F 5	≥ 40	≥ 55	≥ 60	≥ 65
					F 7	≥ 35	≥ 50	≥ 55	≥ 60

Note: In DIN 18560-2, the nominal screed thickness refers to unheated floating screeds.

3

Raised floor slab	Weight	Loadbearing capacity [kN]	Finished tolerance	Dimensional stability	Fire resistance class	Building material class to DIN 4102	Sound insulation	Walk-on comfort level
Wood-based board with aluminium foil backing	very low	1.5–3	low	low	≤F30	B2	average	average
Wood-based board with steel sheet backing	low	3–4.5	low	low	F30	B1	good	average
Fibreboard based on cement, gypsum or calcium sulphite binder	average	3–12	low	very high	F30–F60	A2–A1	very good	very high
Lightweight concrete, natural stone and reconstituted stone	average	5–12	average	very high	F30	A2–A1	very good	very high
Steel tray with mineral filling	average	3–7	very low	high	F30	A2–A1	very good	very high
Steel plate with steel frame	average	2–10	very low	average	–	A1	average	average
Die-cast aluminium plate	low	3–7	very low	average	–	A1	average	average

4 Properties of common raised floor slabs

5 Classification of textile and resilient floor coverings in accordance with EN ISO 10874 use classes.
The classification according to exposure and intensity of use facilitates objective comparison of different floor coverings.

		Class	Exposure	Intensity of use	Example
		Private use (residential)			
		21	moderate/low	low intensity	Bedrooms
		22	normal/medium	medium intensity	Living rooms Entrance areas
		22+	normal	medium to heavy intensity	Living rooms Entrance areas Circulation areas
		23	heavy	heavy intensity	Entrance areas Circulation areas
		Public and commercial use			
		31	moderate	low or part-time use	Cellular offices Meeting rooms Hotel rooms
		32	normal	medium intensity	Classrooms Retail areas
		33	heavy	heavy intensity	Open-plan offices Schools, lobbies Department stores
		34	very heavy	very heavy use	Airports Multi-purpose halls Counter service halls
		Industrial use (light industry)			
		41	moderate	primarily seated activity, occasional vehicular traffic	Electronics or precision engineering workshops
		42	normal	standing activity, vehicular traffic	Storage rooms
		43	heavy	industrial areas	Storage and production halls

FLOOR CONSTRUCTION AND FINISHES
TABLES AND INFORMATION

R value	Angle of incline	Friction coefficient	Displacement class	Examples of use
R9	6°–10°	low		Indoor entrance areas , indoor staircases
				Circulation areas, reception rooms
				Offices, meeting rooms
				Staff/common rooms, first-aid rooms
				Classrooms, auditoriums, reading rooms
				Restaurants, canteens, incl. circulation area
				Retail areas, cash till areas
				Hospitals, wards including circulation areas and operating theatres
				Laboratories
R10	>10°–19°	normal		Public sanitary facilities
				Kitchenettes
				Hospital – sanitary facilities
				Storage rooms
R11	>19°–27°	increased	V4	Entrance areas (external), steps (external)
			V4	Commercial kitchens ≤100 covers/day
				Halls of residence, sanatoria
				Day nurseries
				Retail premises, circulation areas, preparation rooms for packaged goods
				Hospital, rooms for medicinal baths and treatments
			V4/V6*	Workshop/production
R12	>27–35°	high	V4	Commercial kitchens >100 covers/day
				Hospitals
				Retail premises, circulation areas, preparation rooms for non-packaged goods
			V6*	Workshop/production, wet areas
R13	>35°	very high	V10	Slaughterhouses, rooms for fish processing

1   * depending on type of industry and production method in [m³/dm²]

Class	Water displacement [m³/dm²]	Example of use
V4	4	Commercial kitchens
V6	6	Rooms for meat processing: raw sausage department
V8	8	Rooms for meat processing: butchery
V10	10	Slaughterhouses

2

1 Anti-slip properties of floor coverings.
All floor coverings used in public areas and workplaces are classified according to their slip resistance (R value) and floor friction coefficient.
The slip-resistance properties of floor coverings of work rooms and work areas are tested on sloping surfaces in accordance with DIN 511130.

2 Water displacement of profiled floor coverings.
DIN 51130 classifies profiled floor coverings in wet areas according to their water-displacement properties.

3 Common dimensions of ceramic and stone finishes.
As a rule, floor tiles are offered in larger dimensions than wall tiles. The formats of tiles have not been standardised; however, there are some common sizes. Mosaics attached to a backing grid are a special form of tile finish. They are also available as glass mosaics with edge lengths of 1 to 10 centimetres.

Wall tiles	Floor tiles	Concrete paving slabs
Dimensions [cm]	Dimensions [cm]	Dimensions [cm]
10×10	20×20	20×40
13.5×19	20×25	25×25
15×15	25×25	25×50
15×20	30×30	26×48
15×22.5	30×60	33×60
18×18	30.5×30.5	40×40
20×25	32×32	40×60
20×33.3	33×33	50×50
28.4×40.8	40×40	50×75
30×60	41×41	60×60

3

WALLS AND CEILINGS
TABLES AND INFORMATION

4 Ceramic tiles
Classification by manufacturing method and properties.

5 Classification in accordance with EN 14411
Ceramic tiles are classified either by the amount of water retention or by the manufacturing method.

6 Degree of hardness according to Mohs
The Mohs hardness scale divides 10 minerals into the hardness grades MH 1 to 10, in accordance with their resistance to scratching. The Rosiwal absolute hardness scale refers to the grinding of a material, the Vickers hardness to the indentation depth of a material.

7 Plaster mortar groups to DIN 18550-1 and their suitability for internal walls and ceilings

	Classification EN 14441	Forming process	Firing temperature	Frost resistance	Glazing	Degree of hardness (Mohs)	Application area
Earthenware	BIII	dry-pressed	900–1100	–	x	⩾3	Wall
Terracotta							
Stoneware unglazed	BIb BIIa BIIb	dry-pressed	1200–1300	only group BIb	–	⩾6	Wall Floor
Stoneware glazed					x	⩾5	Wall Floor
Porcelain stoneware	BIa	dry-pressed	1200–1300	x	optional	⩾6	Wall Floor Swimming pools

4

By water absorption E as a percentage of weight

Ia	E < 0.5%	frost-proof
Ib	E 0.5 ⩽3%	
IIa	E 3%–⩽6%	not frost-proof
IIb	E 6%–⩽10%	
III	E >10%	

By manufacturing method

A	extrusion moulding
B	dry pressing
C	casting

5

MH	Mineral	Absolute hardness acc. to Rosiwal	Vickers hardness HV [kp³/mm²]	
1	Talcum	0.03	2	can be scored with a fingernail
2	Gypsum	1.25	36	
3	Calcspar	4.50	109	can be scored with a knife
4	Fluorspar	5.00	189	
5	Apatite	6.50	536	
6	Feldspar	37.00	795	will score window glass
7	Quartz	120.00	1120	
8	Topaz	175.00	1427	
9	Corundum	1000.00	2060	
10	Diamond	140000.00	10060	

6

Plaster mortar group	Designation	Binder	Internal wall			Internal ceiling		
			Only light exposure	Standard exposure	Wet rooms (except domestic kitchens and bathrooms)	Only light exposure	Standard exposure	Wet rooms (except domestic kitchens and bathrooms)
PI	Lime plaster	Non-hydraulic lime, hydraulic lime	x	x	x	x	x	x
PII	Lime plaster, render	Hydraulic lime, plaster and mortar binder, lime/cement mixture	Only as scratch coat	x	x	Only as scratch coat	x	x
PIII	Render	Cement	–	x	x	–	-	x
PIV	Gypsum plaster	Gypsum without/with building lime	x	x	–	x	x	–
PV	Gypsum plaster	Anhydrite binder without/with building lime	–	x	–	–	x	–
P Org 1	Synthetic resin render	Emulsions of polymer resin	–	Only as top coat on PII and PIII	Only as top coat on PII and PIII	–	Only as top coat on PII and PIII	Only as top coat on PII and PIII
P Org 2	Synthetic resin render	Emulsions of polymer resin	–	Only as top coat on PII and PIII	–	–	Only as top coat on PII and PIII	x

7

GYPSUM AS BOARD MATERIAL TABLES AND INFORMATION

Type of board	Code in acc. with DIN 18180	Code in acc. with EN 520	Description	Application	Common format thickness × width × length [mm]	Weight per unit area [kg/m²]
Plasterboard	GKB	A	–	Lining of walls and ceilings	* 250mm increments	
Plasterboard, impregnated	GKBi	H2	Delayed absorption of humidity	Lining of walls and ceilings in humid rooms and as substrate for tiling	9.5×1250×2000-4000*	8-10
Fire protection plasterboard	GKF	DF	Increased fire resistance	Lining of walls and ceilings in rooms with stricter fire-resistance requirements	12.5×1250×2000-4000*	10-13
Fire protection board, impregnated	GKFi	DFH2	Increased fire resistance, delayed absorption of humidity	Lining of walls and ceilings in humid rooms with stricter fire resistance requirements	15×1250 x 2000-3500*	13-16
Sound insulation board	GKB	D	Enhanced sound insulation properties	Lining of walls and ceilings in rooms with stricter sound insulation requirements	18×1250 x 2000-2500*	15-19
Perforated plasterboard		DIN EN 14190	Increased sound absorption	Lining of ceilings in order to optimise room acoustics		
Form board		D	Bendable	Lining of concave or convex constructions	20×625×2000-3500*	17-21
Composite board			With thermal insulation backing	Wall lining with thermal insulation	25×625×2000-3500*	20-26
Impact-resistant plasterboard		I	Impact-resistant and durable	Lining of walls in rooms with stricter requirements for impact resistance and durability (e.g. schools)		
Plasterboard, with wood fibre reinforcement		R	Increased surface hardness, compressive strength and rigidity	Linings with stricter structural requirements (e.g. support of larger cantilever loads)		
Gypsum fibreboard	GF		Delayed humidity absorption, increased fire resistance, increased strength	Lining of walls and ceilings in humid rooms and rooms with stricter fire-resistance or strength requirements, bracing function in timber construction, dry screed, floor slabs for raised and cavity floors	10 12.5 15 18	11.5 15 18 21.5
Gypsum fibreboard, high density			Increased load requirements	Lining of walls and ceilings in rooms with stricter requirements	× 625/1000/1250 ×	
Composite board			With thermal insulation backing	Wall lining with thermal insulation	1500-3000* 2540, 2600	

1   Plasterboard and gypsum fibreboard Classification and common formats

Substructure element	Dimensions [mm]	Permissible spacing [mm] for total load of		
		≤0.15 kN/m²	0.15 kN/m² – ≤0.30 kN/m²	0.30 kN/m² – ≤0.50 kN/m²
Timber substructure to DIN 4074-1				
Base batten fixed to structural ceiling	48×24	750	650	600
	50×30	850	750	600
	60×40	1000	850	700
Base batten, suspended	30×50	1000	850	700
	40×60	1200	1000	850
Counter batten	48×24	700	600	500
	50×30	850	750	600
Substructure consisting of steel sheet profiles to DIN 18182-1				
Base profile	CD 60×27×06	900	750	600
Counter profile		1000	1000	750

2   Spacing of fixing battens in suspended ceilings to DIN 18181

Lining	Thickness [mm]	Max. centre-to-centre spacing of counter battens/profiles [mm]	
Plasterboard		across the board	along the board
	12.5	500	420
	15	550	420
	18	625	420
Gypsum fibreboard			
	10	350	
	12.5	435	
	15	525	
	18	630	

3   Maximum spans for plasterboard to DIN 18180 and gypsum fibreboard

4   Overview of common board materials used in furniture and interior construction

WOOD AS BOARD MATERIAL TABLES AND INFORMATION

Designation	Particle board (chipboard)	Oriented strand board	Medium-density fibreboard	Hardboard	Blockboard Lumber core plywood
Abbreviation	–	OSB	MDF	HB	–
Description	Board made of pressed woodchips with synthetic resin impregnation	Board made of oriented wood strands with synthetic resin binder	Wood fibreboard with synthetic resin binder	Board made of pressed lignocellulose fibres (e.g. wood, straw, bagasse) with a low proportion of binding agent	Three-layer plywood consisting of two thin outer plywood layers and a middle layer of glued wood battens
Properties	Easy to process, good dimensional stability; board with 3 or 5 layers of differently sized chips has increased strength and deformation resistance	High flexural rigidity in longitudinal direction owing to the orientation of the strands (lengthways in the outer layers, crossways in the middle layer)	Homogeneous structure, easy to process, good dimensional stability, good strength, average flexural rigidity	Flexible, poor dimensional stability, top face smooth, underside textured	Relatively lightweight, easy to process, not suitable for high-quality surfaces
Surface finishes available	Unfinished, ground, veneered, laminated	Unfinished, primed	Unfinished, pigmented throughout with different colours	Unfinished, paint coated, laminated	With a range of facing veneers, e.g. birch, alder, Gaboon
Thicknesses available [mm]	6, 8, 10, 13, 16, 19, 22, 25, 28, 32, 36, 40, 45, 50, 60, 70	6, 8, 9, 10, 12, 15, 18, 22, 25, 30-40	6, 8,10,12,16,19, 22, 25, 28, 30, 32, 35, 40, 45, 50	1.6, 2, 2.5, 3, 3.2, 3.5, 4, 5, 6, 8	13, 16, 19, 22, 25, 30, 38
Common formats [mm]	4100×1850 2710×2080 5300×2050	625×2500 1250×2500-5000 2500×5000	2200-5600 × 1870-2070	1300-5200 × 1830-2050	1220-4100 × 2440-5400
Density [kg/m³]	550-750	580-700	600-900	700-1000	450
Building material class to DIN 4102	B2, B1 if enhanced with fire-resistant fill material	B2, B1 available	B2, B1 if enhanced with fire-resistant fill material	B2	B2, B1 with fire-resistant coating
Application areas	Furniture construction, interior boarding (floors, walls, etc.)	Board lining, t&g floor panels	Furniture construction	Furniture backing, face layer of door panels	Furniture construction, carcassing

Designation	Blockboard Glued batten core plywood	Veneered plywood	Multiplex board	Concrete shuttering board	Resin plywood
Abbreviation	–	VC	–	–	–
Description	Three-layer plywood consisting of a 24 to 30mm thick middle layer of glued battens and bonded outer veneer layers	Board with symmetric layers of an uneven number of crosswise glued veneer layers (3, 5 or 7 layer board)	Veneer plywood consisting of many crosswise layers	Waterproof plywood board with phenolic resin coating on both sides	Multi-layer board with veneer impregnated with phenolic resin and pressed at high temperatures
Properties	Similar to blockboard (wood core plywood) but for more demanding applications	High strength, dimensional stability and deformation resistance	Very high strength, dimensional stability and deformation resistance Suitable for large spans	Waterproof, high flexural rigidity and dimensional stability	Waterproof, resistant to alkaline and, to a degree, acids; very hard and abrasion-resistant, very high strength and dimensional stability, bullet-proof
Surface finishes available	With a range of facing veneers, e.g. birch, alder, Gaboon	With various facing veneers, including decorative veneers	With various facing veneers, including decorative veneers	In various colours, as vehicle board with textured underside	Unfinished (shades of brown)
Thicknesses available [mm]	13, 16, 19, 22, 25, 30, 38	4, 5, 6, 8, 10, 12	13, 16, 19, 22, 25, 30, 35, 40, 50	6.5, 9, 15, 18, 21, 27-40	5-120
Common formats [mm]	1220-4100 × 2440-5400	1250×2500 1500×3000	1250×2500 1500×3000	2000×3000 2000×5200	1000×1000 1000×2000
Density [kg/m³]	450	400-550	400-550	600-650	1100-1400
Building material class to DIN 4102	B2, B1 with fire-resistant coating	B2, B1 with fire-resistant coating	B2, B1 if enhanced with fire-resistant fill material	B1	B1
Application areas	Furniture construction	Furniture construction, loadbearing elements	Furniture construction, finished fittings	Furniture construction, interior fittings in kitchens and humid rooms	Furniture construction, post-formed plywood seating Various special applications

STANDARDS AND GUIDELINES (SELECTION)

Building Control terminology	Building material class to DIN 4102	EU class to DIN EN 13501-1	Additional requirements	
			No smoke production	No burning droplets or falling parts
Non-combustible, without combustible material content	A1	A1	x	x
Non-combustible, with combustible material content	A2	A2 – s1 d0	x	x
Hardly inflammable	B1	B, C – s1 d0	x	x
		A2, B, C – s2 d0	–	x
		A2, B, C – s3 d0	–	x
		A2, B, C – s1 d1	x	–
		A2, B, C – s1 d2	x	–
		A2, B, C – s3 d2	–	–
Normally flammable	B2	D – s1 d0	x	x
		D – s2 d0	–	x
		D – s3 d0	–	x
		D – s1 d2	x	–
		D – s2 d2	–	–
		D – s3 d2	–	–
		E	–	x
		E – d2	–	–
Highly flammable	B3	F	–	–

FIRE SAFETY
- DIN 4102 Fire behaviour of building materials and components
- DIN EN 13 501 Fire classification of construction products and building elements

BASIS

LIGHT AND LIGHTING
- DIN 5034 Daylight in interiors
- DIN 5035 Artificial lighting of interiors
- DIN EN 12464-1 Light and lighting – Lighting of work places – Part 1: Indoor work places;
- DIN EN 12665 Light and lighting – Basic terms and criteria for specifying lighting requirements

HUMAN BODY DIMENSIONS
- DIN 33402 Ergonomics – Human body dimensions

GRIDS AND DIMENSIONS
- DIN EN ISO 6385 Ergonomic principles in the design of work systems
- DIN 4543 Office work places – Part 1 Space for the arrangement and use of office furniture
- DIN EN 527 Office furniture – Work tables and desks, Part 1 Dimensions (draft)
- DIN EN ISO 9241-5 Ergonomic requirements for office work with visual display terminals – Part 5: Workstation layout and postural requirements
- DIN 16555 Space for communication work places in office buildings
- Safety at Work Framework Directive 89/39/EEC
- Product Safety Directive 2001/95/EC
- Display Screen Equipment Directive 90/270/EEC
- Health and Safety at Work Directive 89/654/EEC
- Workplaces Ordinance (ArbStättV)
- Display Screen Equipment Ordinance (BildscharbV)
- Industrial Safety Regulations (BetrSichV)
- DIN EN 1116 Coordinating sizes for kitchen furniture and equipment
- DIN 18022 Kitchens, bathrooms and WCs in housing

BARRIER FREEDOM
- DIN 18040-1 – Barrier-free Building, Design Criteria Part 1: Public buildings
- DIN 18040-2 – Barrier-free Building, Design Criteria Part 2: Apartments
- VDI 6008 Page 2 – Technical Rules (Draft), 2011-07
- Barrier-free spaces for living – Sanitary equipment options

ACOUSTICS
- ISO 1996-1:2003-08 Acoustics – Description, measurement and assessment of environmental noise – Part. 1: Basic parameters and assessment procedures
- DIN EN 12354-2 Building acoustics – Assessment of the acoustic properties of buildings based on the performance of elements – Part 2: Impact sound insulation between rooms
- DIN EN ISO 717 Acoustics – Rating of sound insulation in buildings and of building elements

SOUND INSULATION
- DIN 4109 Sound insulation in buildings
- VDI Guidelines 2058, 2719 and 4001

ROOM CLIMATE
- DIN 4108 Thermal insulation in buildings
- DIN 18017 Ventilation
- DIN 18164 DIN 18165, Thermal insulation materials

FLOOR CONSTRUCTION AND FINISHES

FLOOR CONSTRUCTION
- DIN 18202 Tolerances in building construction
- DIN 18195 Waterproofing of buildings and impact sound

SCREED

- DIN 18 560 Floor screeds in building construction
- DIN EN 13 813 Screed material and terms
- DIN EN 1264 Water based surface embedded heating and cooling systems
- DIN EN 50559 Electric room heating, underfloor heating, characteristics of performance (replaces DIN 44576-1)

INSTALLATION FLOORS

- DIN EN 13213 Hollow floors
- DIN EN 12825 Raised floors
- VDI 3762 Sound insulation of hollow and raised floors, issue 2012

RESILIENT FLOOR COVERINGS

- DIN EN ISO 24011 Resilient floor coverings Specification for linoleum with and without pattern
- EN ISO 10874 Resilient, textile and laminate floor coverings – classification (replaces DIN EN 685)
- DIN EN 12529 Castors and wheels – Castors for furniture – Castors for swivel chairs – Requirements
- DIN EN 688 Resilient floor coverings – Specification for cork linoleum
- DIN EN 12455 Resilient floor coverings – Specification for corkment underlay
- DIN 12104 Resilient floor coverings – Cork floor tiles – Specification
- DIN EN 12199 Resilient floor coverings – Specifications for homogeneous and heterogeneous relief rubber floor coverings

TEXTILE FLOOR COVERINGS

- DIN ISO 2424 Textile floor coverings – Terminology
- DIN EN 1307 Textile floor coverings- Classification of pile carpets
- DIN EN 1470 Textile floor coverings – Classification of needled floor coverings except for needled pile floor coverings
- DIN EN 13297 Textile floor coverings – Classification of pile floor coverings

WOODEN FLOORING

- DIN EN 13756 Wood flooring – Terminology
- DIN 4072 Boards tongued and grooved, made of coniferous timber
- DIN EN 13226 Wood flooring – Solid parquet elements with grooves and/or tongues
- DIN EN 13227 Wood flooring – Solid lamparquet products
- DIN EN 13228 Wood flooring – Solid wood overlay flooring elements including blocks with an interlocking system
- DIN EN 14342 Wood flooring and parquet- Characteristics, evaluation of conformity and marking
- DIN EN 13990 Wood flooring – Solid softwood floor boards
- DIN EN 1533 Wood flooring – Determination of bending strength under static load – Test methods
- DIN EN 1534 Wood flooring – Determination of resistance to indentation – Test method
- DIN EN 1910 Wood flooring and wall and ceiling linings made of wood – Determination of dimensional stability
- DIN 68702 Wood paving

STONE AND CERAMIC FLOOR COVERINGS

- DIN EN 14411 Ceramic tiles Definitions, classification, characteristics, evaluation of conformity and marking
- DIN 18157 Execution of ceramic linings by thin mortar bed method; hydraulic mortar

ANTI-SLIP PROPERTIES

- DIN 51130 Testing of floor coverings - Determination of anti-slip property - Workrooms and fields of activities with slip danger, walking method - Ramp test
- DIN 51097 Testing of floor coverings; determination of anti-slip properties; barefoot areas exposed to wet; walking method; ramp test

WALLS AND WALL SYSTEMS

NON-LOADBEARING PARTITION WALLS

- DIN 4103 Internal non-loadbearing partitions

SOLID PARTITION WALLS

- DIN 105 Clay masonry units
- DIN V 106 Calcium silicate units with specific properties
- DIN 4166 Autoclaved aerated concrete slabs and panels
- DIN 18162 Lightweight concrete wallboards – unreinforced
- DIN EN 12859 Gypsum blocks – Definitions, requirements and test methods
- DIN 4242 Glass block walls, construction and dimensioning

STUD WALL SYSTEMS/LININGS AND CLADDINGS

- DIN EN 520 Gypsum plasterboards – Definitions, requirements and test methods
- DIN EN 14190 Gypsum plasterboard products from reprocessing – Definitions, requirements and test methods
- DIN 18180 Gypsum plasterboards – Types and requirements
- DIN 18181 Gypsum plasterboards for building construction – Application
- DIN 18182 Accessories for use with gypsum plasterboards
- DIN 18183-1 Partitions and wall linings with gypsum boards on metal framing – Part 1: Cladding with gypsum plasterboards
- DIN EN 622-1 Fibreboards Requirements, Part 1
- DIN EN 1910 Wood flooring and wall and ceiling linings made of wood – Determination of dimensional stability

PLASTERS AND COATINGS

- DIN 18550 Plastering/rendering and plastering/rendering systems – Execution
- DIN 18558 Synthetic resin plasters; terminology, requirements, application
- DIN EN 13300 Paints and varnishes – Water-borne coating materials and coating systems for interior walls and ceilings - Classification
- DIN EN 233 und 234 Wall coverings in roll form
- DIN EN 235 Wall coverings – Terminology and symbols

CEILINGS AND CEILING SYSTEMS

SUSPENDED CEILINGS

- DIN EN 13964 Suspended ceilings – Requirements and test methods
- VDI 3755 Sound insulation and sound absorption of suspended ceilings
- DIN 4074-1 Strength grading of wood – Part 1: Coniferous sawn timber
- DIN EN 1910 Wood flooring and wall and ceiling linings made of wood – Determination of dimensional stability
- DIN 18168 Ceiling linings and suspended ceilings with gypsum plasterboards
- For further standards see above: STUD WALL SYSTEMS/LININGS AND CLADDINGS

WIRE PLASTER CEILINGS/LATH AND PLASTER CEILINGS

- DIN 4121 Suspended wire-plaster ceilings; plaster ceilings with expanded metal fixing substrate, lath and plaster ceilings, execution requirements

FURNITURE AND FIXTURES

- DIN EN 13986 Wood-based materials for use in construction – Characteristics, evaluation of conformity and marking
- DIN EN 312 Particleboards - Specifications
- DIN EN 622 Fibreboards - Specifications
- DIN EN 313 Plywood – Classification and terminology
- DIN EN 635 Plywood – Classification by surface appearance
- DIN EN 636 Plywood – Specifications
- DIN EN 68705-2 Plywood; plywood for general use
- DIN 68360 Veneers
- DIN EN 438 High-pressure decorative laminates (HPL) – Sheets based on thermosetting resins (usually called 'laminates')

ASSOCIATIONS AND MANUFACTURERS (SELECTION)

Associations

Arbeitsgemeinschaft Die Moderne
Küche e.V. (AMK)
Harrlachweg 4
D-68163 Mannheim
Tel. +49 (0) 621 - 8506100
www.amk.de

barrierefrei behindertengerecht
planen - bauen - wohnen
Rigaer Straße 89
D-10247 Berlin
www.nullbariere.de

Beratungsstelle für Handwerk und
Denkmalpflege
Propstei Johannesberg
D-36041 Fulda
Tel. +49 (0) 661 - 9418396
www.denkmalpflegeberatung.de

BetonMarketing Deutschland
Steinhof 39
D-40699 Erkrath
Tel. +49 (0) 211 - 280481
www.beton.org

Bundesindustrieverband
Heizungs-, Klima-, Sanitärtechnik/
Technische Gebäudesysteme e.V
Weberstraße 33
D-53113 Bonn
Tel. +49 (0) 228 - 949170
www.bhks.de

Bine Informationsdienst
Kaiserstraße 185-197
D-53113 Bonn
Tel. +49 (0) 228 - 923790
www.bine.info

Bundesverband der Gipsindustrie
e.V., Forschungsvereinigung der
Gipsindustrie e.V.
Kochstraße 6-7
D-10969 Berlin
Tel. +49 (0) 30 - 311698220
www.gips.de

Bundesverband Deutsche
Beton- und Fertigteilindustrie e.V.
Schlossallee 10
D-53179 Bonn
Tel. +49 (0) 228 - 954 56 56
www.betoninfo.de

Bundesverband Estrich und Belag
Industriestraße 19
D-53842 Troisdorf
Tel. +49 (0)2241 - 3973960
www.beb-online.de

Bundesverband Farbe Gestaltung
Bautenschutz
Gräfstraße 79
D-60486 Frankfurt am Main
Tel. +49 (0) 69 - 66575300
www.farbe.de

Bundesverband Feuchte &
Altbausanierung e.V.
Am Dorfanger 19
D-18246 Groß Belitz
Tel. +49 (0) 38466 - 339816
www.bufas-ev.de

Bundesverband Leichtbeton e.V.
Sandkauler Weg 1
D-56564 Neuwied
Tel. +49 (0) 2631 - 22227
www.leichtbeton.de

Bundesverband Systemboden
(BVS)
Leostraße 22
D-40545 Düsseldorf
Tel. +49 (0) 211 - 9559326
www.systemboden.de

Deutsche Energie-Agentur GmbH
Chausseestraße 128a
D-10115 Berlin
Tel. +49 (0) 30 - 72616560
www.dena.de

Deutsche Gesellschaft für Akustik
Voltastraße 5, Gebäude 10-6
D-13355 Berlin
Tel. +49 (0) 30 - 46069463
www.dega-akustik.de

Deutsche Gesellschaft für Mauer-
werks- und Wohnungsbau e.V.
Kochstraße 6-7
D-10969 Berlin
Tel. +49 (0) 30 - 25359640
www.dgfm.de

Dt. Gütegemeinschaft Möbel e.V.
Friedrichstraße 13-15
D-90762 Fürth
Tel. +49 (0) 911 - 95099980
www.dgm-moebel.de

Deutsche Lichttechnische
Gesellschaft e.V.
Burggrafenstraße 6
D-10787 Berlin
Tel. +49 (0) 30 - 26012439
www.litg.de

Deutsche Wellness Verband e.V.
Neusser Straße 35
D-40219 Düsseldorf
Tel. +49 (0) 211 - 1682090
www.wellnessverband.de

Deutscher Industrieverband
Keramische Fliesen und Platten
Luisenstraße 44
D-10117 Berlin
Tel. +49 (0) 30 - 275959740
www.fliesenverband.de

Deutscher Naturwerkstein-Verband
e.V. (DNV)
Sanderstraße 4
D-97070 Würzburg
Tel. +49 (0) 931 - 12061
www.natursteinverband.de

Deutsches Institut für Bautechnik
Kolonnenstraße 30 L
D-10829 Berlin
Tel. +49 (0) 30 - 78730244
www.dibt.de

Deutsches Lackinstitut GmbH (DLI)
Mainzer Landstraße 55
D-60329 Frankfurt am Main
Tel. +49 (0) 69 - 25561412
www.lacke-und-farben.de

Fachverband Fliesen und
Naturstein
im Zentralverband Deutsches
Baugewerbe e.V.
Kronenstraße 55-58
D-10117 Berlin
Tel. +49 (0) 30 - 203140
www.fachverband-fliesen.de

Fraunhofer-Institut für Bauphysik
(IBP)
Nobelstraße 12
D-70569 Stuttgart
Tel. +49 (0) 711 - 9700
www.fraunhofer.de

Gemeinschaft umweltfreundlicher
Teppichboden
Schönebergstraße 2
D-52068 Aachen
Tel. +49 (0) 2 41 - 968431
www.gut-ev.de

Gesamtverband Dämmstoff-
industrie GDI
Luisenstraße 44
D-10117 Berlin
Tel. +49 (0) 30 - 27594451
www.gdi.de

Gütegemeinschaft Trockenbau am
Institut für Trocken- und Leichtbau
Annastraße 18
D-64285 Darmstadt
Tel. +49 (0) 6151 - 599490
www.trockenbau-ral.de

Hauptverband der Deutschen
Bauindustrie, BFA Akustik- und
Trockenbau
Kurfürstenstraße 129
D-10785 Berlin
Tel. +49 (0) 30 - 21286238
www.bauindustrie.de

Hauptverband der Deutschen
Holzindustrie und Kunststoffe
verarbeitenden Industrie und
verwandter Industrie- und
Wirtschaftszweige e.V. (HDH)
Flutgraben 2
D-53604 Bad Honnef
Tel. +49 (0) 2224 - 93770
www.hdh-ev.de

Institut Bauen und Umwelt e.V. (IBU)
Panoramastraße 1
D-10178 Berlin
Tel. +49 (0) 30 - 30877480
www.bau-umwelt.com

licht.de
Lyoner Straße 9
D-60528 Frankfurt am Main
Tel. +49 (0) 69 - 6302353
www.licht.de

raumPROBE
Hohnerstraße 23
D-70469 Stuttgart
Tel. +49 (0) 711 - 63319980
www.raumprobe.de

SGA-SSA Schweizerische
Gesellschaft für Akustik (SGA)
Postfach 164
CH-6203 Sempach Station
www.sga-ssa.ch

Textiles & Flooring Institute
Charlottenburger Allee 41
D-52068 Aachen
Tel. +49 (0) 241 - 967900
www.tfi-online.de

VDE Verband der Elektrotechnik
Elektronik Informationstechnik e.V.
Stresemannallee 15
D-60596 Frankfurt am Main
Tel. +49 (0) 69 - 63080
www.vde.com

Verband Beratender Ingenieure
(VBI)
Budapester Straße 31
D-10787 Berlin
Tel. +49 (0) 30 - 260620
www.vbi.de

Verband der Deutschen Parkett-
industrie
Flutgraben 2
D-53604 Bad Honnef
Tel. +49 (0) 2224 - 93770
www.parkett.de

Wissenschaftlich-Technische
Arbeitsgemeinschaft für Bauwerk-
serhaltung und Denkmalpflege
Edelsbergstraße 8
D-80686 München
Tel. +49 (0) 89 - 57869727
www.wta.de

Zentralverband Deutsches
Baugewerbe
Kronenstraße 55-58
D-10117 Berlin
Tel. +49 (0) 30 - 203140
www.zdb.de

Zentralverband Sanitär Heizung
Klima
Rathausallee 6
D-53757 Sankt Augustin
Tel. +49 (0) 2241 - 92990
www.shk-portal.de

Manufacturers

OWA Odenwald Faserplattenwerk
Dr.-F.-A.-Freundt-Straße 3
D-63916, Amorbach
Tel. +49 (0) 9373 - 201131
www.owa.de

Richter Furniertechnik
Wallenbrücker Straße 85
D-49326 Melle/St. Annen
Tel. +49 (0) 5428 - 94200
www.richter-furniertechnik.de

Häfele GmbH & Co KG
Adolf-Häfele-Straße 1
D-72202 Nagold
Tel. +49 (0)7452 - 95888
www.haefele.com

Hettich Holding GmbH & Co. oHG
Vahrenkampstraße 12-16
D-32278 Kirchlengern
Tel. +49 (0) 5223 - 770
www.hettich.com

ARDEX GmbH
Friedrich-Ebert-Straße 45
D-58453 Witten
Tel. +49 (0) 2302 - 6640
www.ardex.de

CERESIT/Henkel AG & Co. KGaA
Bautechnik Deutschland
Henkelstraße 67
D-40589 Düsseldorf
Tel. +49 (0) 211 - 7970
www.ceresit-bautechnik.de

Fermacell GmbH
Düsseldorfer Landstraße 395
D-47259 Duisburg
Tel. +49 (0) 203 - 608803
www.fermacell.de

Heidelberger Beton GmbH
Berliner Straße 10
D-69120 Heidelberg
Tel. +49 (0) 6221 - 48139503
www.heidelberger-beton.de

nora systems GmbH
Höhnerweg 2-4
D-69469 Weinheim
Tel. +49 (0) 6201 - 805666
www.nora.com

REHAU AG + Co
Rheniumhaus
D-95111 Rehau
Tel. +49 (0) 9283 - 770
www.rehau.com

Schiefner & Schreiber Asphaltbau
GmbH & Co. KG
Saarstraße 7
D-63450 Hanau/Main
Tel. +49 (0) 6181 - 360120
www.schiefner-schreiber.de

Schlüter-Systems KG
Schmölestraße 7
D-58640 Iserlohn
Tel. +49 (0) 2371 - 9710
www.schlueter.de

Uzin Utz AG
Dieselstraße 3
D-89079 Ulm
Tel. +49 (0) 731 - 40970
www.uzin-utz.com

Forbo Flooring GmbH
Steubenstraße 27
D-33100 Paderborn
Tel. +49 (0) 5251 - 18030
www.forbo-flooring.de

AGROB BUCHTAL GmbH
Postfach 49
D-92515 Schwarzenfeld
Tel. +49 (0) 9435 - 3910
www.agrob-buchtal.de

Casamood
Via Canaletto, 24
I-41042 Fiorano Modenese
Tel. +39 0536 - 840111
www.casadolcecasa.com

Mosa
Meerssenerweg 358
NL-6201 Maastricht
Tel. +31 (0) 43 - 3689229
www.mosa.nl

Porcelaingres Gmbh
Mehringdamm 55
D-10961 Berlin
Tel. +49 (0) 30 - 616753012
www.porcelaingres.de

Admonter STIA Holzindustrie
GmbH
Sägestraße 539
A-8911, Admont
Tel. +43 (0) 3613 - 33500
www.admonter.at

DINESEN
Klovtoftvej 2, Jels
DK-6630, Rødding
Tel. +45 7455 - 2140
www.dinesen.com

Bisazza p.p.A.
Viale Milano 56
I-36041 Alte-Vicenza
Tel. +39 0444 - 707511
www.bisazza.com

Solnhofen Stone Group GmbH
Maxberg 1
D-91807 Solnhofen
Tel. +49 (0) 9145 - 601300
www.solnhofen-natursteine.com

Ströhmann Steinkult GmbH
Nassaustraße 25
D-65719 Hofheim-Wallau
Tel. +49 (0) 6122 - 91070
www.stroehmann.de

Anker-Teppichboden
Zollhausstraße 112
D-52353, Düren
Tel. +49 (0) 2421 - 8040
www.anker-teppichboden.de

Armstrong DLW GmbH
Stuttgarterstraße 75
D-74321 Bietigheim-Bissingen
Tel. +49 (0) 7142 - 71185
www.armstrong.de

Carpet Concept
Bunzlauerstraße 7
D-33719 Bielefeld
Tel. +49 (0) 521 - 924590
www.carpet-concept.de

Interface
Rote-Kreuz-Straße 2
D-47807 Krefeld
Tel. +49 (0) 2151 - 37180
www.interfaceflor.de

OBJECT CARPET
Rechbergstraße 19
D-73770 Denkendorf
Tel. +49 (0) 711 - 34020
www.object-carpet.com

Ruckstuhl AG
Bleienbachstrasse 9
CH-4901 Langenthal
Tel. +41 (0) 62 - 9198600
www.ruckstuhl.com

Vorwerk
Kuhlmannstraße 11
D-31785 Hameln
Tel. +49 (0) 5151 - 1030
www.corporate.vorwerk.de

Baumit GmbH
Reckenberg 12
D-87541 Bad Hindelang
Tel. +49 (0) 8324 - 9210
www.baumit.com

Hasit Trockenmörtel GmbH
Landshuter Straße 30
D-85356 Freising
Tel. +49 (0) 8161 - 6020
www.hasit.de

isofloc Wärmedämmtechnik GmbH
Am Fieseler Werk 3
D-34253 Lohfelden
Tel. +49 (0) 561 - 951720
www.isofloc.de

Knauf Gips KG
Am Bahnhof 7
D-97346 Iphofen
Tel. +49 (0) 9323 - 310
www.knauf.de

Lindner Group KG
Bahnhofstraße 29
D-94424 Arnstorf
Tel. +49 (0) 8723 - 200
www.Lindner-Group.com

MAPEI GmbH
Bahnhofsplatz 10
D-63906 Erlenbach
Tel. +49 (0) 9372 - 98950
www.mapei.de

PCI Augsburg GmbH
Piccardstraße 11
D-86159 Augsburg
Tel. +49 (0) 821 - 59010
www.pci-augsburg.de

Saint-Gobain Rigips GmbH
Schanzenstraße 84
D-40549 Düsseldorf
Tel. +49 (0) 211 - 55030
www.rigips.de

Sika Deutschland GmbH
Kornwestheimer Straße 103-107
D-70439 Stuttgart
Tel. +49 (0) 711 - 80090
www.sika.de

Sopro Bauchemie GmbH
Postfach 420152
D-65102 Wiesbaden
Tel. +49 (0) 611 - 17070
www.sopro.com

Sto AG
Ehrenbachstraße 1
D-79780 Stühlingen
Tel. +49 (0) 7744 - 570
www.sto.de

Tremco illbruck GmbH & Co. KG
Von-der-Wettern-Straße 27
D-51149 Köln
Tel. +49 (0) 2203 - 575500
www.tremco-illbruck.de

DEUTSCHE ROCKWOOL
Rockwool Straße 37-41
D-45966 Gladbeck
Tel. +49 (0) 2043 - 4080
www.rockwool.de

Rieder
Mühlenweg 22
A-5751 Maishofen
Tel. +43 (0) 6542 - 690844
www.rieder.cc

Knauf AMF GmbH & Co. KG
Elsenthal 15
D-94481 Grafenau
Tel. +49 (0) 8552 - 422994
www.knaufamf.de

Sefar AG Architecture
Hinterbissaustrasse 12
CH-9410 Heiden
Tel. +41 (0) 71 - 8985617
www.sefararchitecture.com

Hunter Douglas
Erich-Ollenhauer-Straße 7
D-40595 Düsseldorf
Tel. +49 (0) 211 - 970860
www.hd-as.de

durlum GmbH
An der Wiese 5
D-79650 Schopfheim
Tel. +49 (0) 7622 - 39050
www.durlum.de

Berker
Postfach 1160
D-58567 Schalksmühle
Tel. +49 (0) 2355 - 9050
www.berker.com

Gira
Dahlienstraße 12
D-42477 Radevormwald
Tel. +49 (0) 2195 - 6020
www.gira.de

JUNG
Volmestraße 1
D-58579 Schalksmühle
Tel. +49 (0) 2355 - 8060
www.jung.de

Akzo Nobel Deco GmbH
Vitalisstraße 198-226
D-50827 Köln
Tel. +49 (0) 221 - 5881521
www.akzonobel.com

Brillux GmbH & Co. KG
Weseler Straße 401
D-48163 Münster
Tel. +49 (0) 251 - 7188759
www.brillux.de

Caparol
Roßdörfer Straße 50
D-64372 Ober-Ramstadt
Tel. +49 (0) 6154 - 710
www.caparol.de

Boffi Arredamento Cucina p.p.A.
Via Oberdan 70
I-20823, Lentate sul Seveso
Tel. +39 0362 - 5341
www.boffi.com

Dornbracht
Köbbingser Mühle 6
D-58640 Iserlohn
Tel. +49 (0) 2371 - 4330
www.dornbracht.com

GROHE AG
Feldmühlenplatz 15
D-40545 Düsseldorf
Tel. +49 (0) 211 - 91303000
ww.grohe.com

Hansgrohe SE
Auestraße 5-9
D-77761 Schiltach
Tel. +49 (0) 7836 - 510
www.hansgrohe.de

VOLA
Lunavej 2
DK-8700 Horsens
Tel. +45 (0) 70 - 235500
www.vola.com

PSLAB
P.O.BOX 175636
LB-Beirut
Tel. +961 1 - 442546
www.pslab.net

Artemide
Via Bergamo 18
I-20010 Pregnana, Milanese
Tel. +39 023 - 739750
www.artemide.com

ERCO GmbH
Brockhauser Weg 80-82
D-58507 Lüdenscheid
Tel. +49 (0) 2351 - 5510
www.erco.com

Kreon
Industrieweg Noord 1152
B-3660 Opglabbeek
Tel. +32 (0) 89 - 819780
www.kreon.com

XAL GmbH
Auer-Welsbach-Gasse 36
A-8055 Graz
Tel. +43 (0) 316 - 3170300
www.xal.com

Zumtobel Lighting
Schweizer Straße 30
A-6851 Dornbirn
Tel. +43 (0) 5572 - 3900
www.zumtobel.com

Nimbus Group GmbH
Sieglestraße 41
D-70469 Stuttgart
Tel. +49 (0) 711 - 6330140
www.nimbus-group.com

Kettnaker GmbH & Co. KG
Bussenstraße 30
D-88525 Dürmentingen
Tel. +49 (0) 7371 - 959329
www.kettnaker.com

Vitsoe
Centric Close
GB-London NW1 7EP
Tel. +49 (0) 20 - 74281606
www.vitsoe.com

Arper spa
Via Lombardia 16
I-31050 Monastier di Treviso
Tel. +39 (0) 422 - 7918
www.arper.com

Artek oy ab
Lönnrotinkatu 7
FIN-00130 Helsinki
Tel. +358 10 - 6173460
www.artek.fi

Bene
Schwarzwiesenstraße 3
A-3340, Waidhofen/Ybbs
Tel. +43 (0) 7442 - 5000
www.bene.com

ASSOCIATIONS AND MANUFACTURERS (SELECTION)

Fritz Hansen
Allerødvej 8
DK-3450, Allerød
Tel. +45 (0) 48 – 172300
www.fritzhansen.com

Lista Office AG
Alfred Lienhard Strasse 2
CH-9113, Degersheim
Tel. +41 (0) 71 – 3725252
www.lista-office.com

Thonet
Michael-Thonet-Str 1
D-35059 Frankenberg/Eder
Tel. +49 (0) 6451 – 5080
www.thonet.de

USM
Thunstrasse 55
CH-3110 Münsingen
Tel. +41 (0) 31 – 7207272
www.usm.com

Vitra
Klünenfeldstrasse 22
CH-4127 Birsfelden
Tel. +41 (0) 61 – 3770000
www.vitra.com

Walter Knoll
Bahnhofstraße 25
D-71083 Herrenberg
Tel. +49 (0) 7032 – 2080
www.walterknoll.de

Resopal GmbH
Hans-Böckler-Straße 4
D-64823 Groß-Umstadt
Tel. +49 (0) 6078 – 800
www.resopal.de

EGGER Holzwerkstoffe Brilon
Im Kissen 19
D-59929 Brilon
Tel. +49 (0) 800 – 3443745
www.egger.com

Pfleiderer Holzwerkstoffe GmbH
Ingolstädter Straße 51
D-92318 Neumarkt
Tel. +49 (0) 9181 – 28480
www.pfleiderer.com

Geberit International AG
Schachenstrasse 77
CH-8645 Jona
Tel. +41 (0) 55 – 2216300
www.geberit.de

TECE GmbH
Hollefeldstraße 57
D-48282 Emsdetten
Tel. +49 (0) 2572 – 9280
www.tece.de

Bette
Heinrich-Bette-Straße 1
D-33129 Delbrück
Tel. +49 (0) 5250 – 511175
www.bette.de

DALLMER Sanitärtechnik
Wiebelsheidestraße 25
D-59757 Arnsberg
Tel. +49 (0) 2932 – 96160
www.dallmer.de

wedi GmbH
Hollefeldstraße 51
D-48282 Emsdetten
Tel. +49 (0) 2572 – 1560
www.wedi.de

Agape
Via Alberto Pitentino, 6
I-46037 Mantova
Tel. +39 (0) 37 – 6250311
www.agapedesign.it

Alape
Am Gräbicht 1-9
D-38644 Goslar
Tel. +49 (0) 5321 – 5580
www.alape.de

DURAVIT
Werderstraße 36
D-78132 Hornberg
Tel. +49 (0) 7833 – 700
www.duravit.de

Franz Kaldewei GmbH & Co. KG
Beckumer Straße 33-35
D-59229 Ahlen
Tel. +49 (0) 2382 – 7850
www.kaldewei.de

KERAMAG Keramische Werke AG
Kreuzerkamp 11
D-40878 Ratingen
Tel. +49 (0) 2102 – 9160
www.pro.keramag.de

Laufen Bathrooms AG
Wahlenstrasse 46
CH-4242 Laufen
Tel. +41 (0) 61 – 7657575
www.de.laufen.com

TOTO Europe GmbH
Zollhof 2
D-40211 Düsseldorf
Tel. +49 (0) 211 – 27308200
eu.toto.com

Villeroy & Boch
Saaruferstraße 14
D-66693 Mettlach
Tel. +49 (0) 6864 – 810
www.villeroy-boch.com

VitrA Bad GmbH
Agrippinawerft 24
D-50678 Köln
Tel. +49 (0) 221 – 2773680
www.vitra-bad.de

3M™ Deutschland GmbH
Carl-Schurz-Straße 1
D-41453 Neuss
Tel. +49 (0) 2131 – 142690
www.3m.com

Event Textil Service
Bruno-Dreßler-Straße 9 B
D-63477 Maintal
Tel. +49 (0) 6109 – 7196960
www.event-textil.de

TÜCHLER Bühnen- & Textiltechnik
Rennbahnweg 78
A-1220 Wien
Tel. +43 (0) 1 – 40010
www.tuechler.net

Serge Ferrari, Ferrari p.A
BP 54 F
F-94857 La Tour du Pin – Cedex
Tel. +33 (0) 47497 – 4133
www.ferrari-textiles.com

Georg + Otto Friedrich KG
Waldstraße 73
D-64846 Groß-Zimmern
Tel. +49 (0) 6071 – 4920
www.g-o-friedrich.com

Gerriets GmbH
Im Kirchenhürstle 5-7
D-79224 Umkirch
Tel. +49 (0) 7665 – 9600
www.gerriets.com

Christian Fischbacher
Mövenstrasse 18
CH-9015 St. Gallen-Winkeln
Tel. +41 (0) 71 – 3146666
www.fischbacher.com

Kinnasand
Danziger Straße 6
D-26655 Westerstede
Tel. +49 (0) 4488 – 5160
www.kinnasand.com

SAHCO Hesslein GmbH & Co. KG
Kreuzburger Straße 17-19
D-90471 Nürnberg
Tel. +49 (0) 911 – 99 870
www.sahco.com

acousticpearls GmbH
Am Wall 162/163
D-28195 Bremen
Tel. +49 (0) 421 – 42708780
www.acousticpearls.de

Création Baumann GmbH
Paul-Ehrlich-Straße 7
D-63128 Dietzenbach
Tel. +49 (0) 6074 – 37670
www.creationbaumann.com

Design Composite GmbH
Gewerbegebiet Lengdorf 4
A-5722 Niedernsill
Tel. +43 (0) 6548 – 203970
www.design-composite.com

Kvadrat
Lundbergsvej 10
DK-8400 Ebeltoft
Tel. +45 (0) 89 – 531866
www.kvadrat.dk

Nya Nordiska
An den Ratswiesen 4
D-29451 Dannenberg
Tel. +49 (0) 5861 – 809 0
www.nya.com

Silent Gliss GmbH
Rebgartenweg 5
D-79576 Weil am Rhein
Tel. +49 (0) 7621 – 66070
www.silentgliss.de

Vereinigte Filzfabriken AG
Giengener Weg 66
D-89537 Giengen
Tel. +49 (0) 7322 – 1440
www.vfg.de

abopart GmbH & Co. KG
Eichenweg 4
D-26160 Bad Zwischenahn
Tel. +49 (0) 4486 – 92870
www.abopart.de

feco® Innenausbausysteme GmbH
Am Storrenacker 22
D-76139 Karlsruhe
Tel. +49 (0) 721 – 6289500
www.feco.de

MARBURGER TAPETENFABRIK
Bertram-Schaefer-Straße 11
D-35274 Kirchhain
Tel. +49 (0) 6422 – 810
www.marburg.com

Strähle Raum-Systeme GmbH
Gewerbestraße 6
D-71332 Waiblingen
Tel. +49 (0) 7151 – 17140
www.straehle.de

Vertical Garden Design
Dr Abelins Gata 3nb
SE-11853 Stockholm
Tel. +46 (0) 704 – 979272
www.verticalgardendesign.com

VOMO – Leichtbautechnik GmbH
Borghorster Straße 48
D-48366 Laer
Tel. +49 (0) 25 54 – 9407800
www.vomo-leichtbautechnik.de

RICHTER SYSTEM GmbH &
Co. KG
Flughafenstraße 10
D-64347 Griesheim
Tel. +49 (0) 6155 – 8760
www.richtersystem.com

Lignotrend Produktions GmbH
Landstraße 25
D-79809 Weilheim-Bannholz
Tel. +49 (0) 7755 – 92000
www.lignotrend.com

DuPont Corian
Hugenottenallee 173-175
D-63263 Neu Isenburg
Tel. +49 (0) 6102 – 182527
www.dupont.com

Hasenkopf Holz & Kunststoff
GmbH
Stöcklstraße 1-2
D-84561 Mehring
Tel. +49 (0) 867 – 7984750
www.hasenkopf.de

HI-MACS LG Hausys Europe GmbH
Avenue des Morgines 12
CH-1213 Petit-Lancy Genf
Tel. +49 (0) 711 – 70709511
www.himacs.eu

Pfeiffer GmbH & Co. KG
Emmeliusstraße 21
D-35614 Aßlar
Tel. +49 (0) 6441 – 98330
www.pfeiffer-germany.de

Glas Marte GmbH
Brachsenweg 39
A-6900 Bregenz
Tel. +43 (0) 5574 – 67220
www.glasmarte.at

Glas Trösch Beratungs-GmbH
Benzstraße 13
D-89079 Ulm-Donautal
Tel. +49 (0) 731 – 40960
www.glastroesch.de

Okalux GmbH
Am Jöspershecklein 1
D-97828 Marktheidenfeld-Altfeld
Tel. +49 (0) 9391 – 900 0
www.okalux.de

SCHOTT Architektur
Hattenbergstraße 10
D-55122 Mainz
Tel. +49 (0) 6131 – 661812
www.schott.com/architecture

WEM Wandheizung GmbH
Robert-Bosch-Straße 1-7
D-56070 Koblenz
Tel. +49 (0) 261 – 98339914
www.wandheizung.de

DORMA GmbH + Co. KG
DORMA Platz 1
D-58256 Ennepetal
Tel. +49 (0) 2333 – 7930
www.dorma.de

GEZE GmbH
Reinhold-Vöster-Straße 21-29
D-71229 Leonberg
Tel. +49 (0) 7152 – 2030
www.geze.de

BIBLIOGRAPHY/PICTURE CREDITS

Becker, Klausjürgen; Pfau, Jochen; Tichelmann, Karsten: Trockenbau Atlas Parts 1+2, Cologne 2010

Cheret, Peter (ed.): Handbuch und Planungshilfe Baukonstruktion, Berlin 2010

Ching, Francis D.K.: Architecture: Form, Space and Order, New York 1975, 2nd ed. 1996

Deplazes, Andrea (ed.): Constructing Architecture, 3rd ed., Basel 2013

Dierks, Klaus; Wormuth, Rüdiger: Baukonstruktion, Cologne 2012

Ermel, Horst: Grundlagen des Entwerfens, Volumes 1+2, Darmstadt 2004

Exner, Ulrich; Pressel, Dietrich: Basics Spatial Design, Basel 2008

Feddersen, Eckhard; Lüdtke, Insa: Living for the Elderly: a Design Manual, Basel, Boston, Berlin 2009

Fischer, Joachim; Meuser, Philipp (eds.): Accessible Architecture: Age and Disability-friendly Planning and Building in the 21st Century, Berlin 2009

Fonatti, Franco: Elementare Gestaltungsprinzipien in der Architektur, Vienna 2000

Frampton, Kenneth: The Evolution of 20th Century Architecture, Vienna 2007

Hallschmid, Brigitte: Das Baustellenhandbuch für den Innenausbau, Mering 2012

Hausladen, Gerhard; Tichelmann, Karsten: Interiors Construction Manual, Munich, Basel 2010

Hegger, Manfred; Auch-Schwelk, Volker; Fuchs, Matthias; Rosenkranz, Thorsten: Construction Materials Manual, Basel 2013

Herzog, Thomas; Natterer, Julius; Schweitzer, Roland; Volz, Michael; Winter, Wolfgang: Timber Construction Manual, Basel 2004

Hestermann, Ulf; Rongen, Ludwig: Frick/Knöll Baukonstruktionslehre 1/2, Wiesbaden 2009/2012

Jocher, Thomas; Loch, Sigrid: Raumpilot Grundlagen, Stuttgart 2010

Kummer, Nils: Basics Masonry Construction, Basel 2006

Laasch, Thomas; Laasch, Erhard: Haustechnik – Grundlagen Planung Ausführung, Wiesbaden 2012

Neroth, Günter; Vollenschaar, Dieter (ed.): Wendehorst Baustoffkunde, Wiesbaden 2011

Neufert, Ernst; Kister, Johannes; Brockhaus, Mathias; Lohmann, Matthias; Merkel, Patricia: Architects' Data, 4th ed., Chichester, Ames 2012

Nutsch, Wolfgang: Handbuch der Konstruktion – Innenausbau, Stuttgart 2012

Nutsch, Wolfgang: Handbuch der Konstruktion – Möbel und Einbauschränke, Stuttgart 2011

Pell, Ben (ed.): The Articulate Surface: Ornament and Technology in Contemporary Architecture, Basel, Boston, Berlin 2010

Peters, Sascha: Material Revolution – Sustainable and Multi-purpose Materials for Design und Architecture, Basel 2011

Peukert, Martin: Gebäudeausstattung – Systeme Produkte Materialien, Stuttgart 2004

Pfeifer, Günter; Ramcke, Rolf; Achtziger, Joachim: Masonry Construction Manual, Basel 2001

Pistohl, Wolfram; Rechenauer, Christian; Scheuerer, Birgit: Handbuch der Gebäudetechnik, Neuwied 2013

Pottgiesser, Uta; Wiewiorra, Carsten: Handbuch und Planungshilfe Raumbildender Ausbau, Berlin 2013

Sauer, Christiane: Made of …: New Materials Sourcebook for Architecture and Design, Berlin 2010

Schittich, Christian (ed.): in Detail – Exhibitions and Display, Munich, Basel 2009

Schittich, Christian (ed.): in Detail – Interior Spaces, Munich, Basel 2002

Schittich, Christian (ed.): in Detail – Interior Surfaces and Materials, Munich, Basel 2008

Tichelmann, Karsten; Pfau, Jochen: Dry Construction, Munich, Basel 2008

Wellpott, Edwin; Bohne, Dirk: Technischer Ausbau von Gebäuden, Stuttgart 2006

www.baunetzwissen.de

.PSLAB: p. 98 2; p. 102 1
Aires Mateus: p. 128 2,3; p. 129
abopart: p. 88 3,4
Aldershoff, Roos: p. 24 1
Alma-nac Collaborative Architecture: p. 90 3
Andreas Fuhrimann Gabrielle Hächler Architects: p. 61 4; p. 138 1,2; p. 141 1,2; p. 156
Ano, Daici: p. 77 4; p. 91 8
Baan, Iwan: p. 19 9; p. 41 5
Armando, Salas Portugal: © Barragan Foundation/2014, ProLitteris, Zurich: p. 40 2
bepictures – Mailys Eberlin & Vincent Brunetta: p. 126; p. 148 2; p. 149 5; p. 150 1
Bisig, Tom: p. 13 2; p. 152 1; p. 153 6; p. 155 2, 3
Bitter, Jan: p. 54 2
Boegly, Luc: p. 38 2; p. 65 5
Braun, Zooey: p. 23 4; p. 45 7; p. 67 9; p. 124 2
Bredt, Marcus: p. 113 4; p. 130; p. 133
Campos, José: p. 117 6
Chalmeau, Stéphane: p. 134 2, 3; p. 137 2
Dempf, Christine: p. 95 6; p. 123 8
Dujardin, Filip: p. 116 2
Ebener, Marcus: p. 44 2
Eicken, Thomas: p. 61 6
Emile Ashley/Lignotrend: p. 37 2
EPFL | Alain Herzog: p. 11 4; p. 36 1; p. 67 8
ERCO GMBH: p. 45 3, 4
fermacell: p. 57 4
FG + SG Fotografie de Arquitectura: p. 18 2; p. 112 2

© FLC/2014, ProLitteris, Zurich: p. 10 2
Fujimoto, Sou: p. 14 2
Gambarte, Pascal for Designliga: p. 25 2; p. 69 9
Gee-Ly: p. 124 3
Gonzalez, Brigida: p. 90 4; p. 100 1; p. 144 1; p. 145 4, 5; p. 147 2
Gramazio & Kohler, Architektur und Digitale Fabrikation, ETH Zurich/Alessandra Bello: p. 78 2
h2o_architecture: p. 134; p. 137
Hacker, Christian: p. 31 6; p. 33 4; p. 47 8; p. 95 7; p. 102 2; p. 105 5; p. 123 7
Halbe, Roland: p. 17 8
Heinemann, Oliver: p. 65 4
Heinrich, Michael: p. 13 4; p. 38 1
Helfenstein, Heinrich: p. 41 4
Hempel, Jörg: p. 105 6
Herrmann, Eva: p. 43 9; p. 50; p. 95 5; p. 96; p. 103 4, 5
Holzherr, Florian: p. 16 1; p. 29 4; p. 43 8; p. 94 3; p. 120; p. 123 9
Hufton + Crow: p. 100 2
Huthmacher, Werner: p. 87 6
Institute for Computational Design (ICD), Stuttgart University, Prof. Achim Menges: p. 37 4
Jens Weber&Orla Conolly: p. 92 3
Joos, Luc: p. 101 7
k + w fotografie: p. 119 5; p. 122 3, 5; p. 124 1
KatzKaiser: p. 39; p. 88 3, 4; p. 108 3; p. 117 5; p. 129 4
Kazakov, Nikolay: p. 84 2, 3; p. 87 2
Kirchner, Jens: p. 29 3; p. 49 8; p. 61 7; p. 108 2
Klindtworth, Martin: p. 65 7

Knauf AMF: p. 103 1; p. 106
Knauf Gips KG: p. 81 4
Köhler, Christian: p. 102 5
Kraneburg, Christoph: p. 13 3; p. 25 3
Label Architecture: p. 148 1
Lindman, Åke E:son: p. 41 6
Lindner Group: p. 59 6; p. 62 1, 2; p. 102 3; p. 103 2,3
Lindström, Jesper: p. 114 3
Mair, Walter: p. 86 1
Malagamba, Duccio: p. 72 2
Marburger Tapetenfabrik: p. 94 2
Matthäus, Eckhart: p. 54 1; p. 113 5; p. 114 2
McCarragher, Gilbert: p. 43 6
Miguletz, Norbert: p. 91 7; p. 125 5
Morgado, Joao: p. 67 7
Mørk, Adam: p. 46 4
Mount Fuji Architects Studio: p. 142 2-4; p. 143 3
nora systems GmbH: p. 64 2
Oliv Architects: p. 79 6
Ott, Paul: p. 23 5
Passoth, Jens: p. 53 5; p. 65 6
Philipp Lohöfener/Wüstenrot Foundation: p. 98 1
Markus Palzer: p. 61 8
Probst, Edzard: p. 53 4; p. 65 3; p. 69 10
Projekttriangle Design Studio/ Tom Ziora: p. 119 6
© 2014, ProLitteris, Zurich: p. 40 1
Raab, Emanuel: p. 37 3
Raumprobe: p. 39; p. 67 3-6, p. 82 1; p. 93 5
Régis Golay, FEDERAL Studio, Geneva: p. 31 7
REHAU AG + Co: p. 59 4, 5

Reipka, Dominik: p. 25 4
Richters, Christian: p. 11 3; p. 16 2; p. 23 3; p. 46 3; p. 110
Rintala Eggertsson Architects: p. 16 3
Schiefner & Schreiber Asphaltbau GmbH & Co. KG: p. 57 5; p. 61 5
Schlüter-Systems: p. 71 3
Scholz, Uwe: p. 122 4
Schulz, Kerstin: p. 8
Schumacher, Bernd: p. 92 2
Schwarz, Ulrich: p. 18 3
Sefar AG: p. 101 4; p. 102 4
Sopro Bauchemie GmbH: p. 71 4, 5, 6
Strähle Raum-Systeme GmbH: p. 77 3; p. 87 3
Strobel, Peter: p. 72 3; p. 79 7
Sumner, Edmund: p. 35 3
Suzuki, Hisao: p. 19 8
Suzuki, Ken'ichi: p. 142; p. 143
The International Surface Book: p. 39
The Museum of Decorative Arts in Prague: p. 10 1
UNStudio: p. 21 3
Uzin Utz AG: p. 57 3
Van de Velde, Tim: p. 150 2
Vitsœ: p. 116 3
Voit, Michael: p. 45 6
Weber, Stefan: p. 49 7
WEM Wandheizung GmbH: p. 49 6
www.floorsymbols.com: p. 52 1; p. 64 1; p. 65 1

INDEX

Editors: Alexander Reichel, Kerstin Schultz
Concept: Alexander Reichel, Kerstin Schultz, Andrea Wiegelmann
Authors: Eva Herrmann, Marcus Kaiser, Tobias Katz

Translation from German into English: Hartwin Busch
Copy editing and proofreading: Richard Toovey
Project management: Odine Oßwald

Layout: Eva Maria Herrmann, Marcus Kaiser, Tobias Katz
Drawings: Eva Maria Herrmann, Marcus Kaiser, Tobias Katz, Anna Tschochner
Design concept SCALE: Nadine Rinderer
Typesetting: Amelie Solbrig

The technical and construction recommendations contained in this book are based on the present state of technical knowledge. They should be checked in each case against the relevant instructions, standards, laws etc. as well as local regulations before applying them. No liability is accepted.

Library of Congress Cataloging-in-Publication data
A CIP catalog record for this book has been applied for at the Library of Congress.

Bibliographic information published by the German National Library
The German National Library lists this publication in the Deutsche Nationalbibliografie; detailed bibliographic data are available on the Internet at http://dnb.dnb.de.

This publication is also available as an e-book (ISBN 978-3-03821-267-6)
and in a German language edition (ISBN 978-3-0346-0741-4).

© 2014 Birkhäuser Verlag GmbH, Basel
P.O. Box 44, 4009 Basel, Switzerland
Part of De Gruyter

Printed on acid-free paper produced from chlorine-free pulp. TCF ∞

Printed in Germany

ISBN 978-3-0346-0742-1

9 8 7 6 5 4 3 2 1   www.birkhauser.com